THE CNN EFFECT

The last decade has seen an increased willingness by Western governments to use force to intervene in distant humanitarian crises, and this has been coupled with significant levels of media attention to the human casualties of war and conflict. Central to this new policy of intervention is the so-called 'CNN effect': the saturation of Western viewers with non-stop, real-time news footage of wars and military actions on television and the Internet. In turn, these images constitute a powerful plea for action. But can news media drive foreign policy, or are governments oblivious to partial news coverage? Are there any connections between media coverage of humanitarian crises and Western intervention, and what is the truth behind the 'CNN effect'?

The CNN Effect examines the relationship between the state and its media, and considers the role played by news reporting in a series of 'humanitarian' interventions in Iraq, Somalia, Bosnia, Kosovo and Rwanda. Piers Robinson challenges traditional views of media subservience and argues that sympathetic news coverage at key moments in foreign crises can influence the response of Western governments.

Piers Robinson is Lecturer in Political Communication in the School of Politics and Communication Studies at the University of Liverpool.

D0036807

THE CNN EFFECT

The myth of news, foreign policy
and intervention

Piers Robinson

London and New York

First published 2002
by Routledge
11 New Fetter Lane, London EC4P 4EE

Simultaneously published in the USA and Canada
by Routledge
29 West 35th Street, New York, NY 10001

Routledge is an imprint of the Taylor & Francis Group

Typeset in Times by The Running Head Limited, Cambridge
Printed and bound in Great Britain by
St Edmundsbury Press, Bury St Edmunds, Suffolk

British Library Cataloguing in Publication Data
A catalogue record for this book is available from the British Library

Library of Congress Cataloging in Publication Data
A catalog record for this book has been requested

ISBN 0–415–25905–3 (pbk)

ISBN 0–415–25904–5 (hbk)

This book is dedicated to
Clair, Ira and Louie

CONTENTS

CONTENTS

TABLES

INTRODUCTION

Overview

Since the end of the Cold War the increasing willingness of Western governments to intervene militarily during humanitarian crises, coupled with
significant levels of Western media attention to the human consequences of
'distant' civil wars, raises substantive questions regarding the media–state
relationship. Specifically, it is commonly argued that intervention during the
humanitarian crises in northern Iraq (1991) and Somalia (1992) were partially driven by news media coverage of suffering people, the 'CNN effect'.
The principal aim of this study is to examine the assumptions lying behind
the CNN effect by conducting a search for evidence of news media influence
on intervention during humanitarian crises. The study does not offer a multi-
factor assessment of what causes intervention, although due consideration is
given throughout to the multitude of reasons why intervention might occur.
Rather the focus is on one variable, the media, which are widely understood
to play an important role in influencing US-led intervention. Understanding
what motivates the US to act is central to understanding the CNN effect
because the majority of forcible interventions have occurred under the command and leadership of the US. The study offers substantive conclusions
regarding the significance of news media influence on intervention and
explains why news media can come to affect government policy-making. As
such the research findings are of value to those in humanitarian and foreign
policy circles, those who seek to harness the potential of news media to facilitate humanitarian action or to 'control' the unwanted intrusion of the news
media. In addition to assessing news media influence upon intervention decisions, this study also has the important aim of developing a theoretical
two-way understanding of the direction of influence between the news media
and the state (the 'policy–media interaction model'). This model forms the
core of my analysis of the CNN effect and contributes to our understanding
of media–state relations. As such this study is also of value to those interested
in broader debates over media–state relations and news media power in the
post-Cold War 'real-time TV' environment.

1

Before proceeding five issues require clarification. First, the focus of this study is on the alleged influence of the media upon decisions to intervene during humanitarian crises with the use, or threat of use, of force. As such the research does not examine other types of policy response, for example diplomatic engagement or non-coercive military intervention (peacekeeping), that governments might pursue in response to humanitarian crises (although I do broaden out my research conclusions in the final chapter with a discussion of other types of policy response to humanitarian crises). My focus on forcible intervention is for two reasons. Most importantly I am attempting to address what I believe to be the core of the CNN effect debate that relates to the apparent ability of the media to influence governments to pursue military intervention during humanitarian crises. The idea that the media might have been pivotal in causing governments to pursue such policies, thereby circumventing long-standing notions of non-intervention and state sovereignty, is precisely what is behind talk of a more powerful media and a CNN effect capable of causing governments to pursue the difficult and costly policy of armed intervention. To put this point another way, claims that media coverage inspires aid delivery and diplomatic protests *might* be greeted with little surprise by most in academic and policy circles and certainly would have not led to the kind of widespread debate over media power that characterises the CNN effect and its claimed relationship to military intervention. Also it is good methodological practice when conducting a case study comparison to make sure the phenomenon you are trying to understand – intervention – is sufficiently similar in each case analysed (George 1979). Forcible intervention is quite distinct from diplomatic responses or aid delivery. To have included such cases of a different type would have undermined the research design and made problematic any overall assessment of media influence across the cases. Narrowly defined but precise and defendable research conclusions are the aim here, not broad-ranging and porous claims about the media and international politics.

Second, the phrase CNN effect needs to be defined. The original CNN effect referred to the 'ubiquity of the channel (so that all sides were using the same information source)' (Freedman 2000: 339) and originated during the 1991 Gulf War. Since then the phrase has become the generic term for the ability of real-time communications technology, via the news media, to provoke major responses from domestic audiences and political elites to both global and national events. Debate has not only centred on the role and impact of CNN but also on the impact of the news media in general upon both foreign policy formulation and world politics. In other words, the CNN effect is not synonymous with CNN. Consequently this study focuses upon the impact of both TV news and print media on decision-making. In order to develop a sense of overall political pressure in any given case, a combination of newspapers and TV news outlets were analysed. CBS, CNN, the *Washington Post* and the *New York Times* were the sources selected for analysis. As such the study does not explicitly differentiate between the differing impacts of TV news versus newspapers. Both TV news, because of the visual imagery, and newspapers, because of their greater tendency to express overt political opinion and influence elite opinion, might play an important role in influencing opinion during humanitarian crises. Accordingly both need to be examined in order to offer an assessment of overall political pressure exerted by news media. This said, the method used in this study is sufficiently sensitive to establish whether TV news coverage significantly diverges from print media in any given case. Where this occurs the implications for case study findings are assessed.

The third point of clarification relates to the question of public opinion. In a review article Brenda Seaver (1998: 79) noted that recent literature analysing the relationship between the media and foreign policy-making has largely overlooked 'the entire mass media–public opinion–foreign policy connection'. At first glance this omission appears odd given that the CNN effect is often understood to rest upon a presumed link with public opinion, for example, that graphic images of suffering people provoke outrage amongst the public who in turn pressure government to take action. This study, whilst by no means ignoring the importance of public opinion, does not provide a comprehensive and systematic analysis of the state of public opinion polls in the cases analysed. This is for two interlinked reasons. First, the CNN effect also concerns the direct impact of media coverage on policy-makers and the broader group of politicians, experts and commentators who make up the foreign policy elite. These groups are more attentive than the wider public to foreign affairs news and play a pivotal role in setting both the tone of policy debate and policy options. As such the CNN effect is as much to do with the complex perceptions formed among these groups as it is to do with the immediate impact of public opinion polls. This is not to say that public opinion is unimportant to the elite debate as discussion of policy options will often occur in the context of concern over public opinion. However, and this leads to my second point, available evidence indicates that policy-makers and elite groups do not rely primarily upon opinion polls as evidence of public opinion. Rather they rely upon 'perceived public opinion' (Entman 2000: 21) that in turn is largely formed via the media.[1] In a comprehensive analysis of elite perceptions of public opinion Kull and Ramsay (2000: 105) conclude that 'most commonly, policy practitioners seemed to feel that they could get a sense of public attitudes by reading standard news reporting'. Consequently, focusing analysis on public opinion polls in order to examine the 'mass media–public opinion–foreign policy connection' (Seaver 1998: 79) would provide both an invalid and inaccurate assessment of the CNN effect. Instead, this study focuses upon analysing the amount and form (via framing analysis)of media coverage with the focus upon how a particular humanitarian crisis is represented and the tone of coverage toward official policy. This in turn provides an assessment of the most significant force in shaping policy-makers' perceptions of public and elite opinion and indeed public opinion itself. Notwithstanding this, appropriate secondary sources were drawn upon in order to assess public opinion polls and their relevance to the case study findings.

Fourth, analysing the impact of media coverage upon policy decisions raises the controversial issue of causation. Post-modernism and social constructivism have taught us to be cautious of explaining the world through reference to dependent variables, independent variables and causal links. Inevitably, however, if we are to discuss the impact of media coverage on policy we become involved in making assessments as to whether a particular decision would have been made if media coverage had been different. To my mind this type of question is a reasonable one to ask although I acknowledge some would argue the question is either unanswerable or else ill conceived. More generally academics and researchers have sought to sidestep talk of causation through use of terms such as influence (arguably less deterministic), enabling/disabling and 'transactional outcomes' (for example see Wolfsfeld 1997: 63). In this study I occasionally use the term *cause* (without assuming the phenomenon is overly deterministic) and, more often, *influence*. When I argue that 'A' influenced/caused 'B' to occur I am saying no more and no less than that if 'A' had not been present, 'B' would have been unlikely to occur. In my view, this is equivalent to the implications of much other research that adopts more elaborate phrases such as enabling and disabling effects and transactional outcomes. Also, to say that the media influenced or caused intervention is not to claim that it was the only factor, only a necessary one. As noted before this study does not pretend to offer a multi-factor explanation of intervention.

Finally, recent events following the 11 September attacks on the World Trade Centre and the Pentagon, involving military intervention in Afghanistan and the proclaimed 'war against terrorism', have dominated the international agenda and look set to do so for some time to come. The dramatic visual nature, as well as the human consequences, of the 11 September attacks will undoubtedly be the source of much academic analysis as will the performance of the news media during the subsequent 'war against terrorism'. It is important however, to distinguish this case from those studied in this book. Whilst there are significant humanitarian consequences to this intervention, not least of which is the creation of vast numbers of internally displaced persons (IDPs) and refugees in Afghanistan, the primary motivation for the intervention is rooted in US national security interests. Humanitarian concerns have been clearly secondary to the US goal of destroying the Taliban government and disrupting/destroying the Al-Qaeda terrorist network. As such the case of US intervention in Afghanistan fits the more traditional category of intervention in pursuit of relatively clear-cut national interest/security concerns rather than apparent humanitarian concern for people suffering in 'distant' conflicts. In light of this, I would suggest that the analysis of US media performance during this intervention is likely to indicate the subservience of mass media to US foreign policy objectives rather than any kind of CNN effect whereby the media have influenced the substance of US foreign policy. Whether or not the concept of humanitarian intervention will return to the US foreign policy agenda in any significant way is unknown at the time of writing although it seems likely to be sidelined until the current 'war against terrorism' is over. Having clarified these issues, we can now turn to the organisation of the book.

Organisation of chapters

In Chapter 1 the background to the CNN effect debate is set out and the question of post-Cold War humanitarian intervention assessed. The CNN effect is then contrasted with an existing critical literature on media–state relations that highlights the conformity between the news media and the policy interests of those in power. In particular both the inconsistency between the CNN effect debate and the critical literature, and the tendency of debates regarding media influence to be dogged by an effect/non-effect dichotomy are noted. A section of this chapter is devoted to a review of recent research into the CNN effect, an important aim of which is to establish why this research has failed to clarify the significance of media influence, as well as to establish lines of inquiry for this study.

In Chapter 2 the policy–media interaction model is detailed, including the theory behind it and how it builds upon previous research. The general research design, operationalisation of the model and a typology of media effects are set out in this chapter. The theoretical implications of the policy–media interaction model are then related to other theories of media–state relations (Hallin 1986; Herman and Chomsky 1988; Bennett 1990; Wolfsfeld 1997) in order to demonstrate the two-way understanding of the direction of influence between the media and the state allowed for by the model. In particular the model is used to resolve contrasting claims regarding the impact of news media coverage on the course of the Vietnam War. Also discussed is how the model contributes to Gadi Wolfsfeld's (1997) political contest model of media–state relations. The chapter concludes with the case selection for this study.

Chapters 3 to 5 detail the research findings of the six case studies. Chapter 3 examines the cases of US ground troop intervention in Somalia (1992) and Iraq (1991), Chapter 4 examines two instances of air power intervention during the 1992–5 war in Bosnia whilst Chapter 5 examines two instances of non-intervention or non-influence during humanitarian crises during the 1999 Kosovo air campaign and the 1994 Rwandan genocide. For each case the background to the humanitarian crisis and the policy decisions involved are discussed, an analysis of media influence is provided via the policy–media interaction model and I assess both the type of media effect likely to have occurred and the relative importance of other factors. Chapter 6 draws together the case study findings in order to reach substantive conclusions regarding both the causal link between news media coverage and intervention and the conditions under which news media coverage can influence policy. The chapter also details lines of enquiry for future research and relates the research findings to debates concerning media power, post-Cold War US foreign policy and humanitarian action.

Acknowledgements

My deepest gratitude goes to Dr Eric Herring for the intellectual and personal support he has unfailingly provided me with over the last few years and to my partner Clair McHugh for her sustained guidance, advice and support. Others who have provided me with both ideas and support to whom I am sincerely grateful are Professor Steven Livingston, Professor Phil Taylor, Professor Richard Little, Professor John Corner, Professor Terrell Carver and Dr Jutta Weldes. I also wish to thank in particular Michael Barnett, Robert Gallucci, Arnold Kanter, Anthony Lake, Frank Wisener and Alexander Vershbow. The support from the research communities in the Department of Politics, University of Bristol, and the School of Politics and Communications Studies, University of Liverpool, were also invaluable to this study. The Economic and Social Research Council funded the first two years of this study. Earlier versions of some of the theoretical and case study material were published in the *Review of International Studies*, *Journal of Peace Research*, *European Journal of Communication* and *Political Studies*, for which I would like to thank Cambridge University Press, Sage Publications and Blackwell.

1

THE CNN EFFECT
CONSIDERED

Media power and world politics

During the 1980s the proliferation of new technologies transformed the potential of the news media to provide a constant flow of global real-time news. Tiananmen Square and the collapse of communism, symbolised by the fall of the Berlin Wall, became major media events communicated to Western audiences instantaneously via TV news media. By the end of the decade the question being asked was to what extent had this 'media pervasiveness' (Hoge 1994: 136–44) impacted upon government – particularly the process of foreign policy-making. New technologies appeared to reduce the scope for calm deliberation over policy, forcing policy-makers to respond to whatever issue journalists focused on (Beschloss 1993; McNulty 1993). This perception was in turn reinforced by the end of the bipolar order and what many viewed as the collapse of the old anti-communist consensus which, it was argued, had led to the creation of an ideological bond, uniting policy-makers and journalists. Released from the 'prism of the Cold War' (Williams 1993: 315) journalists were, it was presumed, freer not just to cover the stories they wanted but to criticise US foreign policy as well. For radical technological optimists these developments suggested the realisation of a genuine 'global village' (McLuhan 1964) in which the news media were helping to erode people's identification with the state and instead 'mold a cosmopolitan global consciousness' (Carruthers 2000: 201).

The 1990s and intervention during humanitarian crises

If the 1991 Gulf War reminded observers of the enormous power that governments had when it came to shaping media analysis (e.g. Baudrillard 1991; Philo and McLaughlin 1993; Bennett and Paletz 1994), events after this conflict appeared to confirm the opposite. According to Martin Shaw, emotive and often highly critical media coverage of Kurdish refugees fleeing from Saddam Hussein's forces caused the 'virtually unprecedented proposal for Kurdish safe havens' (Shaw 1996: 88). Operation Restore Hope in Somalia quickly followed and, once again, it was believed that the ill-fated sortie into the Horn of Africa in 1992 had effectively been forced upon the United States by media pressure. The myth of the CNN effect had been born.

These interventions were all the more significant because, to many commentators, they represented a major development in world politics. Earlier Cold War UN peacekeeping operations were normally non-coercive in nature and involved the supervision of *consenting* parties and the reaffirmation of territorial borders and sovereignty. Intervention in northern Iraq and Somalia, however, appeared to represent the development of a norm of *forcible* humanitarian intervention in which state sovereignty could be violated in order to preserve and to protect basic human rights. International society, it was claimed, was undergoing a shift from a state-centric and non-interventionist value system toward a cosmopolitan one in which basic human rights were held to be superior to state sovereignty.[1] It is important to make clear here the distinction between non-coercive involvement in another state, for example peacekeeping or humanitarian aid delivery, and the actual use of military force that occurs either without permission or in direct contravention to the wishes of a state. Many operations during the 1990s involved peacekeeping missions, for example the UN Protection Force (UNPROFOR) in Bosnia.[2] These did not represent, however, intervention as defined traditionally[3] because they occurred with the consent of the host state. Whilst the nature of many of these operations might signal a development in UN peacekeeping toward humanitarian aid relief (rather than policing peace deals and ceasefires) the key development of the 1990s was the willingness to use force in pursuit, purportedly, of humanitarian objectives. Most of these forceful operations occurred with Chapter VII authorisation from the UN Security Council that allowed the use of 'all necessary means'.[4] The focus of debate, and of this study, is on these coercive forms of intervention involving the use or threat of use of force during humanitarian crises.

Beyond the assumed importance of the media in driving these interventions, the question of precisely what underpinned the apparent new-found willingness of Western governments to fight 'humanitarian' wars has become a controversial issue. Before proceeding it is therefore necessary briefly to set out the key arguments pertaining to this issue and the approach toward 'humanitarian' intervention adopted in this study.

For many commentators, as noted above, recent post-Cold War interventions are indicative of a genuine moral development on the part of Western governments whereby military action in order to protect the basic rights of people in other countries has become, to an extent, legitimated. The assumption underpinning this perspective is that, to a significant extent, Western governments are acting with humanitarian motivation and intent. Many, although not all, who adhere to this perspective attribute a significant role to the news media in cajoling Western leaders to 'do the right thing'. Western leaders who subscribe to this 'ethical' agenda offer a slightly more circumspect view of their motives but still claim a concern for the human rights of 'other' people. For example British Prime Minister Tony Blair (1999) merged national self-interest with the pursuit of global justice in his 1999 speech in Chicago:

> Now our actions are guided by a more subtle blend of mutual inter- est and moral purpose in defending the values we cherish. In the end, values and interests merge. If we can establish the spread of values of liberty, the rule of law, human rights and an open society then that is in our national interest.

An alternative and radical interpretation of Western interventionism is that it represents merely a continuation of traditional power politics in which the 'humanitarian' label is used to disguise the selfish pursuit of Western interests (Chomsky 1999; Hammond and Herman 2000a). Although some of these accounts leave unclear precisely how 'humanitarian' intervention serves Western self-interest, the interventionism of the 1990s is understood to be part of a broader hegemonic project aimed at securing Western interests on a global basis. For example Chomsky (1999: 14) paraphrases US National Security advisor Anthony Lake as an example of the agenda lying behind Western actions: 'Throughout the Cold War we contained a global threat to market democracies, but now we can move on to consolidate the victory of democracy and open markets'. This radical perspective fundamentally chal- lenges the assumption of 'pro-interventionists' that Western governments are acting as benign 'Good Samaritans' when intervening in a humanitarian crisis.

To a certain extent, the mainstream and radical interpretations of Western interventionism disagree only on the question of the legitimacy of Western values and actions. For example, Chomsky uses Lake's statement as a critique of Western interventionism whilst Blair's rather similar statement is used and understood as a defence of Western interventionism. Beyond the arguments of pro and anti interventionists there are, however, more immediate motiva- tions that might explain Western intervention during humanitarian crises. For example, controversy surrounds the humanitarian credentials of French intervention in Rwanda in 1994 with some arguing it was motivated more by French geo-strategic goals in Africa than humanitarian concern. Also Howard Adelman (1992: 74) points out in 'The Ethics of Humanitarian Intervention' that geo-strategic concerns over cross-border refugee flows might well be the primary motivation for recent so-called 'humanitarian' interventions. Clearly, the possible presence of such alternative factors makes problematic assumptions behind both mainstream and radical explanations of Western interventionism.

Further alternative explanations for Western action will be considered throughout this study. For now, and given the aforementioned controversies, it is important to set out my position and understanding of the term 'humanitarian intervention" before proceeding. Throughout this study the term humanitarian intervention is understood to mean the use of military force (non-humanitarian means) in order to achieve humanitarian objectives; the interventions in Iraq in 1991 and Somalia in 1992 are commonly understood (although not necessarily accurately) to fit this definition. It should be noted however that, as Eric Herring argues, the term humanitarian intervention is problematic. It is often used in relation to any instance of intervention during a humanitarian crisis. As such the term can gloss over instances of humanitarian means being employed to achieve non-humanitarian ends, and intervention during a humanitarian crisis which is motivated and conducted according to non-humanitarian goals. In order to avoid falling into the trap of assuming humanitarian intent, and therefore prejudicing inquiry into the cause of recent interventions, I adhere both to Herring's phrase 'intervention during humanitarian crises' (rather than humanitarian intervention) and the associated position that humanitarian motivations need to be argued for and demonstrated rather than assumed. Also, whether or not there exists humanitarian intent on the part of policy-makers is not necessarily connected with whether or not the media motivates them to act, as the intention of policy-makers might be to respond to media criticism by intervening rather than to save lives per se. Media motivated intervention is not necessarily synonymous with humanitarian intent. To conclude, by avoiding such prejudgements, I hope to avoid making the assumptions implicit in both the mainstream and radical interpretations of the motivations lying behind Western interventionism.

The CNN effect debate takes off

The two interventions – in northern Iraq and Somalia – triggered a major debate within academic and government circles. Foreign policy 'experts' in particular were dismayed by what they saw as unwarranted intrusion by the Fourth Estate into the policy process. George Kennan argued that media cov-erage of suffering people in Somalia had usurped traditional policy-making channels, triggering an ill-thought-out intervention (Kennan 1993). In other words, Kennan feared that elite control of foreign policy-making had been lost to the media. Other commentators followed Kennan in expressing concern at the dangers of media-dictated foreign policy.[5] James Hoge, for example, observed that 'today's pervasive media increases the pressure on politicians to respond promptly to news accounts that by their very immediacy are incom-plete, without context and sometimes wrong' (Hoge 1994). Working from a realist perspective, critics generally decried the CNN effect and stressed the need for elite control of foreign policy. However, whilst early debate was char-acterised by realist sentiments, the election of Democrat Bill Clinton as US President helped mould a foreign policy community more sensitive to the notion of humanitarian intervention. This in turn reflected the internationalist and Wilsonian temperament of many US Democrats. A similar effect can be observed within the British foreign policy-making community as it has reacted to the proclamations of an ethical foreign policy by the Blair government. As a result of these developments there has been greater appreciation amongst many policy-makers and advisers as to the beneficial role of the news media in promoting Western intervention. For example US Balkans diplomat Richard Holbrooke (1999: 20–1) praised the news media for helping draw attention to the crises in Bosnia and Kosovo, whilst former National Security advisor Anthony Lake welcomed the apparent ability of the media to highlight humanitarian crises around the world.[6] Notwithstanding this development, the prevalent tone within foreign policy circles tends to revolve around concern over the harmful impact of coverage on 'rational' policy-making.

Within humanitarian circles there was also a good deal of debate about the apparent power of the news media to cause intervention. Indeed, ever since the 1984 Ethiopian famine, there has been much discussion about the pur-ported impact the media have on crises in the Third World.[7] Amongst the most significant works in this genre were the 1995 Crosslines Global Report, *Somalia, Rwanda and Beyond*, edited by Edward Girardet and *From Mas-sacres to Genocide* (1996), edited by Robert Rotberg and Thomas Weiss. Both took a decidedly different approach to that of either Kennan or Hoge, and writing from a broadly 'world society' approach applauded the role played by non-state actors in expanding policy debate beyond the narrow corridors of political power. Furthermore, instead of attacking the irresponsible part played by the media, these writer-advocates actually praised the new activism and sought to harness the perceived potential of the media to encourage humanitarian intervention.

To a significant extent the CNN effect debate has persisted throughout the 1990s. For example, members of the policy-making establishment have reasserted their belief in the power of the news media to drive Western responses to humanitarian crises. For example, in his speech during the 1999 air war against Serbia, British Prime Minister Tony Blair (1999) claimed that politicians were still 'fending off the danger of letting wherever CNN roves be the cattle prod to take a global conflict seriously', implying that, if left unchecked, the news media have the power to compel governments to intervene.[8]

Lawrence Freedman (2000) and Nicholas Wheeler (2000) have revisited the CNN effect debate and offered useful insights into the possible scope of media impact. These writers draw upon research into the CNN effect (to be reviewed later in this chapter) and, whilst offering a more cautious assess-ment of media power, still point to the media playing an important role with regard to intervention during humanitarian crises. For example, Freedman (2000: 339) notes that whilst media power might have been exaggerated during earlier phases of the CNN effect debate, policy-makers have in fact come to believe in the power of the media. Freedman (2000: 339) asserts that

US intervention in Kosovo was in part caused by the belief that, if left unchecked, the crisis would generate negative media attention and calls for something to be done.[9]

In his study of humanitarian intervention, *Saving Strangers*, Wheeler (2000: 300) argues that there exist clear limits to the CNN effect, in particular in relation to the deployment of ground troops. He also argues that media coverage does not cause or force policy-makers to intervene but rather enables policy-makers to intervene by building public support. The implication here is that policy-makers are motivated to intervene for non-media related reasons but require dramatic media coverage to help gain domestic support.[10] In short, whilst qualifying straightforward assertions of the media causation which dominate much of the CNN effect debate, these writers still maintain that the media play an important role in facilitating intervention during humanitarian crises. As such their commentaries[11] on media effects fit in with a familiar set of claims regarding the influential role of the media. Notwithstanding the work of Freedman (2000) and Wheeler (2000), rarely during the CNN effect debate was there a critical assessment of the claim that news media influence intervention. More often than not the CNN effect has been asserted rather than demonstrated. The result is continued uncertainty over the scope and significance of the CNN effect, as well as the persistence of an unjustified and widespread assumption that the news media have the power to 'move and shake' (Cohen 1994: 9) governments. In short the CNN effect has become an untested and unsubstantiated 'fact' for many in foreign policy and humanitarian circles.

Manufacturing consent and theories of media–state relations

The undemonstrated assertions within the CNN effect debate sit uneasily with a wealth of critical literature written over the last 25 years in which the political and economic positioning of major news media institutions is seen to lead to a situation in which news accounts tend to support dominant perspectives. More specifically, the 'manufacturing consent' literature emphasises the ability of governments to influence the output of journalists and the tendency of journalists to both self-censor and perceive global events through the cultural and political prisms of their respective political and social elites. Whilst totalising arguments about manufacturing consent (see in particular Herman and Chomsky 1988) are controversial, the thesis that news media coverage of 'foreign' affairs is 'indexed' (Bennett 1990) to the frames of reference of foreign policy elites receives substantial empirical support.[12] Accordingly, the use of the term 'manufacturing consent' throughout this study should be understood as referring to the complete range of arguments that emphasise the power of government to set news media agendas. Whether or not the term 'manufacturing consent' is also taken to mean that all citizens receive and internalise the ideological messages carried in media texts or that journalists serve merely as propaganda agents for the state is irrelevant to my use of the term here.[13] The label is useful because it does, in my view, capture the essence of all elite models of media–state relations: i.e. the understanding that news media are influenced by government policy and only rarely influences government in the way the CNN effect suggests.[14]

Two implicit versions of the manufacturing consent paradigm can be discerned, an *executive* version and an *elite* version.[15] The *executive* version[16] emphasises the extent to which news media content conforms with the agendas and reference frames of government officials where government officials are understood as members of the *executive*. For example Robert Entman (1991) analysed the divergent US news media framing of the Korean Airline and Iran Air shoot-downs that occurred during the 1980s. Both of these international incidents were similar, involving mistakes by the military leading to the destruction of civilian airliners and large loss of life. However, the US news media framed the Iran Air shoot-down, for which the US was responsible, in terms of a technical failure whilst the Korean Airline shoot-down, for which the USSR was responsible, was framed as a moral outrage. According to Entman (1991: 10) overall media coverage was consistent with the policy interests of the respective US administrations. Importantly, according to the executive version, the news media do not function to criticise or challenge executive policy lines. Accordingly this vein of manufacturing consent theory makes a strong implicit claim that the conformity between news media coverage and executive policy interests prevents news media influence on executive policy.

The second elite version of the manufacturing consent paradigm (e.g. Hallin 1986; Bennett 1990) holds that news media coverage conforms to the interests of political elites in general whether they are in the executive, legislative or any other politically powerful position in society. The seminal study of elite manufacturing consent theory is Daniel Hallin's *The Uncensored War*. Examining the claim that during the Vietnam War the news media played an oppositional role to official US policy, Hallin finds that critical news media coverage occurred only after sections of the Washington political elite turned against the war. Hence, perhaps the event most cited as a case of news media influence on government policy actually turns out to be a case of political elites becoming divided over policy with news media coverage simply reflecting this division. Drawing upon these findings Hallin develops the concept of three spheres, one of consensus, one of legitimate controversy and one of deviance. These exist with regard to any given political issue. He argues that the news media, taking their cues from political elites, rarely produce coverage within the deviant sphere but instead either reflect elite consensus on an issue or elite 'legitimated controversy' (Hallin 1986).

Hallin's work receives further conceptual clarification through the work of Lance Bennett (1990). Bennett argues that 'mass media news is indexed implicitly to the dynamics of governmental debate' (Bennett 1990: 108).

When news media coverage highlights *executive* policy problems or failures, that is to say it is critical of executive policy, this simply reflects a 'professional responsibility [on the part of the journalist] to highlight important conflicts and struggles within the centers of power' (Bennett 1990: 110). Bennett's theory receives substantial empirical support via Mermin's (1999) study of news media coverage, elite debate and post-Vietnam US military interventions and Zaller and Chui's (1996) analysis of news media coverage of foreign policy crises between 1945 and 1991. Both Mermin and Zaller and Chui find that, consistent with the predictions of elite manufacturing consent theory, news media reporting rarely moves beyond the confines of 'official' Washington policy debates. An important claim of elite manufacturing consent theory is that news coverage which criticises or challenges executive policy can occur when there exists elite conflict over policy. Hence, contrary to the executive version, the possibility that news media coverage might be *critical* of executive policy is allowed for. An implication of this possibility is that during periods of elite dissensus critical coverage might come to influence executive policy processes. This is an important implication of elite manufacturing consent that contrasts with that of the executive version.

However Hallin (1986), Bennett (1990) and Mermin (1999) do not explore this possibility, at least to any significant degree. The problem here is that elite manufacturing consent theory tends to be rooted in an understanding of the relationship between journalists and official sources (e.g. Hallin 1986; Bennett 1990; Zaller and Chui 1996; Mermin 1999). Finding that news media coverage is indexed to elite opinion is equated, to all intent and purpose, with a passive and non-influential news media. For example, with respect to Hallin's (1986) claim that news media coverage followed elite division over Vietnam, although he is careful not to dismiss out of hand the possibility of media influence, he uses this finding to de-emphasise the possible importance of the news media. Hallin (1986: 213) writes:

> The behavior of the media . . . is intimately related to the unity and clarity of the government itself, as well as to the degree of consensus in the society at large. This is not to say that the role of the press is purely reactive. Surely it made a difference, for instance, that many journalists were shocked both by the brutality of the war and by the gap between what they were told by officials and what they saw and heard in the field . . . But it is also clear that the administration's problems with the 'fourth branch of government' resulted in a large part from political divisions at home . . . In a sense, what is really remarkable . . . is that the press and the public went as far with American policy in Vietnam as they did.[17]

News sources, however, do not disprove news effects and, by focusing upon the relationship between news sources and journalists' elite manufacturing consent 'black boxes' the dynamics between media coverage and any given policy process and, therefore, tends to ignore the possibility that media might influence policy outcomes during elite debate.[18] A further related problem with elite manufacturing consent is the assumption that, because journalists tend only to replicate elite views, they cannot play an independent role during debates between elites. This assumption means that elite manufacturing consent theory tends to ignore the possibility that journalists might actually take sides (either consciously or unintentionally) during elite debates over policy, or even take the side of non-elites (Wolfsfeld 1997), and in doing so become active and powerful participants in political debate. As Timothy Cook (1998: 12–13) argues, 'journalists should not be considered the passive recipients of official information but as active participants functioning as a political institution in their own right'.

A key consequence of these shortcomings is the creation of an effect/non-effect dichotomy in debates about the role of the media. For example historian David Culbert (1998) has directly engaged with Hallin's non-effect claim regarding the Vietnam War and argues instead that news media coverage played a crucial role in helping to change the course of US policy toward Vietnam. Culbert asks: 'how does one reconcile the persuasive conclusions of Daniel Hallin . . . that in general, television followed elite opinion, or had little demonstrable impact on policy-making in Vietnam, with the testimony of those who insist that . . . footage did affect them?' (Culbert 1998: 430). Focusing upon the impact of the infamous footage of General Loan summarily executing an armed civilian and the claims of various actors that they were influenced by the coverage, Culbert (1998: 437) concludes:

> The Loan execution is the most visually significant footage to come out of the war; it merits careful attention precisely because it defines the potential of the medium for influencing elite and mass opinion . . . Its impact related to a changing climate of opinion which found policy-makers as well as average citizens worried as to whether the USA's Vietnam policy merited continued support. In this moment of doubt and uncertainty, a visual microcosm purporting to show the actual practice of justice by the government of South Vietnam offered persuasive . . . evidence which gave people looking for factual reasons to justify a change in policy an opportunity to do so.

The debate between Hallin and Culbert will be returned to, and reconciled, in the next chapter. For now the important point to note is that elite manufacturing consent theory fails to tackle the question of media effects on policy and equates a passive news media with reliance on political elite sources whether executive, legislative or otherwise.[19] As such, to the extent that both deny, or do not explore, the possibility that news media coverage might play a key role in policy formulation, the elite version of the manufacturing consent literature is correctly located alongside the executive version that denies the existence of any independent news media effect on policy.

With respect to the CNN effect debate, the assumption implicit in the CNN effect that news media have the power to move governments literature is clearly at odds with the well-tested manufacturing consent literature. The development of the policy–media interaction model in this study serves to reconcile such contrasting claims and offers instead a more nuanced, two-way understanding of the direction of influence between the news media and the state. This task will be returned to in the next chapter. Our attention turns now to a review of the handful of notable attempts that have been made to subject the CNN effect to careful and considered analysis. These accounts do not constitute, either individually or collectively, a comprehensive assessment of the CNN effect. However, the research does provide important method-ological guidelines and suggested lines of inquiry and these are drawn upon in Chapter 2 when formulating the policy–media interaction model and the research design of this study.

Observing the 'unobservable'

The central aim of CNN effect research has been to establish the degree of media influence on policy-makers when they are deliberating over whether to intervene during a humanitarian crisis. Unfortunately influence cannot be observed in any obvious or straightforward fashion. We cannot see inside the minds of policy-makers and directly observe news media influence at work. This is a point Carruthers (2000: 208) makes when she states that 'debate about the impact of television during humanitarian disasters eludes empirical verification'. The most common approach to observing the 'unob-servable' is via an interview-based research strategy and involves asking policy-makers directly for their assessment of the importance of the news media.[20] This strategy rests upon the assumption that media influence can be observed in a direct manner (by policy-makers) who can then relate the 'truth' of what happened back to the researcher. This work is reviewed first. A second strategy employed involves systematic and theoretically informed case study research. For example Steven Livingston and Todd Eachus (1995), Martin Shaw (1996) and Jonathan Mermin (1997) have conducted in-depth studies pertaining to one case of intervention.[21] These researchers are considered second.

Interview-based research

Nik Gowing (1994 and 1996), Larry Minear, Colin Scott and Thomas G. Weiss (1997) and Warren Strobel (1997) have produced work covering a number of instances of intervention based largely on interview data. Their work is unsystematic in that no explicit research strategy is employed and no specific question is consistently examined. Instead the authors examine a range of relevant questions pertaining to the policy–media relationship. No theory of media–state relations informs the work nor is there any concept of how the news media might come to influence the policy process.

Two things are striking about the interview-based studies: the difficulty each has in measuring the precise impact which the media have on policy, specifically whether or not the media influence humanitarian intervention, and the significance each attaches to policy certainty (and uncertainty) in determining media influence. Let us deal with each in turn.

Starting with the impact that the media are supposed to have on foreign policy, the various authors struggle for intellectual clarity. Gowing[22] for example admits that media coverage can change 'overall [government] strategy', though only on very rare occasions (Gowing 1996: 88). However he never really defines what he means by overall strategy and therefore leaves the reader unsure as to whether the media can influence decisions to intervene during humanitarian crises (Gowing 1996: 86–90). One detects the same lack of precision in Strobel. He argues at one point that there is 'little evidence of a *push* [i.e. cause intervention] effect . . . nor is there evidence of a pull [i.e. cause withdrawal] effect' (Strobel 1997: 212). But elsewhere he speculates that the media 'can exert strong influence' on policy (Strobel 1997: 215–16), that news media reports can play a 'supplementary role' in policy formulation (Strobel 1997: 216), that 'news media reports can have a decided effect on policy and then that news media do not have an independent effect on policy but only facilitate 'others' agendas' (Strobel 1997: 216). This analytical confusion leaves one unsure as to what role the media do play exactly during humanitarian crises. The same lack of precision can be found in the volume, *The News Media, Civil Wars and Humanitarian Action*. The different contributors to the volume look in detail at US intervention in northern Iraq in 1991. They argue that media pressure built upon a perceived Western obligation toward the Kurds in order to create a rationale for humanitarian intervention (Minear *et al.* 1997: 51). Yet once again it is never clear how important the media were. They could get to grips better here if they differentiated between immediate and underlying causes. For example, the perceived Western obligation toward the Kurds could have been described as the underlying causes of the intervention decision. Media pressure would then be understandable as the immediate factor in causing intervention. Instead, what we are presented with is a good deal of loose speculation about 'complex systems' (Minear *et al.* 1997: 57), 'fluid interplay' and a 'rich and diverse relationship' (Minear *et al.* 1997: 46) between media coverage and policy outcomes – all of which sounds reasonable enough but does little to clarify things or prove a direct causal relationship between news coverage and policy decisions.

If the interview-based research fails to offer clear answers regarding the significance of the CNN effect on humanitarian intervention, it does highlight the key role 'policy certainty' plays in determining media influence.

Gowing approvingly quotes Kofi Annan who has observed that 'when governments have a clear policy . . . then television has little impact'; however 'when there is a problem, and the policy has not been thought' through 'they have to do something or face a public relations disaster' (Gowing 1996: 85–6). Strobel is even more certain. He notes that 'the effect of real-time television is directly related to the . . . coherence . . . of existing policy' (Strobel 1997: 219). The contributors to the Minear volume come to much the same conclusion. Indeed, in their view, there is an inverse relationship between policy clarity and media influence. Hence, when policy is unclear or ill defined the media can indeed have some influence on policy; on the other hand, 'the media effect on policy decreases as the clarity of strategic interest increases' (Minear *et al.* 1997: 73). This insight provides an important avenue of inquiry for this study and will be drawn upon when devising the policy–media interaction model. More generally, the research is let down by its failure to offer a clear understanding of the nature and significance of news media impact on the policy process. As I shall explain next these shortcomings are most likely the result of over-reliance on interview data and the absence of a theory-based research strategy. I shall deal with each in turn.

The problem with interviews

As a method of measuring news media influence, the interview approach confronts formidable problems. First, policy-makers are likely to distort the impact of the news media when discussing decisions they have been involved in by either over-estimating or under-estimating media impact. Second, quite apart from the issue of deliberate bias, asking policy-makers to remember events of years past means that research findings are vulnerable to the 'failings and selectivity of memory' (Kramer 1990: 213). Such problems can be compensated for 'if adequate documentary evidence is available [e.g. details of meetings]' (Kramer 1990: 212 and 213) but, because post-Cold War interventions are so recent, classified material is unavailable to the researcher. Finally, and perhaps most seriously, even if memory is free from both the self-interests of policy-makers and the inadequacy of memory, interviews with different actors in the policy process tend to yield divergent accounts of what happened and why.[23] The problem here is that a policy-maker's assessment of what is, and what is not, important with regard to any given decision is largely a matter of interpretation and perspective.

Given these points, a research strategy based *only* on questioning policy-makers directly about levels of news media influence is unlikely to produce reliable or indeed valid research findings. Indeed, in *Impact: How the Press Affects Federal Policy-making*, Linsky (1986: 87) supports this point arguing 'officials cannot be expected to identify instances when they altered their own best judgment about a policy option because of influence they felt from newspapers and television'.

The importance of theory

Theory is crucial to how we understand the social world for three reasons. First, there exists general agreement throughout much of the social sciences that 'a theory of truth based upon correspondence with an external reality' (paraphrased from Hooker 1987: 33) is unavailable. This is the basis upon which positivism rests, at least in its unreconstructed form. Instead, the current state of thinking is that science (natural as well as social) does not explain the reality of the nature of things but rather that it artificially imposes structure by way of theory upon 'facts' or data which in turn enables us to understand the world. If we accept this position, theory becomes crucial to understanding the world. As Waltz argues (1997: 913–14), theory is the primary tool with which social scientists explain a 'circumscribed part of reality of whose true dimensions we can never be sure'. King *et al.* (1994: 8) make a closely related point when they argue that the task of science is to make descriptive and causal inferences 'beyond the immediate data to something broader that is not directly observed'. Accordingly, if we accept this epistemological position, relying upon direct questioning of policy-makers in order to recount the 'truth' of what happened without any theoretical basis is a flawed exercise.

Second, and on a more practical level, theory enables us to generate informed and logically coherent hypotheses about how and why phenomena occur. For example, a theory of the CNN effect can be used to specify the conditions under which the phenomenon occurs. In particular the theory should be built upon, or be consistent with, existing and well-tested theory. Once we have theorised the conditions under which the CNN effect occurs we can specify the observable implications of those conditions, and then search for them in a systematic and rigorous manner.

Third, whilst always acknowledging that our knowledge of a subject is always only partial and potentially subject to refutation at a later date, a theory-based approach to assessing the CNN effect allows for the accumulation and progression of our knowledge. The results of a theoretically informed research design can be used to refine or develop the starting theory whilst other researchers can critique both the theory (for example on grounds of internal consistency) and the research method. In this way, potential is provided for improving what we know about the CNN effect in a systematic and codified fashion. The interview-based research fails to meet any of these theoretical demands and as such hold little potential, on its own, to further our understanding of media influence on foreign policy-making.

Returning to the interview-based research, it is clear from the preceding discussion that the work is seriously undermined by its over-reliance on interview data and failure to employ a theoretical framework. Whilst the work gleans important and useful insights into the CNN effect, it is necessary, if we are to improve our understanding of the phenomenon, to develop a theoretically

19

informed approach to the question which does not involve journalistic quizzing of policy-makers as to their considered opinions.

Theory-based research

Martin Shaw's (1996) *Civil Society and Media in Global Crises* is a close analysis of the impact of news media coverage on the 1991 decision to intervene in northern Iraq during the Kurdish crisis. His work is based on an analysis of news bulletins and he describes how news media coverage of the plight of Kurdish refugees became increasingly critical of Western inaction. The qualitative analysis of news reports is juxtaposed with statements by Western leaders, also mainly taken from news bulletins, showing that they at first refused to intervene and then, when news media criticism reached a crescendo, altered policy and decided to intervene. The central claim Shaw makes is that 'news media coverage of suffering Kurdish refugees caused the unprecedented proposal for Kurdish safe havens' (Shaw 1996: 79). Importantly, Shaw's work highlights the importance of news media framing. He argues that it was a particular type of coverage that placed pressure on Western leaders to intervene:

> The graphic portrayal of human tragedy and the victims' belief in Western leaders was skilfully juxtaposed with the responsibility and the diplomatic evasions of those same leaders to create a political challenge which it became impossible for them to ignore.
>
> (Shaw 1996: 88)[24]

He also alludes to the importance of policy uncertainty arguing that 'it may be that the loss of policy certainty over strategy in the aftermath of the Cold War opened up a particular window for news media influence' (Shaw 1996: 181).

In general Shaw's work is more systematic than the interview-based research as it is based upon a thorough content analysis of news media reports. Refreshingly, he is also willing to make explicit whether or not the news media played a key role in producing an intervention and he attributes significant power to the news media, at least in the Kurdish intervention case. The drawback is Shaw's failure to analyse the policy processes involved in the Kurdish intervention decision. As noted above, the politicians' statements that he draws upon are taken from news media broadcasts. Shaw does not review either official statements or the work of commentators that might illuminate the reasoning behind the decision. Consequently other possible motivations for the intervention are left unexplored. This omission is particularly problematic in the case of US intervention in Iraq because some policy-makers claim that the primary motivation for the intervention revolved around geo-strategic concerns over cross-border refugee flows into

Turkey (Livingston 1997: 10). As such Shaw's causal inference that the news media precipitated intervention in northern Iraq during 1991, whilst plausible, is less than convincing.

Similar to Shaw, Steven Livingston and Todd Eachus (1995) and Jonathan Mermin (1997) offer sophisticated and in-depth analyses of the CNN effect, published in *Political Communication* and *Political Studies Quarterly* respectively. In their cases, however, the focus is instead on US intervention in Somalia during 1992. Their research analyses both news media content and the relevant policy process via consideration of official statements, documents and interviews with officials.[25] These two studies are by far the most methodologically and theoretically exacting considered so far and therefore have the potential to gain a level of insight that cannot be achieved either by broad-ranging and theoretically uninformed interview-based research or the analysis of news media content alone (Shaw 1996). Interestingly and importantly, both pieces of work conceptualise the CNN effect as a question of 'political control'.

The CNN effect as political control

For Mermin (1997) and Livingston and Eachus (1995), the CNN effect is not about whether the news media can influence policy-making but rather who is responsible for setting the news agenda:

> The question at the heart of the CNN effect is, who controls that capacity [to influence]. Believers in the CNN effect claim that the roles of the professional policy expert and diplomat have been undermined by media. To the degree that foreign policy is reactive to news content, the key decisions are those made by reporters, producers, and editors. In this view, foreign policy decision has become epiphenomenal to new decision-making.
>
> (Livingston and Eachus 1995: 415)

By defining the CNN effect in this manner the task of the authors is then to determine who was setting the news agenda. If it were the case that journalists alone had been setting the media agenda, then the CNN effect would have been present regarding US intervention in Somalia. If, on the other hand, it was politicians or particular policy-makers setting the news agenda then the CNN effect would not be present in the case in hand. As such their work analyses news sources rather than news media effects on the policy process.

This conceptual approach reflects elements of the CNN effect debate and manufacturing consent theory discussed earlier. First, the debate within foreign policy circles, which as we saw was motivated by a concern over loss of policy control to actors outside government, was very much concerned with who is setting the news media agenda. By analysing the sources of news media reports this conceptual approach can determine if it really is the case that non-governmental actors have gained control of the policy process. Second, the elite version of the manufacturing consent paradigm equates media reliance on elite sources with a passive and non-influential media. This is similar to the conceptualisation by Livingston and Eachus and Mermin where the CNN effect is deemed not to exist if *elites* are setting the news agenda and, conversely, to exist if *non-elites* are setting the media agenda. The question of the utility of this conceptualisation of the CNN effect will be returned to shortly.

The research conducted by these authors convincingly highlights how an array of political actors (including middle-ranking executive officials, members of Congress and aid workers) set the news media agenda on Somalia. Mermin (1997: 403) concludes:

> It is likely that television news contributed to the decision of the Bush administration to act in Somalia . . . yet if television contributed to the emergence of Somalia as a political liability for the President in August and a threat to his legacy in November, it had powerful outspoken allies in Washington, whose efforts to get Somalia on to the news in the first place appear to have been indispensable.

Having defined the CNN effect as a question of political control they therefore conclude that, because it was officials setting the news media agenda and not the journalists, the US decision to intervene in Somalia is not a case of the CNN effect. As with elite manufacturing consent theory, media reliance on elite sources is, with respect to the CNN effect, equated with a passive and non-influential news media. By adopting this conceptualisation of the CNN effect their work successfully debunks both the myth that journalists alone 'discovered' the crisis in Somalia and the simplistic notion that political actors in Washington were merely passive receivers of the issues raised by journalists. As noted earlier when discussing elite manufacturing consent, however, news sources do not disprove news effects and their work only partially challenges the CNN effect because they do not directly address the question of whether or not news media coverage caused senior policy-makers to intervene in Somalia. Surprisingly, even though they argue Somalia was not a case of the CNN effect, according to their conceptualisation of it, they assume that news media coverage *was* a factor in influencing senior policy-makers to intervene in Somalia (Livingston and Eachus 1995: 427; Mermin 1997: 402). Specifically, Mermin (1997: 386) writes:

> The argument that television contributed to US intervention is supported by the chronology of events and news stories presented in this study; there is no reason to doubt that the appearance of Somalia on American television just before major changes in US policy in

August and November of 1992 influenced the decision of the Bush administration to act.

The CNN effect as political control reconsidered

It is contended here that the definition employed by these researchers of the CNN effect is inadequate. By failing to question if news media coverage influenced senior policy-makers and assuming instead that it did, their research 'black boxes' the dynamics between news media coverage and the policy process. In doing so their work masks two important and unanswered questions regarding the purported power of the news media. First, Mermin (1997) and Livingston and Eachus (1995) cannot provide evidence either for or against the thesis that, by compelling senior policy-makers to respond to emotive reporting of suffering people, news media coverage actually influences intervention during humanitarian crises. This is particularly important for those in humanitarian circles who wish to know why Western states intervene during humanitarian crises. Second, whilst news media coverage has been associated with recent interventions it has also accompanied instances of non-intervention, for example, non-intervention during the 1994 genocide in Rwanda. Analysing the sources of news reports might be able to explain why journalists covered, for example, both Rwanda and Somalia. But it cannot explain why news media coverage appeared to influence intervention in Somalia but was unable to in Rwanda. Answering this question requires us to move beyond news sources to an analysis of news media content and its influence on the policy process. In short, the definition of the problem in hand adopted by Mermin, Livingston and Eachus tends to sidestep the question of actual news media impact on the policy process.

The need for systematic and theoretically informed research

Reviewing the debate outlined so far, the ending of the Cold War and with it the 'Cold War prism' (Williams 1993: 315) imposed on news reports, coupled with the arrival of real-time media technologies, has offered at least a prima facie case for the existence of more powerful and influential news media. Current debate, however, has been hampered by undemonstrated assertions concerning the CNN effect. It is perhaps of no surprise then that several key commentators have noted the lack of progress made in understanding the CNN effect. Writing in *The Media at War*, Carruthers (2000: 207) states 'most agree that television coverage of foreign events has some impact on policy-making. The dispute is over when, why and to what degree.' More forcefully Livingston (1997: 1) states 'despite numerous symposia, books, articles, and research fellowships devoted to unravelling the CNN effect, success at clarifying it . . . has been minimal'. Specifically, what is required, and what this study aims to do, is to conduct research in order to establish the scope and significance of media influence upon decisions to intervene during humanitarian crises. In order to do this it is necessary to conduct a systematic and theoretically informed analysis of intervention cases which employs a variety of research strategies, rather than relying upon interview data only, and focus upon the actual influence of news coverage on the policy process, rather than news sources. The task we turn to next is the development of a theory of media influence, the policy–media interaction model, which will form the basis of this study.

2

DEVELOPING A THEORY
OF MEDIA INFLUENCE

Taken together the studies reviewed in Chapter 1, coupled with the insights provided by manufacturing consent theory, provide a basis for devising a theoretical model of news media influence. The idea of policy certainty as a key factor in determining whether or not the news media influence the policy process was widely referred to throughout much of the CNN effect research (Gowing 1996: 85–6; Shaw 1996: 219; Minear *et al.* 1997: 73; Strobel 1997: 219). Specifically, it appears that, as policy certainty decreases, news media influence increases and that, as policy becomes more certain, the influence of news media coverage is reduced. The idea of media influence at points of policy uncertainty is also consistent with the broader policy studies literature that points to a correlation between dissensus amongst policy-making elites and the ability of 'external' actors to influence policy formulation (see for example Baumgartner and Jones 1993). Drawing upon this insight, we can theorise that news media impact on the policy process is greatest when policy is uncertain.

A second key insight of the research was the importance of the way in which news media coverage was framed in determining the political impact of that coverage (Shaw 1996: 88). The crucial point here is that news media reports do not 'objectively' reflect humanitarian crises. Rather, they report crises in particular and often very different ways. The emotive and graphic coverage of the Kurds in 1991 clearly pressured politicians to 'do something'. This pressure would not have existed if news media reports had been framed in a less emotive and more distancing manner. Accordingly we can theorise that news media influence is greatest when coverage is framed so as to criticise existing government policy and empathise with the plight of suffering people. Conversely, when coverage is framed so as to produce an emotional distance from the plight of suffering people, the likely political effect will be to deter politicians from intervening. These two insights provide us with the starting point for devising the policy–media interaction model. Before proceeding, however, policy uncertainty and media framing need to be clearly defined and operationalised.

Policy uncertainty

Unfortunately, policy uncertainty remains an underdeveloped concept in CNN effect research. For example Minear *et al.* (1997: 73) refer to news media impact when 'policy-making is weak or cynical' whilst Gowing (1996: 86) refers to policy uncertainty in terms of 'moments of policy panic'. Alternatively, Shaw's use of the term is far more general, noting that the whole post-Cold War era is characterised by uncertainty over foreign policy. In terms of providing evidence of policy uncertainty, the researchers considered either tend to rely on their own considered opinion of levels of policy certainty or to refer to anecdotal evidence provided by policy-makers. This failure to define and operationalise policy uncertainty has meant that its utility, in terms of assessing news media power, is limited. For example, Gowing (1996: 86) understands policy uncertainty (or policy panic) as occurring when the news media covers unexpected events and politicians literally do not know how to respond. It seems likely that this narrow definition leads him (1996: 86) to argue that news media impact is rare. Alternatively, Shaw (1996: 181) notes that the whole post-Cold War era is characterised by uncertainty regarding the foreign policies of Western governments. Understanding policy uncertainty in these broad terms allows Shaw to argue that news media impact is far more profound. Without defining, conceptualising and then specifying the observable implications of policy uncertainty, it is difficult even to start to determine levels of policy certainty and, therefore, the scope of news media influence on policy. This study intends to rectify this nebulous state of affairs with regard to our understanding of policy uncertainty.

Drawing upon the work of Allison (1971), George (1989), Smith and Clarke (1985), Hilsman (1987) and Welch (1992) we can conceptualise policy-making as the outcome of a complex bargaining process between a set of sub-systems in government (for full details of this literature and its contribution to the definition of policy uncertainty see Appendix A). Building upon this theory we can define policy uncertainty as a function of the degree of consensus and co-ordination of the sub-systems of the executive with respect to an issue. If an issue suddenly arises and no policy is in place, or if there is disagreement, conflict of interest or uncertainty owing to an ambiguous policy between the sub-systems of the executive, there can be said to be policy uncertainty. Conversely policy certainty is the result of agreement and co-ordination between the sub-systems of the executive.

Observing policy uncertainty

In order to ground this theoretical discussion it is necessary to place it in the context of the US executive. The key decision-making body in the US government regarding the use of force is the executive with the Constitution allocating the President as Commander in Chief of US forces. Here we might reasonably expect disagreement on policy to manifest itself at two levels: the first level occurring within the key policy-making sub-system in the White House and the second level occurring between the collection of sub-systems making up the executive. I shall deal with each in turn.

In terms of policy sub-systems the most important (i.e. powerful) sub-system is that of the President and his immediate group of 'favoured' policy advisers. With respect to any given policy we might expect the degree of agreement and consensus between these 'players' to vary across time. Importantly, disagreement will not necessarily be due to the bureaucratic position of any given player, for example the Secretary of State for Defense promoting the interests of the military. Rather, within the context of crisis decision-making we might expect that, at least some of the time, disagreement and agreement will develop from the desire of individuals to achieve the 'best outcome' in terms of US interests.

In addition to the White House, the other key policy sub-systems in the US executive are the Pentagon, State Department, National Security Council, the Joint Chiefs of Staff and the CIA. In broader terms we might expect to observe varying degrees of consensus between all these sub-systems with respect to a given issue. Disagreement might manifest itself within the White House sub-system, where heads of each department are present, but it might also manifest itself in terms of different sub-systems pursuing different agendas. Finally, we need to define a typology of policy states in order to specify precisely the observable implications of policy uncertainty (this is developed from the work of George (1989); for full details see Appendix A). First, policy might be 'unstable . . . [and] contradictory' (George 1989: 114) when sub-systems are in disagreement with each other. This type of policy can be defined as an *inconsistent* or *undecided policy*. Second, the idea of 'no policy' (George 1989: 114) would appear to be useful, especially in the context of crisis policy-making where unexpected events frequently occur. We can define this type of policy simply as *no policy*. Finally, policy might be expected to change frequently when there exists a lack of commitment amongst the policy sub-systems to that policy. We can define this as *wavering policy.*

Taken together these three types of policy, if observed either within a policy sub-system or between sub-systems, can be taken to be indicative of policy uncertainty within the executive. In order to assess levels of policy certainty a variety of sources was drawn upon including US executive sub-system press briefings (White House, Pentagon and State Department), published documents, secondary accounts and primary interviewing. For further details on the approach to gauging policy certainty, see Appendix A.

Media framing[1]

With respect to this study a key task is to establish precisely what kind of pressure news media coverage might have been exerting. To date a considerable literature on news media framing of disasters and humanitarian crises has accumulated which can be drawn upon in order to guide our operationalisation of news media framing. News media coverage of humanitarian crises tends to fall into one of two distinct forms. With respect to the 'post-Cold War [dis]Order', a series of researchers and commentators have highlighted how the theme of 'ancient ethnic hatreds' has been a common interpretive framework for journalists seeking to explain crises (for example see van der Gaag and Nash 1987; Myers *et al.* 1996; Campbell 1998: 51–4; Allen and Seaton 1999; Beattie *et al.* 1999). Indeed, policy-makers have regularly invoked the discourse of 'ancient ethnic hatreds' in order to justify non-intervention. For example, William Shawcross (2000: 83) describes how US Secretary of State Warren Christopher employed this language when justifying US non-involvement during the early part of the Bosnian War:

> Christopher told Congress that the conflict had 'evolved into a war of all against all . . . a struggle between three groups . . . each possessing deep distrust and ancient hatreds for each other'. He believed that the Bosnian combatants were not ready to make peace and that it would therefore be dangerous for Clinton to insert US troops between them.

In addition to the 'ancient ethnic hatreds' frame, Alison Preston has also described how much coverage of the war in Bosnia focused on questions of diplomacy and 'high' politics. She refers to this kind of reporting as a narrative template of *distance*. She argues (1996: 112) that 'the template of "distance" can be laid over the subject matter of diplomacy or politics; dispassionate documentation as a reporting style; a target audience of elites; and an emphasis on the complicated or difficult'. If there is elite consensus over an issue this kind of coverage tends to defer to official policy in accordance with Bennett's indexing hypothesis and there is unlikely to be a significant level of coverage that challenges or criticises official policy.

These two modes of reporting can be suitably labelled as

1 *distance framing* in that the style of coverage creates emotional distance between the audience and the people suffering in a conflict and
2 *support framing* in that official policy is, in effect, deferred to. Distance and support framing is implicitly supportive of a government policy opposed to military intervention and as such either implicitly or explicitly promotes a policy of non-intervention.

A second and radically different way of framing conflicts focuses instead on the victims of crises. The pre-eminent example of this style of journalism is the famous BBC report by Michael Burke and Mohammed Amin of the 1984 Ethiopian famine in which graphic footage of starving people in refugee camps shocked TV audiences around the world. This kind of coverage tends to focus upon the suffering of individuals, identifying them as victims in need of 'outside' help, although it only occasionally highlights the political dimension of their struggle (for example see van der Gaag and Nash 1987; Benthall 1993; Preston 1996; Philo *et al.* 1999). Indeed, as Philo *et al.* (1999: 218) argue in relation to UK news media coverage of the refugee crisis at Goma in Zaire in 1994, such coverage tends to avoid underlying political and social issues preferring instead a discourse of simple humanitarianism which focuses on the requirements of aid agencies and short-term relief. Preston describes this type of framing as a 'narrative template of proximity' (Preston 1996: 112). She argues:

> The narrative template of 'proximity' can be laid over humanitarian issues, which in turn emphasised the geographic and societal closeness of the war [in Bosnia]. The ordinary individual was highlighted, encouraging empathy and also clarity: the simple imperative of personal suffering.

Policy-makers invoke this kind of framing when seeking to justify intervention during a humanitarian crisis. For example, in his 4 December 1992 live televised address to the Nation, George Bush Snr employed such framing when justifying the decision to send US troops to Somalia:

> The people of Somalia, especially the children of Somalia, need our help. We're able to ease their suffering. We must help them live. We must give them hope . . . Only the United States has the global reach to place a large security force on the ground in such a distant place quickly and efficiently and thus, save thousands of innocents from death.[2]

In addition, in situations where no government action is forthcoming, empathising coverage will often be accompanied by strong criticism of policy-makers. For example, as we saw in Chapter 1, Martin Shaw described how journalists juxtaposed news media coverage of suffering Kurds with the 'diplomatic evasions' (1996: 88) of Western leaders and in doing so created coverage that was critical of the non-intervention policy. These modes of reporting are labelled here as *empathy* and *critical* framing because the coverage encourages viewers to associate themselves with the suffering of people and criticises government inaction. With respect to this study, it is precisely this kind of coverage that creates a political imperative on policy-makers to 'do something'. Indeed, with respect to critical framing, Linsky (1986: 119) notes that negative coverage is one of the 'most important variables for big press impact' to occur because it demands the attention of policy-makers. It should also be noted that in situations where governments have already decided, for reasons unrelated to the media, to intervene, empathy coverage functions to support the policy of intervention.

In terms of measuring media frames, a combination of approaches was adopted involving both interpretive analysis and more systematic keyword analysis. In particular keywords relating to empathy/distance framing and critical/support framing were quantified. (Full details of the keywords and their justification are provided in Appendix B and in the individual case studies.) In summary, keywords such as 'women', 'children', 'elderly', 'people' and 'refugee' were associated with empathy framing whilst keywords such as 'fighter', 'men', 'soldier' and (for example 'Muslim') were some of the keywords associated with distance framing. Keywords associated with critical framing included negative descriptions of policy such as 'failing' whilst keywords associated with support framing included positive descriptions of policy such as 'succeeding'. For full details on the framing analysis and keyword test, see Appendix B.

Developing the policy–media interaction model

Having defined policy certainty and media framing we are now in a position to set out a theory of media influence. We can start by theorising that, in accordance with manufacturing consent theory, when there exists elite consensus over an issue the news media are unlikely to produce coverage that challenges that consensus. Here official government policy is, in effect, deferred to as described by executive manufacturing consent (see row 1 of Table 2.1). However, when there exists elite dissensus with respect to an issue, as predicted by elite manufacturing consent, news media coverage reflects this debate and we can expect to observe a variety of critical and supportive framing in news reports (see row 2 of Table 2.1). It is in this scenario that the news media have the potential, at least, to start to play a more active and influential role in policy debate. If journalists reflect the reference frames of one side of an elite debate they can become promoters, either consciously or otherwise, of the policy preferences of one particular elite group (see row 3 of Table 2.1).

If, however, there exists a high level of policy certainty within government we can theorise that the government will draw upon both its substantial resources and credibility as an information source in order to influence news media output (see row 3 of Table 2.1). Here we would expect news media to fall into line with official policy and elite dissensus might dissipate (Hallin 1986; Bennett 1990; Mermin 1999). If elite dissensus persisted, critical news media coverage might come head to head with policy certainty within the executive. However when policy-makers are set on a particular course of action they are unlikely to be influenced by news media coverage. Anthony Lake (former National Security advisor to the Clinton administration) asserts this point noting that, when policy is decided upon, news media coverage has little influence on the policy process.[3] Instead policy-makers are more likely to ride out the criticism and work harder to promote their chosen course of action

Table 2.1 The policy–media interaction model and theories of media–state relations

Level of elite consensus	Media–state relationship	Role of the media
Elite consensus	The media operate within 'sphere of consensus' and coverage reflects elite consensus on policy (Hallin 1986)	*Executive manufacturing consent:* the media remain uncritical and help build support for official policy
Elite dissensus	The media operate within 'sphere of legitimate controversy' (Hallin 1986) but overall coverage does not favour any side of the elite debate	The media reflect elite dissensus as predicted by Hallin (1986) and Bennett (1990) but remain non-influential
Elite dissensus but policy certainty within executive	The media operate within 'sphere of legitimate controversy' (Hallin 1986) but coverage, overall, becomes critical of government policy	Although coverage pressures government to change policy, policy certainty within executive means that media influence is resisted
Elite dissensus *plus* policy uncertainty within government	The media take sides in political debate and coverage becomes critical of government. The media are now active participants influencing elite debate	*'The CNN effect':* in conditions of policy uncertainty, critical media coverage provides bargaining power for those seeking a change in policy or makes policy-makers feel pressured to respond with a policy or else face a public relations disaster. Here the media can influence policy outcomes

through press briefings and public announcements. This notwithstanding, we should remain open to the possibility that, in a scenario where news media pressure is head to head with official policy, policy-makers might feel forced to change course especially if other factors are in play such as public or congressional pressure. This possibility will be evaluated in the conclusion through reference to the case study findings. For now the working assumption is that the media cannot influence policy-making when policy certainty exists.

Alternatively, if policy uncertainty in government combines with elite dissensus and critical and empathy-framed media coverage (in the case of a humanitarian crisis, see row 4 of Table 2.1) the conditions exist under which the CNN effect might occur. Set in this context of negative news media coverage, government is confronted with

31

1   the possibility that public opinion might be influenced by the negative media coverage
2   associated damage to government image and credibility caused by the 'bad press' and
3   the fact that policy-makers might themselves start to question the cogency of existing government policy.

Crucially, the greater the level of uncertainty over policy within the executive, the more vulnerable the policy process is to the influence of negative media coverage. In this scenario, a number of factors related to the existence of policy uncertainty might come into play. First, if it is disagreement between executive policy sub-systems that is the cause of policy uncertainty (i.e. policy is *inconsistent* or *undecided*), critical media coverage might provide additional bargaining power to those policy-makers seeking a change in policy direction. As Strobel (1997: 211) notes, 'at times, media reports become an ally for an entire administration, or individual members of it, seeking to pursue new policies'. Linsky (1986: 114) makes a similar point in his study of media impact on policy-making, noting that the press can 'have an influence on the capacity of policy-makers to turn their ideas into policies that are adopted and implemented'. Second, if it is the case that policy uncertainty is the result of there simply being *no* policy in place, policy-makers are liable to feel pressured to respond to critical coverage or else face a public relations disaster and criticism for being 'caught on the hop'. Here policy might be formulated, at least in the first instance, primarily as a way of counteracting negative publicity. Finally, not only does policy uncertainty make policy-makers susceptible to media influence, it also means that government is ill-equipped to respond to journalists by drawing upon its substantial public relations apparatus. In other words, without a clearly articulated policy line with which to respond to critical coverage, policy-makers become even more vulnerable to a hostile press, the so-called feeding frenzy (Sabato 1991). As O'Heffernan (1994: 241) argues

> a condition that can be even more important is the cohesion of the executive. Mixed messages or disagreement from within the executive that makes its way to the media seriously undermines public-relations efforts and enhances the opportunity and likelihood of adversarial treatment of real policy positions.

The policy–media interaction model: offering an advanced two-way understanding of media–state relations[4]

By way of example, we can apply this model of influence to US policy toward the Vietnam War. As described in Chapter 1, Hallin (1986) argues that because news media coverage only followed elite dissensus over the war it played little part in influencing US policy. At the same time Culbert (1998) claims the media played a far more significant role than that suggested by Hallin. The policy–media interaction model offers a way of reconciling these contrasting claims.

Hallin's analysis highlights how news media coverage of the war in Vietnam, up until 1968, was largely supportive of the war and rarely published material that criticised or questioned official US policy. This, according to Hallin, reflected elite consensus regarding US policy toward Vietnam. During this period we can characterise media coverage as manufacturing consent for executive policy. During 1967 and 1968, however, concern was growing amongst foreign policy elites and within the US administration as to the viability of US intervention in Vietnam. As Culbert points out, '[l]arge numbers of Americans – policy-makers, soldiers in the field and average citizens – had serious doubts about the wisdom of America's Vietnam policy by Autumn 1967' (Culbert 1998: 434). More specifically, Hallin (1986: 159–60) argues:

> A basic disagreement had . . . emerged over US strategy. Westmoreland and the Joint Chiefs believed increased military pressure would raise North Vietnamese and NLF losses to the point that they could no longer go on with the war. Their civilian opponents, concentrated primarily in the Office of Systems Analysis, argued that the North Vietnamese could sustain indefinitely the losses they would suffer even with substantial increases in US military activity.

On 31 January 1968, the forces from northern Vietnam combined with National Liberation Front (NLF) resistance forces throughout southern Vietnam to launch the Tet Offensive. Although technically speaking a military failure, the offensive was an embarrassment for the US government which had been maintaining that the war was being won. The offensive also provided a wealth of dramatic and shocking news reports as the war spilled over on to the streets of Saigon. The execution of an armed civilian was the most graphic and brutal image of this offensive, and also perhaps of the whole war. One of the most notable journalistic judgements during this period was made by CBS commentator Walter Cronkite:

> To say that we are closer to victory today is to believe, in the face of the evidence, the optimists who have been wrong in the past. To suggest we are on the edge of defeat is to yield to unreasonable pessimism. To say that we are mired in stalemate seems the only reasonable, yet unsatisfactory, conclusion. But it is increasingly clear to this reporter that the only rational way out then would be to negotiate, not as victors, but as honorable people who lived up to their pledge to defend Democracy, and did the best they could.
>
> (CBS special broadcast, 27 February 1968,
> quoted in Culbert 1998: 430)

In short, during this period of crisis, elite dissensus started to be reflected in media coverage (see row 2 of Table 2.1). However, the divisions within the sub-systems of the US executive detailed above suggests that dissensus (policy uncertainty) was also present within the US executive itself. In terms of the theoretical model, this suggests that the policy process would have been susceptible to outside (i.e. media) influence. With respect to media coverage, whilst much coverage clearly challenged official policy, in effect adopting the perspective of those opposed to escalation in Vietnam, whether or not overall news media coverage took sides in the debate over Vietnam is beyond the scope of this speculative exercise. Some of the evidence provided by Hallin, however, does suggest media coverage reflected the perspective of those opposed to official policy. For example, Hallin's framing analysis indicates twice as many unfavourable editorial commentary *vis-à-vis* administration supporters as there were against the critics of the war (Hallin 1994: 44). Also, after the Tet Offensive, there were ten times as many negative references to the democratic credentials of the US-sponsored government in southern Vietnam as there were positive and 5.8 times as many negative references to the morale of US troops as there were positive (Hallin 1994: 45). Hallin's figures also show that during the Tet Offensive, critics of the administration were quoted twice as often in comparison with supporters of the administration. Overall, whilst this evidence is not conclusive it does suggest a prima facie case that media coverage during and after the Tet Offensive took sides in the elite debate over whether to escalate or seek negotiation and withdrawal. In short, the conditions of policy uncertainty and critically framed media coverage appear to have been present in this case, therefore indicating the possibility of media influence on policy.

We can now reconcile Hallin's thesis that media coverage did not influence US policy with Culbert's claim that it did. The combination of policy uncertainty and critical news media coverage meant that policy-makers were susceptible to news media influence during this period. Culbert documents the influence of media in the following quote:

> Harry McPherson, counsel to the President . . . feels that the Cronkite special 'had a huge impact on Johnson and his sense of crumbling public support for the war'. McPherson feels that Johnson 'liked and trusted' Cronkite, a fellow Texan . . . McPherson thinks that Johnson watched television not so much for information as to 'gauge what its impact on the public would be'.
>
> (Culbert 1987: 227 cited in Culbert 1998: 432)

In doing so media coverage, having passively reflected elite consensus prior to 1968, became an active participant in elite debate by adopting the side (whether deliberately or not) of those opposed to the war and, in the presence of executive policy uncertainty, influencing key policy-makers to move to withdrawal. In short, Hallin is most likely correct in arguing that critical news media coverage followed rather than caused elite dissensus over Vietnam. But Culbert might also be correct because this coverage actually took sides during the elite debate over policy and, in doing so, helped shift US policy toward withdrawal. In short, by theorising the conditions under which the media influence policy and building upon manufacturing consent theory, the policy–media interaction model enables us to make sense of both arguments.

Wolfsfeld's political contest model of media–state relations

In his 1997 work, *The Media and Political Conflict*, Wolfsfeld develops a political contest model of the media and offers a development of elite manufacturing consent theory. As we shall see shortly, when combined with the policy–media interaction, Wolfsfeld's model facilitates a more comprehensive overview of the ways in which the media might play a more influential role than is suggested by manufacturing consent theory.

Wolfsfeld's goal is to identify the conditions under which news media coverage comes to play an active role in political debate and, in doing so, achieve a more nuanced understanding of the relationship between the news media and government. Wolfsfeld's focus of concern is the relationship between non-elite groups in society that seek to challenge government and political change. His central claim is that, whilst the news media normally function to reflect, and even mobilise support for, dominant views in society, there are times when they serve the interests of marginalised groups. The bulk of the first section of his book is devoted to specifying more precisely the conditions under which marginalised groups, to which he refers to as 'challengers', can come both to set media agendas and to influence political outcomes. Out of a number of variables which determine whether or not challengers are able to seize control of the media agenda, he argues that '[t]he authorities' degree of control over the political environment is the key situational variable that determines whether the news media will play an independent role in a political conflict' (Wolfsfeld 1997: 24). He also employs the concept of framing in order to highlight how media coverage can effectively take the side of challengers by promoting their particular perception of the political issue at stake.

As one example of an instance during which a challenger was able to attain control of both the media agenda and the way in which media coverage was framed, Wolfsfeld analyses the case of the Palestinian Intifada during 1987. Summarising, Wolfsfeld (1997: 167–8) argues that during this period of unrest in the occupied territories, the Israeli government lost control of the media agenda because

a   'they were unable to take control over the political environment' b   the internationalisation of the Palestinians' struggle levelled the balance of power between Palestinians and the Israeli government and

c   the access of journalists to the sites of civil unrest meant that the resulting footage of unarmed Palestinians engaging with Israeli soldiers cast the Israelis, on balance, in a negative light.

As a result, a frame of 'injustice and defiance' (Wolfsfeld 1997: 168) prevailed in media reports that favoured the cause of the Palestinians. However, whilst Wolfsfeld's study aims to develop an interactive theory of media–state relations, his political contest model focuses primarily on explaining when and how challengers can come to set the media agenda.[5] As such, the model relates largely to the question of the relationship between news sources and the news. For example, the entire chapter detailing his study of the 1987 Palestinian Intifada deals with explaining how and why the Palestinians were able to secure favourable media coverage. The question of whether this favourable (from the Palestinians' point of view) coverage actually influenced political outcomes is tackled in Wolfsfeld's conclusion. However, even here Wolfsfeld does not consider in any significant depth the question of whether official Israeli policy was changed by the pro-Palestinian media coverage. He does highlight how the actions of the Israeli authorities, in particular the military, were shaped by concern over media coverage (Wolfsfeld 1997: 206):

> Israeli authorities were especially concerned with the damage the Intifada was doing to their image . . . the Israelis spent a considerable amount of time and effort attempting to control the damage from the news reports coming out of the territories . . . One of the clearest examples of Israeli adaptation to the news media occurred in the field. The presence of the news media had a direct influence on restraining soldiers' behaviour.

Wolfsfeld also highlights the influence of the media coverage on the Palestinians (Wolfsfeld 1997: 207–8). However, he only starts to tackle the question of media impact on policy on the last page of his discussion regarding the Intifada (Wolfsfeld 1997: 208–9) when he claims that

1   media coverage changed the balance of power between the Palestinians and the Israelis and

2   that it was media coverage which caused the US to intervene diplomatically in the crisis (although he references another researcher's study as evidence for the latter claim).

However, at no point does Wolfsfeld make explicit the effect the media coverage had on the actual substance of Israeli policy. In short, Wolfsfeld's political contest model and case studies provide a strong theoretical account that explains why challengers can come to set the media agenda, but it does not theorise the link between the resulting media coverage and actual policy outcomes.

This is where the policy–media interaction model illuminates a further dimension of the media–state relationship by theorising precisely when media coverage might influence policy outcomes. By providing an understanding of the conditions under which media coverage might influence policy outcomes, the policy–media interaction model, in combination with Wolfsfeld's political contest model, offers the potential of a more complete theory of media–state relations. Whilst Wolfsfeld's model explains the sources of elite dissensus, identifying when challengers can come to set media agendas, the policy–media interaction model explains the precise conditions under which critical news coverage influences and shapes policy outcomes. With respect to the frequency and significance of media influence, the policy–media interaction model would suggest that media influence is likely to be a frequent occurrence within the context of elite debate over policy. In contrast, Wolfsfeld's analysis of non-elites securing the media agenda is likely to occur more rarely although, when it does, the significance of media influence (in terms of causing large-scale political change) might well be argued to be greater. In either instance, the importance of the media regarding political outcomes is far greater than allowed for by existing manufacturing consent theory.

To summarise, the policy–media interaction model offers a two-way understanding of media–state relations which advances media theory beyond a simple effect/non-effect dichotomy, helping resolve debates such as those between Hallin and Culbert over the Vietnam War. When combined with recent work by Wolfsfeld (1997) the model offers a more complete theoretical understanding of media–state relations.

Types of effect

The policy–media interaction model is designed to help identify instances when media coverage comes to play a significant role in persuading policy-makers to pursue a particular policy. As such the model is designed to capture instances where media reports helped drive or push policy-makers down a particular path. This type of effect is suitably labelled a strong CNN effect because media coverage is a significant influence on the policy process and might operate as either a necessary or even sufficient factor in producing a particular policy outcome. It is crucial to note that describing the media as a necessary or sufficient factor (and therefore using the problematic language of causality) should not be taken to suggest that media coverage can necessarily force policy-makers to take a particular course of action. Rather the implication here is that media coverage becomes a significant factor in influencing policy-makers' decisions to act. The decision ultimately rests with the policy-makers but, without media coverage, the decision would not have been reached. In terms of defining the amount of coverage necessary in order to create pressure on policy-makers to act, a reasonable benchmark would be at least one front-page newspaper story per day and a major news segment on the evening news run within the opening ten minutes of the news. This level of coverage would have to be sustained over at least three or four days in order to force executive attention. It is hard to imagine anything less than this (i.e. stories relegated to the foreign news section or the tail-end of the evening news) being sufficient to influence a government to change policy. The possibility of a small number of reports creating a weak CNN effect will be considered shortly.

The strong CNN effect overlaps, but is not synonymous with, Steven Livingston's (1997: 6) agenda-setting effect. The difference between the two relates to the stage of the policy process. An agenda-setting strong CNN effect occurs during a 'problem identification stage' (Linsky 1986: 137) when media coverage helps place an issue on the policy-making agenda. Alternatively the strong CNN effect can also occur after an issue is on the policy agenda when media coverage influences policy-makers over the appropriate course of action to take. This might occur during 'solution formulation . . . when policy-makers are developing and sorting out the possible responses' or policy adoption when 'the options are being assessed and a choice is being made and disclosed' (Linsky 1986: 137). Beyond a strong CNN effect there are, however, other types of effect media might have with respect to humanitarian crises decision-making and these must be set out clearly before proceeding. These are a weak CNN effect, Livingston's (1997: 2) 'accelerant and impediment effects', a potential CNN effect and the enabling effect. In addition, and moving clearly away from the CNN effect and toward manufacturing consent, media coverage might simply report, in a relatively straightforward fashion, elite debate (Hallin 1986; Bennett 1990) or act so as to help build support for executive policy (Herman and Chomsky 1988).

The weak CNN effect

Livingston and Riley (1999) hypothesise that a media effect might occur when policy-makers are *personally* affected by random media reports that highlight a particular crisis (Livingston and Riley 1999). The implication of this hypothesis is that media coverage is not so much creating a *political imperative* for policy-makers to act, but rather serves to cause a politician to be *inclined* to take a particular course of action. Given the bureaucratic and political constraints upon policy-makers, the publication of only a few news reports is unlikely to have a large effect on any policy process. This does not, of course, apply to situations where a one-off shocking event hits the news headlines such as the fall of the Srebrenica 'safe area' in Bosnia in 1995 or the image of the dead US marine being dragged through the streets of Mogadishu,

Somalia. Clearly these events become major news stories instantaneously and have the potential to influence policy (i.e. these instances belong in the strong CNN effect category). Rather, with respect to just a handful of reports, say in the back pages of a newspaper or at the tail-end of the news, the idea of a policy-maker formulating policy, to any significant extent, based on such coverage is unlikely. This said, this type of coverage might be described as a weak CNN effect whereby media reports might incline policy-makers to act rather than create a political imperative to act. With respect to the thesis that media coverage influences intervention, the weak CNN effect thesis suggests the media play only a marginal role during intervention decisions. Certainly coverage would not be sufficient on its own to cause intervention and is unlikely even to be a necessary factor in influencing policy-makers to act. This notwithstanding, in cases where a strong CNN effect is not indicated either by the policy–media interaction model or additional research strategies, the possible presence of a weak CNN effect will be evaluated.

Accelerant and impediment effects

Livingston (1997) also notes the possibility of an accelerant[6] and impediment effect. An accelerant effect can occur when the media speed up the policy process and is particularly associated with the impact of real-time communication technologies and the concern that decision-making has been speeded up in today's real-time environment. This is an interesting and oft-cited effect of news media, especially during fast-breaking crises. It should, however, be kept conceptually distinct from the strong CNN effect for the following reason. In a particular case media coverage might well increase the speed with which policy-makers respond. But this possibility assumes, logically, that policy-makers would have acted in any case (only at a later date). If this is the case it does not make sense to understand the media as influencing actual policy outcomes, only the process of policy (specifically the timing of the policy process). In the context of trying to establish whether the media are a factor in causing intervention, an accelerant effect would suggest the media not being, in any meaningful sense, a cause of the intervention. Whether or not the media simply brought forward the inevitable or actually helped influence a policy outcome needs to be considered when evaluating instances of the strong CNN effect. In particular, consideration of alternative factors will help evaluate the causal significance of the media in these circumstances. If other factors appear insufficient to have produced a particular policy outcome, then our confidence in the causal role of the media will be increased.

The impediment effect, also labelled the 'body-bag effect' by Freedman (2000), relates to the fear of policy-makers that, once casualties are taken, public support for an intervention will rapidly wane. This is often labelled the Vietnam syndrome as it reflects the deeply held conviction within military and foreign policy circles, born out of their perception of the Vietnam war, that Western domestic populations are unable to tolerate casualties especially when perceived core national interests are not at stake. Clearly the impediment effect operates in opposition to the CNN effect with one pushing policy-makers to intervene during a humanitarian crisis and the other urging caution against involvement in one. It is important to note that the impediment effect works at two levels. The first relates to concern over the impact on domestic opinion of media coverage of US casualties. The second relates to the straightforward fact that if US casualties are taken, according to the Vietnam syndrome, public support is undermined whether or not there exists media attention. Again, when assessing media influence *vis-à-vis* intervention, due consideration must be given to the extent to which any possible CNN effect might be countered by the impediment effect.

Potential CNN effect

To an extent the strong CNN effect is concerned only with 'uni-linear media influence' (Carruthers 2000: 210) and does not take into account the possibility that policy-makers might consider potential future news media coverage when formulating policy. The impediment effect can operate at the potential level with policy-makers being deterred from intervention owing to fear of the potential negative news media coverage of casualties. This phenomenon is labelled the potential impediment effect. In addition policy-makers might decide to intervene during a humanitarian crisis in the expectation that ensuing positive news media coverage of humanitarian endeavour will reap political and electoral advantage. More plausibly, perhaps, policy-makers might decide to intervene because they believe that inaction will ultimately lead to negative news media publicity and public reaction. In cases where it is possible that potential news media coverage has shaped policy outcomes, this possibility will be evaluated.

Enabling effect

Another possible route via which media coverage might affect the policy process is through the process of enabling policy-makers to pursue a particular course of action. For example Frank Wisener, Under Secretary of State in the Bush Administration during the Somalia crisis, argues that media coverage 'enables and creates conditions . . . [by building] a domestic constituency for intervention'.[7] As noted in Chapter 1, Wheeler (2000: 165) makes a similar point suggesting that the media cannot force policy-makers to intervene during a humanitarian crisis but can enable policy-makers to act by creating a constituency for intervention. It is important to keep the enabling effect distinct from the strong CNN effect for the following reason. It is certainly possible that media coverage opens up the options for policy-makers and whether or not any given intervention was simply enabled by media coverage needs to be considered. However, enabling is not the same as setting the policy-making agenda or helping persuade policy-makers to take action where they would otherwise not. Indeed, in terms of media–state relations, the enabling effect is much closer to the manufacturing consent model in which policy-makers utilise the media to their own ends. This point is reinforced by the fact that policy-makers, in any case, can do much to set the media agenda if they wish to act in particular crises and are not hostage to whether or not the media choose to cover a conflict as implied by the enabling effect. Accordingly the enabling effect is conceptually distinct from the CNN effect and does not describe instances when policy-makers are forced or pressured to take action. The possibility of coverage having enabled policy-makers to pursue a particular course of action is considered where appropriate. To a large extent, however, the policy–media interaction model helps distinguish instances of the enabling effect from the strong CNN effect. For example, the presence of critical coverage and uncertain policy is indicative of policy-makers being persuaded or caused to act. Alternatively, the presence of policy certainty in favour of intervention and empathy framing with no criticism of government would be indicative of policy-makers having exploited pro-intervention media coverage in order to pursue their policy objectives. At the same time additional research strategies are employed in order to assess whether coverage simply enabled policy-makers to intervene or caused a strong CNN effect to occur.

This leads us to a final point, that above and beyond the aforementioned effects, media coverage can, of course, function simply to reflect policy debate (Hallin 1986; Bennett 1990) or function to manufacture consent (Herman and Chomsky 1988) for executive policy. When assessing the role of the media all the aforementioned media effects and roles need, where appropriate, to be considered.

Testing the CNN effect

The policy–media interaction model serves, in effect, as a measure of news media power and provides us with a basis from which to test the claim that media coverage influences intervention decisions. Applying the model to instances of humanitarian intervention, if we observe substantial amounts of empathy-framed media coverage containing implicit or explicit criticism of government inaction, combined with policy uncertainty within the executive, we expect media coverage to have been a factor in producing the policy outcome. In this situation, media coverage can influence the policy process via the mechanisms outlined earlier, for example, by providing additional bargaining power to those policy-makers seeking intervention or as a result of policy-makers being pressured to come up with a response to critical coverage. However, if we find either distance-framed media coverage or low levels of empathy-framed media coverage, media coverage is unlikely to have been a major factor in causing the intervention. With respect to the latter, media coverage might still have had a small *weak* effect on the policy process, *minding* policy-makers to act, but other more significant factors are expected to have moved policy-makers to intervene.

Alternatively, if a decision has been taken to intervene for non-media-related reasons, we would expect to observe high levels of policy certainty with the executive drawing upon its substantial resources in order to try to influence the news agenda. In this scenario, we expect to observe either

1 supportive and empathetic coverage which helps build support for the policy of intervention or
2 critical coverage if there exists elite dissensus regarding the intervention (Hallin 1986; Bennett 1990).

In the latter scenario, as noted earlier, with policy-makers set on a particular course of action, critical media coverage is unlikely to influence policy. In short, by measuring policy certainty and news media framing in any given case, the model allows us to make a theoretically informed assessment of whether or not news media coverage was a factor in a given policy process.

In cases of non-intervention we would expect to observe either policy certainty against intervention coupled with distance framing (which implicitly supports a policy of non-intervention) or else critical and empathy-framed coverage coming head to head with policy certainty against intervention. In this scenario, again, policy certainty prevents media influence on policy.

In any given case, however, it is likely that a series of factors either individually or combined might be responsible for an intervention. Here additional research strategies and the employment of counter-factual analysis is necessary in order to facilitate an approximation of the importance of other factors relative to the news media. However, without a systematic and theoretically informed approach to measuring alternative factors (such as national interest or credibility) it will not be possible to determine whether news media coverage was a minor as opposed to a major factor in any given decision. Given the failure thus far to establish any 'convincing, non-anecdotal validation' (Carruthers 2000: 205) for the news media being a factor in causing intervention, this limitation is not serious. In other words, before we can start engaging in multi-factor analysis in order to assess the relative significance of the news media, we need to establish exactly what factors actually are relevant to intervention decisions. By establishing whether or not the news media is a factor in causing intervention, this study takes this important first step.

As part of a case study comparison, if uncertain policy and pro-intervention framing are found to be associated with cases of intervention, theoretical support will be found for the claim that the media causes humanitarian intervention. This case study methodology reflects the logic of Alexander George's (1979) 'structured, focused comparison' method. This method entails asking a set of standardised questions across a series of cases that focus on a particular aspect of that case. The standardised questions are levels of policy certainty and news media framing. The focus is on the question of news media impact in cases of intervention during humanitarian crises. By focusing case study research in this way the method enables us to detect causal patterns by establishing correlations between independent and dependent variables in a manner akin to large-scale statistical studies. The more cases in which we find variables to be correlated, the greater the confidence we have in there being a causal link between them. As well as facilitating an analysis of the CNN effect, the case study research will also facilitate a limited test of the policy–media interaction model itself. Full details regarding this limited test can be found in Appendix C.

Additional research strategies

Whilst the policy–media interaction model is the primary tool for gauging news media influence, a number of additional strategies need to be employed in order to cross-check inferences made on the basis of the model. In each case, process tracing was conducted in order to examine further evidence for the causal links indicated by the model. For example, in each case careful attention needed to be paid to the timing of news media coverage, policy uncertainty and intervention. In particular it was necessary to establish precisely when policy-makers decided to intervene. Otherwise empathising 'do something' coverage might actually be following a decision to intervene and therefore tend to mobilise support for an intervention rather than cause it. As well as establishing the chronology of events, each case study involved an assessment of both primary and secondary data. Whilst details of actual policy meetings remain unavailable for some considerable time, official documents including press statements, press briefings, policy documents and news media reports are available. A wealth of secondary data is also available via the work of commentators, academics and policy-makers' written accounts. Importantly, this material is a rich source of statements and opinions made by policy-makers at the time of the decisions concerned. This material was examined in order to establish further evidence, either for or against, news media influence in any given case and also to establish the presence of alternative factors that might have triggered an intervention. In addition primary telephone interviewing, involving discussion with officials involved with the relevant policy process, was employed. In each case, inferences based on the model were cross-referenced with the findings of these additional research strategies. Only if there was consistency between the two sets of data were claims about the impact of news media made with confidence.

Case selection

The final issue to be covered in this chapter is that of case selection (see also Appendix D). The central requirement guiding the selection of cases was to avoid biasing overall research findings. This involved ensuring a balance between hard and easy cases with respect to the central research question. The principal aim was to test the claim that news media coverage is a key factor in influencing intervention decisions where intervention is defined as the use, or threat of use, of force during a humanitarian crisis. This required, therefore, selecting a case in which it appeared that news media-triggered intervention (an easy case for the media-driven intervention thesis) and a case of intervention in which it appeared unlikely that news media coverage was a major influence (a hard case). These two cases (alongside two secondary case studies detailed below) focus on analysing the influence of media coverage on intervention decisions. In addition, two cases in which the media did not appear to influence policy during humanitarian crises were selected for analysis. These cases allow us to observe if the factors hypothesised to lead to news media influence (the level of policy uncertainty and media framing) do indeed vary in cases where the media failed to influence policy-makers to intervene. This is good methodological practice and strengthens the validity of claims made in other case studies that these variables lead to media influence on policy.

With respect to the number of cases that should be studied, the study comprises three core case studies, each of which involved extensive and systematic primary research. These cases are selected according to the hard/easy case criteria. In addition three further secondary case studies were selected. These involved primary research but were also reliant upon secondary sources in order to make inferences with confidence. For example, the secondary studies did not employ a systematic check on the framing analysis but rather compared results with other studies in order to confirm or refute frame inferences. These secondary cases were selected according to their comparability with the core case studies. This helped in further identification of patterns across cases and provided a test of any inferences made in the primary case studies.

A full explanation and justification of the case selection process can be found at Appendix D. Briefly, Operation Restore Hope (involving ground troops) in Somalia in 1992 was the easy case selected for analysis owing to the absence of geo-strategic and national interest motivations that might otherwise have accounted for the intervention. Operation Provide Comfort (also involving ground troops) in Iraq in 1991 was the secondary case selected. The decision to threaten the use of air strikes in Bosnia in order to defend the Gorazde 'safe area' following the fall of Srebrenica in 1995 was selected as the hard case owing to the strategic and national interest factors which were thought to have underpinned policy-making. The secondary case study was a

decision to defend Sarajevo (also involving the threat to use air strikes) following a mortar bombing of a market place in February 1994. Finally, the
cases of non-influence were non-intervention during the Rwandan genocide
in April 1994 and the failure to intervene with ground troops, in the face of
widespread criticism of the adequacy of the air war, during the 1999 air war
against Serbia.[8]

Conclusion

The policy–media interaction model provides a systematic and theoretically
informed measure of news media impact on any given policy process. By specifying the conditions of news media influence, the model also goes some way
to reconciling the contrasting claims of the CNN effect and manufacturing
consent theory and to contributing to a more comprehensive understanding
of media–state relations. Overall, the theoretical model and research design
set out in this chapter should go some way to providing a clearer assessment
of media power than that offered by research to date outlined in Chapter 1, as
well as offer a solid foundation for further theory development and research.

3

THE CNN EFFECT MYTH

Overview

Operations Provide Comfort in northern Iraq (1991) and Restore Hope in Somalia (1992–3) were both seminal events in terms of 'humanitarian' intervention. For many commentators the emergent norm of 'humanitarian intervention' witnessed in northern Iraq (1991) was cemented, at least initially, by intervention in Somalia. US willingness to deploy forces in combat conditions in which there existed no apparent national interest appeared to have become a post-Cold War reality. Both interventions were also major news events remembered perhaps most for the graphic scenes of Kurds freezing in mountains in the case of Iraq and, for Somalia, US marines being greeted on the beaches of Mogadishu, not by hostile gunmen, but by the world's press. But by the end of Operation Restore Hope, with the world-wide broadcast of a dead US marine being dragged through the streets of Mogadishu, the future of Bush's 'New World order' and humanitarian intervention appeared to be fatally undermined. As we shall see with the Rwanda case study, the perceived failure in Somalia had a substantive subsequent impact on the type of forcible intervention deemed tolerable. But precisely what form did the press–state relationship take with respect to these interventions? Were these allegedly norm-creating operations in any sense a product of media coverage?

Each case is analysed in turn starting with the core case study concerning the decision to deploy ground troops in Somalia. For each a brief background is provided before a more focused examination of the period leading up to and surrounding the critical decision period is given. Key arguments put forward to explain the intervention decision are detailed before the policy–media interaction model is applied. The results are then detailed before an assessment is made regarding the likelihood and types of media influence in each case.

The 1991–2 civil war in Somalia

Located close to strategically important Middle East oil fields and key sea-lanes, Somalia was of importance to both the USSR and the US during the

46

Cold War. Siad Barre, who took power in a military coup in 1969, initially moved the country into the Soviet sphere of influence but, by the 1980s, Somalia had become a US client state and, between 1980 and 1987, was one of the largest recipients of US aid on the African continent (Cusimano 1995: 2). When the Cold War ended, however, US support for Barre's dictatorship evaporated and, in turn, the regime became unstable. General Aideed of Ethiopia led rebel forces against Barre whilst business elites within Somalia sought to remove him from power. By January 1991 fighting between rebel and government forces had reached the capital Mogadishu. On 6 January 1991 the United States abandoned Somalia and evacuated its embassy staff along with diplomats from ten other foreign nations (Cusimano 1995: 2). By 28 January Siad Barre had also fled the country. What followed was a rapid descent into anarchy as the conflict mutated from one of rebels versus government to one of clan and sub-clan warfare. In this context, the success of UN and aid agency relief efforts was limited and these were withdrawn in January 1991. By the end of 1991 all UN officials had left Somalia.

US re-engagement in Somalia

Though Somalia had effectively been abandoned by both the international community and its former US ally, elements of the US executive and aid agency network continued to pay attention, albeit from afar, to the crisis in Somalia. The US response can be split into two distinct phases. The first, detailed next, occurred between January 1991 and August 1992 when the US executive ordered an airlift of relief supplies into Somalia. The second relates to the lead-up to the decision to deploy ground troops in Somalia. I will discuss each phase in turn.

The lead-up to the August 1992 airlift

In fact, in March 1991, one and a half years prior to intervention, Assistant Secretary of State Herman Cohen declared Somalia a civil strife disaster at which point the Office of Foreign Disaster Assistance (OFDA) began to fund relief efforts. Hence, well in advance of the decision to intervene, elements of the US executive were responding to the war and famine in Somalia. It was not until the spring and summer of 1992, however, that Somalia became a major political issue in Washington. A combination of concerted lobbying by officials within the US executive (Livingston and Eachus 1995: 422–6) coupled with increased news media attention (Livingston and Eachus 1995: 419) raised the profile of Somalia during this period. A diplomatic cable titled 'A Day in Hell', written by US Ambassador to Kenya, Smith Hempstone Jr, is reputed to have secured Bush's own personal attention to the crisis (Oberdorfer 1992). By 14 August the Bush administration had ordered a major airlift of relief supplies (Operation Provide Relief) to Somalia. The airlift represented a major escalation in US involvement and symbolised the political commitment of the Bush administration to acting in Somalia.

Operation Restore Hope

Whilst the August airlift increased the flow of aid into Somalia, the security conditions within the country remained difficult. In particular, a situation of bribery and theft had developed whereby rival gangs demanded bribes for allowing food aid to pass through their territory. At the same time food convoys were regularly looted. In addition aid agencies had become reliant on hired gun-men for protection. Owing to this situation, 500 UN troops were sent to Somalia in September 1992 with the support of four US warships and 2,100 marines (Schraeder 1994: 177). At around the same time Bush publicly supported the use of security forces in Somalia (Livingston and Eachus 1995: 423). Despite these developments, and the on-going airlift, news media attention very quickly peaked and after the 1992 presidential election campaign started, Somalia almost disappeared from the news. Between 19 September and 8 November research by Jonathan Mermin (1997: 400) shows that only 250 seconds of Somalia news appeared on the major networks.

By the time the presidential election was over in early November, the situation in Somalia had worsened with much of the food aid failing to move beyond the port of Mogadishu. As calls for the international community to protect relief supplies from the gangs increased and pressure intensified for more effective action in Somalia the attention of senior administration officials turned to the problem (Cusimano 1995: 6). On 9 November Senators Paul Simon, Nancy Kassebaum and Harris Wofford called for further action (Mermin 1997: 400). At this point Assistant Secretary of State Robert L. Galluci drafted 'two pieces of paper' to advise Secretary of State Lawrence Eagleburger on the need for intervention in both Somalia and Bosnia. Gallucci met with Eagleburger and stated 'we believe we can stabilise the situation' in both Bosnia and Somalia. Gallucci states that 'Eagleburger then listened to the argument on Bosnia', for which he had 'not much time for', and said he would take the reports to the President.[1] By 12 November Assistant Secretary of State Robert L. Galluci had persuaded Secretary of State Lawrence Eagleburger 'that the United States lead a coalition to save Somalia from starvation under a UN Security Council authorisation to use "all necessary means"' (Oberdorfer 1992). In addition US aid agencies and members of Congress stepped up their lobbying of the executive to take greater action in Somalia. On 16 November senior representatives of US relief organisations working in Somalia met with UN officials in New York and appealed for greater protection. The next day 11 relief groups began drafting a joint letter to the Bush administration declaring that humanitarian agencies could not work effectively in Somalia without greater security. At about the same time a Senate delegation headed by Senator Paul Simon and a House delegation under Republican John Lewis, after visiting Somalia, called for more security (Oberdorfer 1992). On 18 November Bush and President-elect Bill Clinton met. According to Mermin (1997: 401) Somalia was one of four areas of the world discussed and the Clinton camp was struck by the depth of Bush's concern over Somalia (Mermin 1997: 401). Between 18 and 20 November Fred Cuny of the United States Agency for International Development (USAID) argued in public that 'the situation [was] so dire and the UN so slow and ineffectual that US forces [had to] intervene immediately without waiting for UN approval' (Gelb 1992).

By 20 November the attention of senior policy-makers had been secured and the first of a series of inter-agency meetings occurred. These meetings were called in order to develop policy options. Cuny had briefed Pentagon and State Department officials prior to the meetings (Cusimano 1995: 7). According to Oberdorfer (1992) the second of these meetings marked a turning point regarding the possibility of deploying troops: 'Jeremiah, who co-ordinates with the Joint Chiefs of Staff chairman Powell daily, startled the group by saying that "if you think US forces are needed [on land in Somalia] we can do the job"' (Oberdorfer 1992). According to Frank Wisener, Under Secretary of State, this change of heart was driven by desire to involve US forces in an 'easy' mission rather than a more complicated intervention in Bosnia which, it was feared, would be ordered by the incoming Clinton administration.[2] Oberdorfer (1992) argues that 'Jeremiah's statement transformed the use of US ground troops – an option that previously had been considered "fantasy land" by non-military policy-makers – into a leading possibility'. By 24 November, the day UN Secretary General Boutros Boutros-Ghali wrote to the Security Council urging intervention, the inter-agency meetings had come up with three options. The first involved continuing with the on-going aid operations and seeking to enhance the UN presence in Somalia. The second involved organising an international coalition of forces under UN command in which US military airlift, sealift, logistical and communications support would be offered, but not ground troops. And third, the option of sending in a division or more of US troops under US command and control (Cusimano 1995: 10) was discussed. On 25 November a National Security Council meeting occurred at which point the third option, to offer the United Nations up to 28,000 US troops to spearhead an intervention aimed at protecting the delivery of food supplies, was agreed upon. By 4 December the UN Security Council had voted to support an intervention and President Bush, in a televised address to the nation, announced that US troops would be sent to Somalia. By 9 December, the first US troops arrived in Somalia.

Possible causes of intervention

The most common explanation put forward for Operation Restore Hope is that emotive news media coverage of suffering people caused policy-makers to decide to intervene; in short that the intervention decision was a straight-forward case of the strong CNN effect. For example Bernard Cohen argued that TV coverage of Somalia 'mobilised the conscience of the nation's public institutions, compelling the government into a policy of intervention for humanitarian reasons' (Cohen 1994: 10).[3] Research by journalists Nik Gowing (1994) and Warren Strobel (1997), whilst highlighting the multipli-city of factors that came together to cause the intervention, also supports the strong CNN effect thesis in the case of Somalia. Gowing (1994: 68) argues that the 'well-worn phrase "television got the US into Somalia . . . and got the US out" . . . stands up to examination'. He cites White House press secretary Marlin Fitzwater on the decision to deploy ground troops in Somalia:

> After the election, the media had free time and that was when the pressure started building up . . . We heard it from every corner, that something had to be done. Finally the pressure was too great . . . TV tipped us over the top . . . I could not stand to eat my dinner watch-ing TV at night. It made me sick.
>
> (Fitzwater cited in Gowing 1994: 68)

Eagleburger also noted the importance of television. He stated: 'I was one of those two or three that [sic] was strongly recommending he do it, and it was very much because of the television pictures of these starving kids' ('Reliable Sources: How Television Shapes Diplomacy', CNN, 16 October 1994, cited in Minear et al. 1997: 55). Finally, in 1999, George Bush himself asserted that it was news media coverage that motivated him to intervene in Somalia:

> Former President Bush conceded Saturday that he ordered US troops into Somalia in 1992 after seeing heart-rending pictures of starving waifs on television . . . Bush said that as he and his wife, Barbara, watched television at the White House and saw 'those starving kids . . . in quest of a little pitiful cup of rice', he phoned Defense Secretary Dick Cheney and General Colin Powell, chairman of the Joint Chiefs of Staff. 'Please come over to the White House', Bush recalled telling the military leaders. 'I – we – can't watch this anymore. You've got to do something.'
>
> (Hines 1999)

As discussed in Chapter 1, research by Livingston and Eachus (1995) and Mermin (1997) does not address the question of whether or not news media coverage caused senior policy-makers to intervene in Somalia. Rather they assume that news media coverage was a factor in causing senior policy-makers to intervene (Livingston and Eachus 1995: 427; Mermin 1997: 402). The picture therefore emerging from their work is one of middle-ranking officials, Congress persons and aid workers using news media coverage of suffering people in order to force more senior policy-makers to take action in Somalia. Finally, a different explanation for intervention, that still incorporates the news media as a factor, is put forward by Cusimano (1995: 8). She argues that senior aides claimed that Bush believed the Somali situation presented him with the opportunity to 'exit in glory' and 'leave office on a high note' (Cusimano 1995: 8). If this is the case, Somalia might well be a case of the potential CNN effect whereby policy-makers decided to intervene in the expectation that ensuing positive press coverage would reap political rewards.

However there are alternative explanations for the decision that are not necessarily connected with news media coverage. First and foremost, given the degree of congressional and aid agency lobbying (detailed earlier) in the run up to the intervention, the decision can be explained in terms of the outcome of domestic political and interest group pressure. Alternatively, Brent Scowcroft argued that the Bush administration was 'faced with acknowledging defeat and letting all of the areas where the refugees were starving to death . . . or do[ing] something' (Strobel 1997: 139). Here the motivation would seem to be not so much the immediate news media pressure but a concern over the US having to accept failure, and therefore loss of face, in Somalia. Another possible explanation is that the idea of humanitarian intervention in a 'failed' state conformed with Bush's internationalist 'New World order' vision in which the international community had a duty to uphold international law including those pertaining to basic human rights. Other explanations offered include Bush's own Christian principles that led him to believe that if the US could make a difference in saving lives it should do so. In particular Andrew Natsios (assistant administrator for the Bureau of Food and Humanitarian Assistance at USAID) recalls the powerful personal motivation of President Bush toward the famine in Somalia:

> I sat through a discussion in December 1992 between President Bush and Phil Johnson [president of Care] . . . in which President Bush described his visit with the First Lady and Johnston to a CARE feeding center for starving children in the middle of the Sahelian famine in the mid-1980s in the Sudan. He said that he and his wife would never forget the scenes of death he witnessed then, a memory he said had clearly affected his decision to send troops into Somalia.
>
> (Natsios 1996: 168)

Finally, the desire within the Bush administration to deflect congressional pressure to intervene in Bosnia has also been suggested as a possible cause of the intervention.

It is important to note that none of these alternative non-media based explanations for intervention are necessarily unassociated with news media coverage. For example, desire to avoid loss of face in Somalia could be argued to make sense only if there was news media attention. I say 'could be argued' because concern over loss of face owing to failure to control gunmen might be underpinned by concern over US military credibility. Alternatively media coverage of the crisis in Bosnia could have reinforced congressional pressure to intervene there. However, the important point is that each of these alternative factors could have influenced the policy process whether or not there was news coverage of Somalia (or of Bosnia in the case of the Bosnia explanation).

In order to test the claim that the decision to intervene in Somalia was the result of media coverage we need to apply the policy–media interaction model to the decision period. According to the model, if critical and empathy-framed news media coverage ran alongside policy uncertainty preceding the decision to intervene, then media coverage is likely to have been a factor in policy deliberations. Alternatively, if policy certainty and supportive and empathy-framed news media coverage was present in the run up to interven-tion then the media coverage is more likely to have simply reflected, and perhaps even helped build support for, the policy of intervention. It is to the analysis of policy certainty and media framing that we now turn.

Applying the policy–media interaction model

The analysis is split into two periods. The first is between 5 November and 25 November 1992, the period prior to Bush's decision to deploy ground troops. The second period is between 26 November and 9 December 1992. This relates to the period between Bush's decision to deploy ground troops, the official announcement that troop deployment was going ahead (Bush's address to the nation on 4 December) and the arrival of the first US marines in Mogadishu on 9 December.

5 November to 25 November 1992: press lack of interest versus persistent State Department attention to Somalia

Prior to the decision to deploy ground troops on 25 November media cover-age of Somalia was scant (see Table 3.1).[4] The *Washington Post* ran only six articles (none were editorials) over a 21-day period (0.29 articles per day) pri-marily concerning Somalia with only one being run on the front page.[5] Of these articles only three can be described as promoting a policy of interven-tion via empathising reporting and, moreover, only one ran on the front page.[6] The *New York Times* devoted slightly more attention with ten stories (0.48 per day) primarily concerning Somalia.[7] Of these, two were editorials and only one a front-page article. In terms of content the two editorials were clearly of an empathising nature. The first, run on 19 November, was titled 'Shoot to Feed Somalia' (by Leslie Gelb) and the second, on 20 November, was titled 'Action or Death' (by Anthony Lewis). Of the seven articles, all focused upon the crisis *vis-à-vis* relief supplies in Somalia although only one

Table 3.1 Total *New York Times, Washington Post*, CBS and CNN coverage of Somalia

	5–25 Nov.	*26 Nov. – 4 Dec.*	*5–9 Dec.*
No. of articles	16	50	76
Average no. of articles per day	0.76	5.5	15.2
CBS coverage	3 min. 30 sec.	46 min. 30 sec.	85 min. 10 sec.
CNN	5 news segments* (av. 0.24 per day)	169 news segments (av. 16.9 per day)	238 news segments (av. 47.6 per day)

Note
*Figures for CNN are given in terms of number of segments rather than length because Lexis-Nexis transcripts do not provide times.

front-page article, titled 'How One Somali Family, Some of It, Survives' by Jane Perlez, was clearly empathy framed:

> In August, after three of their children had died and the last of the grain was gone, Mr Omer and his wife, Fatima Ali Abdi, bundled up their favourite cooking pots, collected their three starving children and shuffled, stooped and weak, for three days to this bush outpost. For three months, the couple and their children have lived in a disease-infected camp for the displaced.

Similar to the print media, CBS evening broadcasts paid a low level of attention to Somalia. For the 21 days analysed, CBS ran only five news segments on Somalia. None of these were at the top of the news bulletin and only one was run within the first ten minutes of the news starting. The total airtime devoted to Somalia was a mere 3 minutes and 30 seconds. This equated to just 10 seconds of airtime per day to Somalia. In terms of content, all of these reports concerned the famine and/or the refugees from Somalia and as such served, at least implicitly, to highlight the on-going crisis and suffering in Somalia. Finally CNN coverage mirrored that of CBS. Only five news segments[8] (0.24 per day) were run on Somalia although four of these could be described as promoting intervention in Somalia.

Contrasting with the low levels of media attention was the fact that during this period the US executive was actually trying to draw attention to Somalia. For example the State Department ran ten press briefings in which Somalia was mentioned usually in the context of the press briefer disseminating information regarding aid flights to Somalia.[9] For example on 10 November press briefer Richard Boucher declared:

> The US-contracted civilian aircraft have been flying on behalf of the World Food Program and the International Committee of the Red

Cross since September. The combined US military and civilian airlift has now delivered a total of 17,539 metric tons of relief assistance in Somalia and Kenya . . . That's worth noting.[10]

These announcements, reflecting the State Department's desire to advertise the aid flights, started back in August. However, as a general rule, the briefer's repeated references to Somalia were rarely picked up and normally journalists swiftly changed the subject.[11] In fact, the only sustained attention to Somalia during the 5 November to 25 November period is on 12 November and 16 November when Boucher issued a warning to the Somali warlord Aideed to stop disrupting food deliveries.[12] However even in these unusual instances of press attention to Somalia, journalists quickly moved on to asking questions about other issues. Regarding levels of policy certainty during this period, the absence of any mention of a humanitarian intervention in the press briefings indicates that no decision had yet been made. This inference is consistent with other accounts of the policy process that indicate no decision regarding intervention was made during this period (Oberdorfer 1992; Cusimano 1995; Mermin 1997: 399–403). According to the typology outlined in the methodology section, the existence of no policy with regard to an intervention indicates policy uncertainty during this period.

Media coverage and briefings following the intervention decision: 26 November to 9 December 1992[13]

Compared with 5–25 November, press attention to Somalia dramatically increased after 25 November (see Table 3.1). This followed the leaking of Bush's decision to offer US troops to the UN. Between 26 November and 4 December *Washington Post* coverage increased to an average of 2.7 articles per day on Somalia, a huge increase over the 0.29 articles per day between 5 November and 25 November. Almost every day at least one article was on the front page. For the *New York Times* the average daily article rate increased to 2.9 from the 0.48 rate in the preceding period. CBS evening news, contrasting with the limited attention in the 21 days leading up to Bush's intervention decision, covered Somalia as the leading headline story every day except on two occasions (27 November and 3 December 1992). On these days Somalia was still covered within the first ten minutes of the news starting. CNN coverage made a similar leap with 169 news segments mentioning Somalia during this period. Somalia had now become a major news story.

After 4 December, following the go ahead from the UN Security Council and President Bush's live address to the nation, media coverage took another major leap. Between Bush's address and US troops landing in Somalia the *Washington Post* ran 39 articles on Somalia (7.8 per day) and the *New York Times* ran 37 articles (7.4 per day). Looking at the combined *Washington Post* and *New York Times* figures in Table 3.1 we can see an article rate of 15.2 per day for this period. This is substantially greater than the 5.5 articles per day for the 26 November to 4 December period and an order of magnitude greater than the 0.76 articles per day prior to Bush's decision to offer ground troops. CBS coverage also increased after Bush's address to the nation with over 85 minutes of airtime devoted to Somalia in just five days. This compares with 46 minutes of Somalia news between 26 November and 4 December and only 3 minutes and 30 seconds over the 21-day period running up to Bush's decision. Finally, CNN coverage increased similarly and averaged over 47 news segments per day on Somalia. By the period 5 to 9 December, Somalia dominated the news.

Following the decision to intervene, the US executive worked hard to promote the policy of intervention with eight State Department briefings, five Pentagon briefings and nine White House briefings. This reflected the high levels of policy certainty following the 25 November decision to intervene. In particular, both Bush and Clinton made public announcements in order to promote the policy of intervention. For example, Bush declared:

> There is no government in Somalia. Law and order have broken down. Anarchy prevails . . . It's now clear that military support is necessary to ensure the safe delivery of the food Somalis need to survive . . . And so, to every sailor, soldier, airman, and marine who is involved in this mission, let me say you're doing God's work. We will not fail. Thank you, and may God bless the United States of America.[14]

Other notable features were set-piece briefings by the Pentagon to explain the upcoming military operation. For example, on 4 December there was a Pentagon briefing with both Secretary of Defense Cheney and chairman of the Joint Chiefs of Staff Colin Powell alongside the regular briefer Pete Williams. Half of the following 8,000-word briefing was a well-prepared and detailed presentation from Cheney.[15] Again on 7 December there was another similar style of press briefing with the briefer spending almost one-third of an 8,000-word briefing disseminating details about Operation Restore Hope.[16]

Media framing after the intervention decision[17]

With respect to the framing of reports the bulk of reports supported the policy of intervention using positive language such as 'Mission to Somalia'[18] and 'extraordinary actions to save hundreds of thousands of lives'.[19] For example, out of 45 articles containing significant reference to the intervention decision, 30 were supportive of the intervention whilst only eight were largely critical. In terms of the empathy versus distance framing, most reports empathised with the suffering people of Somalia using emotive

Table 3.2 A selection of descriptors associated with the empathy and support frames taken from *Washington Post* and *New York Times* articles

Support descriptors	Empathy descriptors
Mission to Somalia	Nation's hungry
Safe delivery of aid to the starving	Gather in hope of nourishment
Worthy purpose	Appalling situation
Landmark change of policy	Historic disaster
Strong support	People are starving
Strong action warranted	Stench of death
Strong case for humanitarian	Merciful deliverance
intervention	Suffering of Somalia
We must help	Descent into anarchy
We cannot stand by	Mass starvation and bloodshed
Something needs to be done, let's do it	in Somalia
Deliver food and suppress the warlords	Somalis in need of help
An historic step	Starving Somalis
Brake Somalia's descent into anarchy	Chaotic conditions
Landmark in the development of	Death and starvation
humanitarian law	Emaciated children and elders
Safe delivery of aid	Somalia's misery
Save starving women and children	Famine and war ravaged country

language such as 'starving Somalis gather in the hope of nourishment'[20] and 'Somalia's misery'.[21] Overall, of the 16 articles making significant reference to the famine and war in Somalia, 12 were empathy framed whilst only two were distancing. A selection of descriptors associated with empathy and support framing can be seen in Table 3.2.

The framing inferences were then checked by a keyword systematic.[22] Here media texts were analysed for keywords predicted to be associated with both the *supportive* and *empathy* frames and the opposite *critical* and *distancing* frames. Starting with the supportive/critical frames the keywords 'save', 'protect' and 'help' were counted. One would expect to find a predominance of such terms in reports that supported the intervention because they tend to emphasise the positive and worthy dimensions of intervening in Somalia. Conversely, the keywords 'national', 'US/American interest', 'unclear/uncertain' and 'danger' were counted. One would expect to find a predominance of such terms in reports that opposed the intervention because they highlight both the risks of the operation and the debate over whether or not US troops should be sent into action when there was no perceived national interest at stake. With regard to the empathy/distance framing, the keywords 'people', 'starving,' 'dying' and 'dead' were counted. By identifying the Somali population as people and highlighting their suffering, these keywords encourage identification between the reader and the people of Somalia. Conversely the keywords 'Somali', 'fighting', 'warring' and 'killing' were counted. These terms do not encourage close identification or sympathy from the reader but rather help frame the crisis in Somalia as a distant civil war and not as a humanitarian crisis that demands the help of the US.

The results of the keyword analysis confirm the inferences of a support and empathy frame predominating in media reports made during the interpretive section of the framing analysis. Examining Table 3.3, we can see that keywords predicted to be associated with supportive framing clearly outnumber those predicted to be associated with a critical frame (112 to 87). With respect to the empathy frame, we can see that the keywords predicted to be associated with the empathy frame outnumber those predicted to be associated with a distance frame by almost two to one (409 to 249). Overall then, the keyword analysis supports the interpretive inference that media reports were supportive of the intervention in Somalia and empathised with the suffering people of Somalia.

News media and US intervention in Somalia: a case of manufacturing consent or indexing and not the strong CNN effect

The hypothesis of the policy–media interaction model is that news media influence is likely during times of policy uncertainty and critical and empathy-framed news media coverage. Hence if the news media were a factor in causing the decision to intervene in Somalia, we would have expected to observe substantial amounts of critical and empathy-framed media coverage and

Table 3.3(a) Media coverage of the intervention decision, 26 November to 9 December 1992

Support frame		Critical frame	
Keyword	Frequency	Keyword	Frequency
Save/saving	33	Interest	26
Protect	25	Uncertain/unclear	19
Help	54	Danger	42
Total	112	Total	87

Table 3.3(b) Media coverage of Somali population, 26 November to 9 December 1992

Empathy frame		Distance/neutrality frame	
Keyword	Frequency	Keyword	Frequency
People	185	Somali	157
Starve/starving	174	Fight/fighting	39
Dying/die/dead	50	Warring/killing/ killed	53
Total	409	Total	249

Sources: Washington Post, available online at http://www.washingtonpost.com; *New York Times* and CNN search available via Lexis-Nexis; and *CBS* evening news segments available via Vanderbilt TV News Archive.

policy uncertainty preceding the decision to intervene. Alternatively, if the relationship between news media coverage and the decision to intervene is more accurately described as one of manufacturing consent or indexing, we would expect to observe policy certainty with a clear policy line being fed to the news media after the decision to intervene, combined with supportive and empathy-framed media coverage.

In terms of understanding Somalia as a case of the CNN effect, the findings here offer little support. Prior to the 25 November decision to offer ground troops, US policy toward Somalia was uncertain in that no decision had been made regarding the intervention. Although policy-makers were theoretically open to news media influence during this period of policy uncertainty, journalists paid only scant attention to Somalia. The combined average number of articles per day for the *Washington Post* and *New York Times* was 0.76 and Somalia received front-page coverage on only two occasions. CBS devoted a mere three minutes of airtime to Somalia for the whole 21-day period. Even though *some* of the reports were empathy framed, it is difficult to imagine this level of coverage being sufficient to 'mobilise the conscience of the nation's public institutions' (Cohen 1994: 10) or 'create a political clamour to feed Somalia' (Mandelbaum 1994: 16). If we understand the CNN effect as a barrage of press attention influencing policy-makers to alter course, nine seconds of airtime per day and less than one newspaper article per day relegated to the inside pages seems unlikely to have compelled politicians to act. Certainly the image offered by Marlin Fitzwater of news media coverage tipping policy-makers 'over the top' (Gowing 1994: 68) and making it difficult to eat his dinner 'watching TV at night' (Gowing 1994: 68) is not supported by the actual level of media attention to Somalia. Others involved in the policy process, interviewed for this study, also have little recollection of media coverage being a major factor at this point. Under Secretary of State Frank Wisener does not 'recall news pressure being a big issue in any policy meeting' and states that 'we were responding less to the imperatives of news pressures . . . than to the reality of the situation'.[23] Also Robert Gallucci had no recollection of the quantity or nature of media coverage during this period.[24] He agreed that the decision to intervene in Somalia was not an instance in which media coverage helped push policy-makers to act. Also Arnold Kanter does not recall a 'precipitating media event'[25] in the lead-up to the decision to intervene. In short, extensive news media attention to starving people in Somalia (the strong CNN effect) was not a factor in producing the decision to deploy ground troops in Somalia. This finding is reinforced by the almost total disregard that journalists showed to State Department information regarding aid flights to Somalia. Indeed, the press briefing analysis indicates that, rather than news media coverage drawing the attentions of officials to Somalia, press briefers were, if anything, trying to encourage press attention to Somalia.

Overall the research indicates that substantial media attention to Somalia followed increased levels of policy certainty when Bush had decided to offer ground troops to the UN. Once this decision was leaked, media coverage increased dramatically. By 4 December the Security Council had given the go-ahead for Operation Restore Hope. During this period of policy certainty the executive started in earnest to sell the policy of intervention via presidential announcements and set-piece press briefings. Levels of media coverage reflected this public relations exercise with a large increase in the number of articles and airtime devoted to Somalia. But media coverage did not simply follow the official agenda. Journalists also framed reports in a particular way. Rather than challenging executive policy, or even reporting equally the views of those for and against the intervention, journalists overwhelmingly framed reports in a way that was supportive of Bush's decision. By both empathising with the people of Somalia and choosing to highlight the positive aspects of the intervention decision, rather than the potential pitfalls, journalists produced coverage that favoured Bush's policy of intervention whilst marginalising those in Washington who opposed such a move. In short, rather than helping cause the Bush administration to intervene in Somalia, media coverage actually turns out to have helped build support for the policy of intervention. If we are to place a theoretical label to the media's role, it is more accurately described as one of manufacturing consent (Herman and Chomsky 1988) or indexing (Bennett 1990), rather than the CNN effect.

Consideration of other possible routes of media influence

Whilst finding that Somalia is not a case of the strong CNN effect, we need to consider three alternative possibilities through which the news media might have become a factor in policy deliberations. These are the weak CNN effect, the potential CNN effect (including the potential impediment effect) and the enabling effect. I shall deal with each in turn.

If news media coverage did not create a political imperative to intervene in Somalia, could it have been a case of the weak CNN effect whereby a few media reports served to incline policy-makers to act? The interpretive analysis of the handful of news media reports during the run up to the intervention did indicate that some of the reports advocated intervention. The most notable of these were the two *New York Times* editorials that openly called for US action in order to prevent starvation in Somalia. There is no reason to doubt, therefore, that at least some of those involved in the policy process read these, and other, reports and perhaps saw some of the very brief TV news stories devoted to Somalia. Accordingly, it is possible that these media reports had an effect on policy-makers whilst they deliberated over whether to act. Marlin Fitzwater, although clearly exaggerating the quantity of coverage, and George Bush clearly believed in retrospect that media reports had motivated them to act. However, if this was the case, two issues suggest only minimal causal significance should be attributed to the weak CNN effect in terms of explaining why intervention occurred in Somalia.

First, the possible effect of these few reports must be set against the wealth of additional factors that were pressing for US involvement at that time. As detailed earlier, Senators Simon, Kassebaum and Wofford were lobbying the administration over ten days before Bush called the inter-agency meetings. At the same time, relief agencies wrote to the Bush administration asking for help whilst Fred Cuny of USAID, a powerful advocate of intervention, was actually briefing key policy-makers. So both Congress and interest groups (i.e. aid agencies) were working hard to move the Bush administration toward greater involvement. Outside of domestic and internal political pressure, the UN Secretary General was also pushing for intervention in Somalia.

Second, as outlined at the start of this chapter, elements of the US executive had been responding to the crisis in Somalia one and a half years prior to the intervention. In March 1991, Assistant Secretary of State Herman Cohen declared Somalia a civil strife disaster and, in August 1992, Bush ordered a major airlift of relief supplies, an operation that was still going on come November. Accordingly the Bush administration was already substantially engaged with the crisis in Somalia by the time of the policy deliberations about intervention. Set in this context, and bearing in mind the array of other factors, the idea that a handful of media reports had anything more than a minor effect on the policy process is unpersuasive. Certainly President Bush's recollection – that it was one night's TV viewing that caused him to order the intervention in Somalia – appears far less plausible. Certainly without the presence of these other pressures pushing for intervention and the Bush administration's close involvement in the on-going crisis the smattering of media reports could not, in and of themselves, have caused policy-makers to deploy 28,000 US troops. Instead, policy-makers would have been able to ignore the small number of reports just as they do when other 'distant' civil wars and crises sporadically make the news. At the very most the news reports might have had a mild effect, inclining policy-makers already on the path to intervention to act, but it is unlikely to have been a significant factor overall. Congressional and aid agency lobbying, coupled with existing policy engagement, offer more immediate, substantiated and plausible explanations for the intervention.

Another possible, though indirect, way through which media coverage might have influenced the decision to intervene in Somalia was via media coverage of the crisis in Bosnia. As mentioned earlier, some argue that Bush intervened in Somalia in response to a failure to act in Bosnia. If this is so, then media coverage of the crisis in Bosnia might have *indirectly* caused intervention in Somalia. A brief review of media coverage of Bosnia during this period indicates that coverage of Bosnia was only slightly greater than that of Somalia. For example, CBS evening news devoted only ten minutes of news coverage to Bosnia over the entire 21 days, giving less than 30 seconds per day on average to it. In terms of headline articles, the *Washington Post* ran only four articles on its front page about Bosnia and the *New York Times*, ten.

Whilst this attention is not insignificant it does not constitute the kind of coverage one would expect to see if a strong CNN effect has occurred. As with the low levels of media attention to Somalia, the attention to Bosnia might have had a weak effect, inclining policy-makers to act (although obviously not enough to actually take action in Bosnia). If this is the case, and there is no reason to think this did not occur, the causal significance of a weak CNN effect should not be over-stated, especially when there also existed the same kind of congressional and executive pressure to intervene in Bosnia as there was with Somalia.

But what of the possibility that policy-makers decided to intervene in Somalia owing to a potential CNN effect? Here policy-makers might have believed either that inaction would lead to negative publicity or that political rewards could be reaped owing to positive media coverage once the intervention to save lives was underway. I shall consider each in turn. With regard to the possibility that senior policy-makers acted in order to forestall future negative coverage no evidence during the research was found to support this possibility. Moreover, the above mentioned series of factors in the run up to the intervention are likely to have been sufficient in their own right to move policy-makers to act. Regarding the possibility that the intervention was designed to reap political rewards, this remains a possibility and evidence provided by Cusimano (1995: 8) supports this thesis. The argument requires important qualification, however. When the Bush administration made the decision to intervene, Bush was a 'lame duck' president, having already lost the presidential election to Clinton. No immediate political rewards could therefore be obtained from action in Somalia. It is still possible, as Cusimano (1995: 8) relates, that Bush saw it as a way to exit the presidency in glory and as such we should therefore remain open to the possibility that media influence occurred via this potential CNN effect route. Overall, however, it seems unwise to over-emphasise the importance of either of these possibilities. For example, with respect to potential future critical coverage, the logic is unclear as to why the Bush administration would be blamed for failing to act anymore than the incoming Clinton administration. Perhaps more significantly deploying 28,000 US troops in a potentially hostile environment (however 'doable' the mission may appear to be) is a high-risk approach to securing positive media coverage. Here it is reasonable to assume that any such potential CNN effect would have been cancelled out by a potential impediment effect whereby policy-makers would have taken into account the possibility of US troops being killed in action. Of course, any impediment effect was not sufficient to prevent the deployment of ground troops as intervention went ahead. The crucial point here, rather, is that a desire to secure future positive coverage is unlikely to have mobilised policy-makers to act because they would have been aware that potential casualties would lead quickly to negative coverage. In support of this argument Robert Gallucci recalled that he felt at the time that the administration might be 'in for criticism . . . [and that] everyone knew that if we had troops dying there would critical press coverage'.[26] In short, the presence of a potential CNN effect in this case must not be overstated both because no evidence was found to support such a claim and because it is counteracted, in any case, by the potential impediment effect. Again, as with the weak CNN effect, congressional and aid agency lobbying (as well as Bush's personal convictions detailed earlier in this chapter) offer more immediate and substantiated explanations for the intervention than does the thesis that policy-makers acted in the hope of securing favourable media coverage in the future.

Finally, media coverage might have had an enabling effect, allowing policy-makers to take action in Somalia, by helping to build a domestic constituency for the action. Certainly calculations over domestic support for action in Somalia would have helped policy-makers feel able to launch an intervention. It is important to note, of course, that such an effect is unlikely to have come from the low level of coverage in November 1992. Rather policy-makers would have been aware from the substantial media attention in the summer surrounding the August airlift that the public and media paid significant and positive attention to Somalia. In support of this effect Frank Wisener recalls that he was aware of a 'substantial amount of sentiment' amongst journalists in favour of acting in Somalia. He stated: 'I think it was less of an effect on policy . . . but what I think it really did was provide a certain conditioning effect for the US public . . . the CNN effect conditions Americans to welcome the intervention.'[27] Arnold Kanter made a similar point noting that 'in trying to build support for the [intervention], the ground work had already been laid by the vivid pictures'.[28] Finally, at the time an administration official, responding to a criticism that the Bush administration had failed to build support for the intervention policy, declared: 'There is already public support for helping the people of Somalia', thus indicating that policy-makers were well aware of the existence of public support for intervention.[29] Overall, media coverage might have caused a weak CNN effect in this case and also had an enabling effect. It seems less likely that any kind of potential CNN effect occurred.

The myth of the strong CNN effect and Somalia

The decision to deploy 28,000 US troops in Somalia was not prompted or 'caused' by media attention to the starvation in Somalia. In fact, the media did not pay any significant level of attention until after Bush had decided to send in US troops. Other factors, such as aid agency and congressional lobbying and President Bush's own personal conviction, offer more immediate and empirically substantiated reasons for the intervention. At the very most there might have been a weak CNN effect whereby a handful of reports *might* have inclined some policy-makers to act. If, however, the media played any significant role at all *vis-à-vis* the policy process it was as an enabler and then as a builder of support. Policy-makers, aware of prior sympathy toward the suffering in Somalia amongst journalists and the public, could act confidently in the knowledge that an intervention could easily be sold to the public. Once the decision was made, positive and pro-intervention coverage helped mobilise support for Operation Restore Hope.

If the media played such a supportive, not pressuring, role in what was apparently an easy case for the CNN effect, the question is raised as to the validity of this thesis. In order to offer a comparison to Somalia we move to the secondary case study involving an examination of a similar instance of ground troop deployment in northern Iraq during 1991.

Intervention in northern Iraq: the case of the Kurds[30]

Operation Provide Comfort was launched in the aftermath of the 1991 Gulf War and involved the deployment of both US air power and ground troops in northern Iraq. The officially stated aim of the operation was to guarantee the safety of Iraqi Kurds. Following the defeat of Iraqi forces by the allied coalition, Iraqi Kurds in the north of Iraq and Shi'ite Muslims in the south mounted armed uprisings against the Iraqi authorities. By late March 1991 both uprisings had been crushed and hundreds of thousands of Iraqi Kurds fled toward the Turkish and Iranian borders in order to escape the retribution of the Iraqi authorities. Whilst Iran was, in comparison with Turkey, willing to offer safe haven to at least a number of the Iraqi Kurds, the Turkish authorities sought to prevent the flow of refugees across the Iraq–Turkey border. Trapped in the mountainous border region between Iraq and Turkey, in freezing weather conditions, a vast humanitarian disaster rapidly developed. During this period the UN Security Council passed Resolution 688 that ordered the Iraqi authorities to allow the provision of humanitarian relief within Iraq. This intervention sparked major controversy over whether it represented the legitimating of forcible humanitarian intervention[31] and also represented an apparent 'about turn' by the Bush administration that had previously resisted involvement in Iraq's 'internal affairs' (i.e. there existed policy certainty against intervention). It also paved the way for the creation of an air exclusion zone over northern Iraq (still in place today), the air dropping of supplies into northern Iraq and the deployment of coalition troops within Iraq.

A closer examination of these policy developments will be made when analysing the US policy response to this crisis. For now it is sufficient to note that the intervention in northern Iraq has become understood, if not entirely accurately, as the first major instance of forcible intervention during a humanitarian crisis. With respect to our focus of concern on intervention involving the deployment of ground troops, this case is widely understood to have been precipitated, at least in part, by news media coverage (Gowing 1994; Shaw 1996; Minear *et al.* 1997; Strobel 1997).

With respect to this study we need to establish whether US intervention in Iraq was indeed driven by news media coverage. If this is the case, we have a case in which media coverage would not only appear to have overcome policy certainty against intervention but also have influenced the deployment of ground troops. In short we would have an instance of unprecedented media influence on foreign policy. In order to assess this possibility we need to analyse closely the events surrounding the intervention, including levels of policy certainty and the quantity and framing of news media coverage.

From policy certainty against involvement, to US ground troops in northern Iraq

Throughout the month of March, when the Kurdish and Shi'ite rebellions were underway, the Bush administration decided against any attempt to provide support to the rebels, refusing even to stop Iraqi helicopters from flying. Indeed, as Hurst (1999: 122) points out, perceived US national interest lay in the maintenance of a unified Iraq in order to balance the power of Iran. In addition, Turkey, a key NATO ally, opposed the formation of an independent Kurdish state in northern Iraq through fears that its own Kurdish minorities in southern Turkey, many of whom had been fighting for independence, would be strengthened by such a development.[32] Even when the rebellions collapsed and the humanitarian disaster started to unfold, the Bush administration adhered to its policy line of non-involvement. On 3 April President Bush declared:

> Of course I feel a frustration and a sense of grief for the innocents that [sic] are being killed brutally. But we are not there to intervene. That is not our purpose; it never was our purpose. I can understand the frustration of some who think it should have been our purpose, some who never supported this in the first place on military action. I share their frustration, but I am not going to commit our forces to something of this nature. I'm not going to do that.[33]

On 2 and 3 April, as the number of refugees on the Iraq–Turkey border started to swell, the Turkish National Security Council was convened. According to Kirisci (1995) it was decided 'to keep the border closed until a reaction could be solicited from the UN Security Council'. On 3 April, the same day that the UN Security Council passed the Gulf War ceasefire Resolution (SCR687), a letter was drafted to the UN Security Council stating:

> The Iraqi government forces are deliberately pressing these people towards the Turkish border in order to drive them out of their country. These actions violate all norms of behavior towards civilian populations and constitute an excessive use of force and a threat to the region's peace and security.
>
> (UN Security Council Document S22433,
> 3 April, cited in Kirisci 1995)

By 5 April, against a backdrop of continued refusal to involve US personnel in the crisis,[34] Turkey and France convened a meeting of the UN Security Council in order to address the flood of refugees 'threatening' Turkey (Ramsbotham and Woodhouse 1996: 70). Earlier that day Turkish diplomats had met with their European counterparts in Ankara during which, according to Kirisci (1995), 'a draft version of the eventual Resolution 688 seems to have been agreed'. By the end of the Security Council meeting the innovative Resolution 688 was voted on and accepted. This both defined the crisis in Iraq as a threat to international peace and security in the region and demanded that Iraq allow humanitarian relief to be delivered in northern Iraq. On the same day President Bush announced his intention to launch a relief effort. This involved the air dropping of food and relief supplies to the Kurdish refugees, providing 'economic and food assistance' to Turkey and the deployment of a US military medical unit to the 'border area in southern Turkey'.[35]

On 6 April, according to some newspaper reports, the Bush administration warned Iraq not to interfere with relief operations in northern Iraq. In a *New York Times* article Elaine Sciolino (1991) wrote: 'President Bush's spokesman, Marlin Fitzwater, told reporters that in the message to Baghdad [sent Saturday, 6 April], the Administration said "no ground or air forces" would be allowed to function in the area involved, adding that their use would constitute a threat to relief operations.' This development by the Bush administration, in conjunction with Resolution 688, also suggested the beginning of a policy reversal away from strict adherence to the non-intervention policy.

The following week, commencing Monday, 8 April, international engagement in northern Iraq expanded significantly. On the Monday, having met with President Ozal of Turkey on the Sunday evening,[36] Secretary of State James Baker visited refugee camps along the Iraq–Turkey border. Martin Shaw's analysis of UK media coverage of this visit captures well the dramatic nature of this visit during which Baker was confronted with the realities of the unfolding humanitarian disaster:

> A Kurdish man appealing to Baker directly made the media's pitch to the statesman as well as his own: 'and we have been on the ice all these days, and we are suffering, our children are suffering, from hunger and starvation. So you have got to make for us something, to help us.' Baker could only agree: 'We know that and we're going to do that . . . We are going to mount a very large international effort just to do that.'
>
> (ITN, *News at Ten*, 8 April 1991, cited in Shaw 1996: 91)

The same day the idea of 'safe areas'[37] within Iraq was aired of which British Prime Minister John Major was a leading advocate. (The initial idea for 'safe areas' came from President Ozal on Sunday, 7 April (Freedman and Boren 1992: 160, cited in Wheeler 2000: 148)). Although initially resisted by the US, by Wednesday, 10 April, the No Fly Zone north of the 36th parallel had been established[38] indicating both the development of a forcible dimension of the international involvement in northern Iraq and the willingness of the US to enforce a safe area policy. Indeed US spokespersons confirmed on Thursday, 11 April that threats had been issued to Iraq to avoid military operations in refugee areas. For example, Richard Boucher (State Department spokesman) stated '[t]he overall thing that we've said to the Iraqis is that Iraqi forces should take no actions in any part of the country, including southern or northern Iraq, which might interfere with the provision of humanitarian services'.[39] Also Pentagon briefer Pete Williams stated 'We are not disengaged from the region . . . We would still have the capability to deliver on our statement that if they interfered with the humanitarian effort, they would do so at their own risk.'[40] That same day Bush confirmed that he was in 'total agreement'[41] with the safe area policy. The threat of air power was soon complemented by the planned deployment of ground troops in northern Iraq. Exactly at what point it was decided to deploy US ground troops within northern Iraq is slightly unclear. The *New York Times* reported that on 12 April US officials had started to set out plans for US troop deployment in order to secure the refugee safe areas within Iraq.[42] Conversely a *Washington Post* article on the same day described US officials as declaring US involvement would end at the Iraq–Turkey border:

'We've got thousands of people involved, hundreds of aircraft', Defense Secretary Richard B. Cheney told reporters in Washington yesterday. But officials stressed yesterday that direct US involvement would end at the Iraqi border, saying that international relief organisations – not US personnel – would be responsible for establishing planned refugee camps in Iraq. 'Our policy is that we are getting ourselves out of Iraq,' a senior administration official said.[43]

In fact, it was not until 16 April that President Bush announced that US troops would enter Iraq in order to police the safe areas. The wording of his statement, in particular the reference to the inadequacy of relief operations, indicates that troop deployment was decided some time after the initial relief effort and only when it became apparent that aid could not be effectively provided to the Kurds in the mountains along the Iraq–Turkey border:

Eleven days ago, on April 5th, I announced that the United States would initiate what soon became the largest US relief effort mounted in modern military history. Such an undertaking was made necessary by the terrible human tragedy unfolding in and around Iraq as a result of Saddam Hussein's brutal treatment of Iraqi citizens . . . But despite these efforts, hunger, malnutrition, disease, and exposure are taking their grim toll . . . It is for this reason that this afternoon, following consultations with Prime Minister Major, President Mitterrand, President Ozal of Turkey, Chancellor Kohl this morning, UN Secretary General Perez de Cuellar, I'm announcing a greatly expanded and more ambitious relief effort. The approach is quite simple: if we cannot get adequate food, medicine, clothing, and shelter to the Kurds living in the mountains along the Turkey–Iraq border, we must encourage the Kurds to move to areas in northern Iraq where the geography facilitates rather than frustrates such a large-scale relief effort . . . I can well appreciate that many Kurds have good reason to fear for their safety if they return to Iraq. And let me reassure them that adequate security will be provided at these temporary sites by US, British, and French air and ground forces, again consistent with United Nations Security Council Resolution 688.

Bush also alluded to the fact that Saddam Hussein had given assurances to the UN on 16 April that Iraqi forces would not oppose the aid efforts: 'I don't think Saddam Hussein, given the assurances he made today to the United Nations in Iraq . . . would venture to use force. But the problem isn't what we think about it; the problem is what do these Kurdish refugees . . . think. And what they think is . . . [we] need some security.'[44] On 17 April there were media reports of US special forces scouting refugee camps in northern Iraq[45] and, significantly, on 18 April a memorandum of understanding (MOU), negotiated by Saddam Hussein, Eric Suy (personal representative of the Secretary General) and Prince Sadruddin Aga Khan (executive delegate for the UN Humanitarian Programme), was agreed by the UN and Iraq. Overriding Iraq sovereignty, this MOU asserted the right of all civilians in Iraq to humanitarian assistance (Ramsbotham and Woodhouse 1996: 81). However, whilst the understanding signalled Hussein's agreement to extensive humanitarian involvement by the international community within Iraq, he continued to protest at the violation of Iraqi sovereignty by allied forces in northern Iraq. By 19 April, US TV news was reporting meetings between US and Iraqi generals in northern Iraq aimed at finalising an agreement for US troops to set up refugee camps within Iraq. At this point US, French and British forces started moving in significant numbers beyond the Iraq–Turkey border and into Iraq in order to police the refugee camps.

US media coverage of the Kurdish crisis: emotive and critical of Bush

Media coverage of the Kurdish crisis was intensive. Between 26 March and 15 April, the day before Bush announced the deployment of ground troops in Iraq, the *New York Times* published over six articles per day whilst the *Washington Post* published almost four articles a day on the crisis.[46] The crisis was the headline news on most days throughout this period on ABC, CBS and

NBC evening news.[47] For example, on ABC the crisis was the top headline story on 17 out of 21 days. By any yardstick, this represented a significant and rarely seen level of sustained coverage.

In terms of content[48] coverage both empathised with the plight of the Kurds and much of it either explicitly or implicitly demanded that something be done. A good example of empathy framing can be seen in the following exchange between Pat Buchanan and Julie Flint on CNN's *Crossfire*:

> *PB:* Good evening and welcome to *Crossfire*. A vast tragedy is unfolding tonight as millions of Kurds flee to the mountains to escape the murderous revenge of Saddam Hussein. Pregnant women, old men in wheelchairs, children with no shoes in a caravan 50 miles long are being strafed by helicopter gunships.

> *JF (journalist):* And they're running for their lives. There's millions of refugees; there's very little food. They've had no water or electricity since the beginning of the bombing by the Americans, absolutely desperate. In the few weeks of the uprising they've seen the full extent of the atrocities Saddam committed against them, and they're absolutely terrified.[49]

Editorial comment in the *New York Times* and *Washington Post* was particularly critical, although not in all cases, of the Bush administration and its refusal both to aid the Kurdish rebellion and for its dogmatic adherence to a policy of non-interference. Out of 22 editorials on the Kurdish crisis published between 1 and 15 April in the *New York Times*, 16 were, either or both, critical of the Bush administration and called for some kind of action to be taken to help the Kurds.[50] In the *Washington Post* [51] nine out of 15 either clearly called out for something to be done or criticised the Bush administration. Of the remaining six editorials only two spoke out against US involvement in the Kurdish crisis with the rest being ambiguous or unclear *vis-à-vis* the intervention/non-intervention question. The following opinion-editorial (op-ed) by William Safire is indicative of the kind of criticism levelled at President Bush in editorial sections:

> George Bush's answer to genocide is to insist angrily that 'our kids' – his new term of juvenile vulnerability for what he used to call America's armed forces – will not be 'sucked' or 'shoved' by some sinister outside pressure into anybody else's civil war. That's the old straw man trick. Three weeks ago, when urged to order Saddam Hussein to freeze all movement of aircraft and armor – which could have saved thousands of innocent lives without a single US casualty – Mr Bush chose instead to go fishing. Now the bloody consequences of his moral failure are on view: Americans watch in dismay as helpless

and terrified millions are driven into exile, babies dying on the way. Perhaps to assuage his guilt, the US President now creates a straw man: he accuses those who urged a freeze three weeks ago of having wanted to send our ground troops into an endless, millennium-old battle to end Arab tyranny.[52]

In short, media coverage functioned to highlight the plight of the suffering Kurds through empathy framing and was deeply critical of the Bush administration's policy toward the crisis.

Assessing the impact: was Operation Provide Comfort motivated by media coverage?

According to the policy–media interaction model, media influence on policy is unlikely to occur when policy-makers are set upon a particular course of action. In this case, the Bush administration was firmly set against involvement in Iraq. This policy of non-intervention applied to both the question of helping the Kurdish and Shi'ite uprisings in March and the humanitarian disasters that occurred in the wake of the collapse of the rebellions in April. Despite the critical and empathy-framed coverage, we would not expect the media to have influenced policy under these conditions. Why then did the Bush administration appear to change policy and initiate a forcible humanitarian intervention in Iraq? Given that the model indicates influence is unlikely to have occurred and yet intervention did occur, it is particularly important to search for further evidence in this case. After all, as noted in Chapter 2, the theoretical claim that policy certainty prevents media influence on policy could simply be incorrect. Specifically, in order to cross-check the inferences based on the policy–media interaction model, we need to consider whether any other factor can plausibly account, on its own, for the intervention.

On the first count, those involved in the policy process hold divergent views on the significance of the media. For example US Under Secretary of Defense Paul Wolfofitz has stated: 'I do think the vividness of television images probably heightened the sense of urgency.'[53] Alternatively many down-play the importance of the media, arguing instead that geo-strategic concerns over refugee flows into Turkey were the reason for the intervention. For example, according to Strobel, Andrew Natsios (then director of the Office of Foreign Disaster Assistance (OFDA)) claimed that 'major geopolitical considerations drove policy at the time . . . The first was concern for Turkey, one of Washington's closest Muslim allies . . . Turkey, with its own Kurdish "problem", had no desire to take in hundreds of thousands of destitute Kurdish refugees . . . Even if the cameras had not been there, the Bush administration would have made the same decision' (Natsios, paraphrased in Strobel 1997: 130). Similarly Brent Scowcroft has claimed that 'Without

Turkey factored in, with just television pictures, I don't know what our response would have been. We were very sensitive to Turkey's anxiety about allowing the Kurds to stay. That was fundamentally what motivated us' (Livingston 1997: 10).

So, notwithstanding the ambiguity of the anecdotal data, the possibility that the intervention was motivated over concerns with refugee flows into Turkey serves as a plausible and alternative explanation for the intervention. This explanation also fits well with the chronology of events detailed in this study. First and foremost it should be noted that President Ozal of Turkey and President Bush had met in late March in the US during which the US president had thanked Ozal for Turkish loyalty during the Gulf conflict.[54] Moreover, it was President Ozal of Turkey who first drew the attention of the international community to the burgeoning refugee crisis by tabling Resolution 688. As Kirisci (1995) details, this in turn came after several unsuccessful attempts by Turkey to prevent refugees crossing its border. Indeed, the clearest expression of the geo-strategic issues at stake came in the wording of Resolution 688 itself:

> The Security Council . . . Gravely concerned by the repression of the Iraq civilian population . . . which led to a massive flow of refugees towards and across international frontiers and to cross-border incursions, which threaten international peace and security in the region . . . decides to remain seized of the matter.

Also, Brent Scowcroft states 'the first problem [with] the Kurds is that they tried to flee into Turkey and Turkey didn't want them'[55] whilst Baker's visit to the refugee camps on 8 April was preceded by a visit to Turkey and a meeting with President Ozal. As the scale of the intervention increased the focus of the international effort evolved around a 'safe area' policy, itself devised by President Ozal of Turkey, which was designed to draw Kurdish refugees out of the mountainous border region and back into refugee camps within Iraq. In addition Wheeler (2000: 151), drawing from a *Time* magazine article and a *Sunday Times* article,[56] notes that Bush was in telephone contact with President Ozal on 15 April, the day before the announcement of ground troop deployment. Wheeler (2000: 151) writes: 'Baker reportedly told Bush that the Turkish government was particularly worried about the scale of the catastrophe and President Ozal confirmed this in a telephone conversation on Monday, 15 April.' In short, driven by the desire to avoid an influx of unwanted Kurdish refugees, Turkey was clearly closely involved in lobbying the Bush administration for greater intervention.

Overall the evidence suggests that the intervention in northern Iraq was probably not a case of the strong or indeed weak CNN effect. First and foremost the Bush administration clearly had a decided policy line against involvement in Iraq and, under these conditions, the theoretical insight of the media influence model is that media influence is unlikely. Instead the sequence of events, the close contact between President Ozal of Turkey and Bush, the stated objectives of the intervention (e.g. Resolution 688), plus most of the anecdotal evidence all indicate that the intervention decision was grounded in geo-strategic concerns regarding the vast number of unwanted Kurdish refugees that threatened to flood into southern Turkey. It is contended here that, given Turkey's membership of NATO, its loyalty (particularly during the Gulf War) to the US and its on-going 'problem' with Kurdish separatists in southern Turkey, geo-strategic concerns rather than media-inspired humanitarian intent or media–public relations are sufficient to explain the intervention. At the very most the critical and empathy-framed coverage would have had an enabling effect, helping to explain and justify the deployment of ground troops in Iraq to the US public, but the decision itself was most likely motivated by non-media related concerns. In short, the claim that ground troop intervention in northern Iraq was a case of the strong CNN effect is not born out by this case study.

The myth of the CNN effect

The interventions in northern Iraq in 1991 and Somalia in 1992/93 are the two most high profile instances of ground troop deployment during humanitarian crises. Moreover, in both cases it had been widely asserted that news media coverage, to a greater or lesser extent, helped push policy-makers to take action. The findings here indicate that in neither case did media coverage play this galvanising role. At most media coverage enabled policy-makers, who had decided to intervene for non-media-related reasons, by building domestic support for action. But in no sense did media coverage drive or compel policy-makers into taking action where they would have otherwise not.

4

THE CNN EFFECT IN ACTION

Overview

This chapter analyses two instances during the 1992–5 war in Bosnia when the US intervened directly during a humanitarian crisis. The core case is the decision to defend the Gorazde 'safe area' through the threat of air strikes in July 1995 which occurred shortly after the fall of the Srebrenica 'safe area'. This decision also involved a commitment to respond to further attacks on any 'safe area' with extensive air strikes. The secondary case study is that of the US response to a market-place bombing in February 1994. With respect to the core case study, the decision to defend Gorazde in 1995 was set against the broader context of growing US involvement in the Bosnian War. This included a renewed diplomatic initiative in August and a bombing campaign (Operation Deliberate Force) in late August/early September which in turn flowed from military commitments made following the fall of Srebrenica to defend 'safe areas' from further attacks. The US brokering of the Dayton peace talks in October/November 1995 finally secured a tentative peace throughout Bosnia.

The chapter starts by detailing the background to the 1992–5 war in Bosnia and the initial international response to the crisis. The events surrounding growing US involvement during the summer of 1995, in particular the lead-up to the initial US military engagement following the fall of the Srebrenica 'safe area', are detailed. The policy–media interaction model is then used to evaluate the likelihood of media influence. The relative importance of other factors is then considered before the 1995 intervention is compared with the secondary case study. This comparison enables further evaluation of the causal inference made in the core case study.

Background

The war in Bosnia was the bloodiest conflagration to emerge from the dissolution of the Federal Republic of Yugoslavia (FRY). Following the death of Tito in 1980 a combination of economic crisis, resurgent nationalism and the broader decay of communist ideology throughout Eastern Europe desta-bilised the FRY. By the early 1990s several of its republics were seeking independence. At first the European Union favoured the maintenance of the FRY whilst the US remained aloof seeing the growing crisis as a matter of European concern. In 1991, however, both Slovenia and Croatia declared independence whilst Germany broke ranks with 'official' EU policy by recog-nising Croatian claims to statehood. This was quickly followed by votes in Bosnia to break away from the FRY. Fighting between supporters of the FRY (including the Serb-dominated Yugoslav army and Bosnian Serbs) and those loyal to the fledgling states broke out. In Croatia a short but bloody war led to the first deployment of UN peacekeepers in the region. Within Bosnia, Bosnian Serb nationalists, with the support of the Yugoslav army, attempted to create an ethnically pure region of Bosnia.

As the conflict in Bosnia escalated, the EU sought to contain the war by deploying a 'peacekeeping' force UNPROFOR (United Nations Protection Force) and subjecting the region to an arms embargo. The immediate effect of this policy was to disadvantage Bosnian government forces against the well equipped Bosnian Serb nationalists and Yugoslav army (Herring 1997). A combination of murder, rape, intimidation and fighting were the primary mechanisms by which regions of Bosnia were made 'ethnically pure'. As the war continued however, pressure grew in the US for more direct involvement. Shocked at the gross violation of human rights and attacks on civilians because of their perceived ethnic identity, many in the US advocated stronger action. Elements of both Congress and the US executive (particularly the State Department) supported either direct intervention to defend the Bosnian government or, at the very least, the lifting of the arms embargo so that the Bosnian government could defend itself. The Clinton administration fought hard to deflect such pressures, often expressing outrage at what was happen-ing but then failing to carry through with substantive engagement (Gow 1997: 208). But, as the war continued, US involvement did gradually increase. During 1994 the US started to focus on the conflict by altering the balance of forces on the ground through both retraining and rearming the Croatian army and fostering an alliance between Bosnia and Croatia. At the same time the UN mission was, after well-publicised atrocities and crises, edged toward a more forceful posture and at various points air strikes were threatened and authorised in response to violations of UN directives. However, it was not until 1995 that the US engaged directly with the war in Bosnia.

US involvement in 1995[1]

In both diplomatic and military terms, US policy toward the war in Bosnia in 1995 underwent a dramatic reversal and it became directly involved with the international response to the war. It is important to note that US involvement did not occur all at once, but rather developed over the course of several months, often reacting to changing events on the ground. Initial military engagement came in July 1995 after the fall of the Srebrenica 'safe area' to Bosnian Serb nationalist forces and involved a threat to bomb Bosnian Serb Army (BSA) targets if the Gorazde 'safe area' was attacked. Diplomatic engagement did not come until early August when the US used the Croatian offensive to take the Krajina region. In a White House press conference (WHPC) on 10 August 1995 Clinton declared:

> This is an important moment in Bosnia, and it could be a moment of real promise. Because of the military actions of the last few days, the situation on the ground has changed. There is some uncertainty and instability. It could go either way. But I think it's time we should try to make a move to make peace.[2]

As Richard Holbrooke (chief US negotiator) notes (1998: 73), the Croatian offensives altered the 'diplomatic landscape' and placed Bosnian Serb nationalists in a position of weakness. Actual military intervention did not occur until several weeks later when a Sarajevo market place was mortar bombed. This triggered Operation Deliberate Force, a sustained bombing of Bosnian Serb targets.

Despite the belief of many at the time, however, Operation Deliberate Force was not part of a co-ordinated and pre-planned attempt to force the war in Bosnia to an end. As Holbrooke (1998: 104) notes 'almost everybody came to believe that the bombing had been part of a master plan . . . but it simply did not happen that way. It took an outrageous Bosnian Serb action [a mortar bombing of a Sarajevo market place] to trigger Operation Deliberate Force'. Instead the authority to launch air strikes had 'already been pre-delegated to the respective NATO and UN commanders' (Daalder 1999: 131) following the fall of Srebrenica when policy-makers decided to defend Gorazde by threatening extensive air strikes. As such Operation Deliberate Force, whatever effect it might have had on the course of the Bosnian War, was primarily aimed at enforcing Bosnian Serb compliance with NATO and UN directives set out following the fall of Srebrenica. It started in response to a violation of the UN 'safe area' of Sarajevo and was suspended, on 14 September, when an agreement was reached to withdraw Bosnian Serb nationalist heavy weaponry from around the city.[3] This suspension was followed by a 144-hour deadline for the removal of the weaponry.[4] By 21 September the deadline had expired, NATO was satisfied the Bosnian Serb nationalists had withdrawn heavy weaponry, and the air strikes were stopped indefinitely. Overlapping with the bombing campaign were Croatian and Bosnian government offensives that forced the Bosnian Serb nationalists out of 20 per cent of Bosnian territory thereby returning the territorial division of the country to the 51:49 per cent split that was the focus of Western diplomacy with regard to any peace settlement. By the end of September the war in Bosnia had come to an end.

The following analysis assesses whether news media coverage influenced initial US military engagement in Bosnia in 1995, specifically the decision to defend Gorazde following the fall of Srebrenica. Although this initial intervention set the conditions for Operation Deliberate Force in late August and early September, the findings of this case study are not *primarily* aimed at explaining either this later bombing campaign (although the two are clearly closely linked according to Daalder's comments outlined above) or indeed US diplomatic engagement. As we shall see when discussing the details of the policy process, the decision to defend Gorazde was, to an extent, distinct from the decision to try to bring the war to an end via US led diplomacy.

US military engagement[5]

As Tihomir Loza (1996: 28) explains, by 1995, despite years of fierce warfare, the Bosnian conflict was largely deadlocked militarily and diplomatically in the same configuration as in October 1992. Bosnian Serb nationalists possessed 70 per cent of Bosnian territory and the French and British governments continued to command the international response to the war. This military and diplomatic continuity, however, masked more substantial changes in the geo-strategic situation. In fact, by spring 1995, the Bosnian Serb nationalists were militarily and diplomatically isolated. As noted earlier, with the support of the United States the Croatian army had retrained and rearmed since 1994. In May 1995 they successfully demonstrated their military capability when 'Operation Flash captured . . . Sector West in Western Slavonia' (Strategic Survey 1995–6: 131). The formation of the military alliance between the Muslim Croat Federation and the Republic of Croatia in March, coupled with Serbian President Milosevic's increasing unwillingness to offer support, compounded the Bosnian Serb nationalists' diplomatic and military isolation.

From this position of weakness the Bosnian Serb nationalists stepped up an aggressive and desperate policy that sought to 'twist . . . [Izetbegovic's] arm . . . by giving both his civilians and the UN forces a hard time' (Loza 1996: 31). As UN designated 'safe areas' were subjected to increasingly ferocious attack, a few limited NATO air strikes were authorised. In response Bosnian Serb nationalists took UNPROFOR personnel hostage. According to Alexander Vershbow (senior director for European Affairs at the time) images of the UNPROFOR hostages broadcast around the world 'really shook policymakers to change policy' and helped initiate moves toward a more forceful stance in Bosnia.[6] With UNPROFOR humiliated and the viability of French and British leadership in Bosnia in question, the two governments responded to the crisis with a decision in June to deploy the Rapid Reaction Force (RRF). This force was to be important in reducing the vulnerability of the ground troops and opening up the possibility of stronger military action. It was to be the last significant move by the European powers however before US leadership took over the international response to the war.

By June several issues had forced Bosnia to the top of the US foreign policy agenda. First, the Bosnian Self-Defence Act, already passed by the House of Representatives, was to be considered by the Senate in July (Daalder 1999: 61). If passed it would represent a major challenge to the Clinton administration's foreign policy. Second and more seriously, the US had committed itself to the NATO extraction plan Determined Effort, which required the deployment of US ground troops in Bosnia to support UNPROFOR's withdrawal if it were ordered (Loza 1996: 38; Woodward 1996: 257; Holbrooke 1998: 65–7; Daalder 1999: 56–61). Third, and at the same time, following the hostage-taking crisis, a debate had broken out within the Western alliance over whether or not to stay in Bosnia (Holbrooke 1998: 65). Consequently, the US faced the growing possibility of an UNPROFOR withdrawal triggering the deployment of US troops. On this issue Loza (1996: 38) cites National Security advisor Anthony Lake: 'We all agreed that collapse would mean that American troops would have to go into Bosnia in order to rescue UNPRO-FOR, which meant that we were going in the context of a defeat. And nobody wanted that. It would have had huge consequences.' Holbrooke also concurs with Lake's position arguing that rescuing UNPROFOR was considered an unacceptable option (Holbrooke 1998: 38). Of course the option of simply not rescuing UNPROFOR, and in doing so reneging on the agreement with Britain and France, would have damaged the credibility of the NATO alliance. So, facing the unwelcome possibility of a UN withdrawal, coupled with US ground troops in Bosnia, Lake started creating policy alternatives (Loza 1996: 38; Woodward 1996: 254–60). According to Loza, Lake proposed two parallel actions: the strengthening of UNPROFOR and the launching of an American peace initiative – both of which were to be supported by a decisive threat of NATO air strikes (Loza 1996: 38). According to Woodward, Lake's policy was entitled the 'end-game strategy' and, consistent with Loza's account, involved carrots and sticks for all sides to force a negotiation (Woodward 1996: 259). At this point US policy toward Bosnia was clearly under review. However, as Holbrooke describes, events in Bosnia were moving 'faster than the policy-review process in Washington. As the administration deliberated, the Bosnian Serbs attacked. This time their action would go down in history' (Holbrooke 1998: 68).

The fall of the Srebrenica 'safe area' on and around 11 July, the ensuing massacre of upwards of 8,000 inhabitants[7] and the expulsion of its remaining population had a galvanising effect on the Western alliance. According to Holbrooke (1998: 70) 'everywhere one turned, there was a sense of confusion in the face of Bosnian Serb brutality. On ABC's *Nightline* programme Holbrooke declared: 'We agree that Srebrenica is an absolute disaster . . . [and the situation] is the worst mess we have seen in Europe since the end of World War II. It is . . . the greatest collective failure of the West since the 1930s.'[8] Not only did the taking of Srebrenica reveal the fundamental flaws of existing Western policy toward Bosnia but it also caused French President Chirac publicly to demand military action to retake the enclave and deride the in-action of his British and American counterparts. He declared: 'I owe it to the truth to say that up until now the contacts the French government has made have not been positive. I deplore that. For the moment, we are alone.'[9] According to Daalder (1999: 69) Clinton's senior National Security advisors spent two-and-a-half hours debating Chirac's demand to retake Srebrenica. Two distinct decisions were made following the fall of Srebrenica. The first related to Lake's end-game strategy. Lake used Clinton's frustration at not being in control of the situation to move his end-game strategy forward. On 17 July Lake presented the end-game to Warren Christopher, William Perry, John Shalikashvili, Madeleine Albright and Sandy Berger (Woodward 1996: 261). Christopher, Perry and Shalikashvili 'showed minimal interest in the ideas Lake had laid before them' (Daalder 1999: 101), preferring instead to deal with more immediate pressures, specifically the need for a response to the French demands made in the wake of the Srebrenica débâcle (Daalder 1999: 101). However, Lake arranged for Clinton to enter the meeting in order to make clear the need for a long-term approach toward Bosnia. Daalder notes that 'the principals left, taking the end-game strategy with them' (Daalder 1999: 101). Over the next two weeks an informal inter-agency group developed strategy papers, some of which built upon Lake's 'end-game' strat-egy, others of which challenged Lake's general thrust. It was not until 9 August that Lake's strategy, involving a last ditch diplomatic effort to be backed by the use of force if necessary, had fully taken shape and been accepted by US policy-makers (Daalder 1999: 101–12).

The second key decision, made on 18 July (Daalder 1999: 72–3), related to the defence of the threatened Gorazde 'safe areas'. According to both Hol-brooke and Daalder the key decision made at this point was to 'draw a line' at Gorazde by threatening a disproportionate response to any further attacks on 'safe areas' (Holbrooke 1998: 72; Daalder 1999: 71–2). Clinton declared that 'the situation underscores the need for robust airpower being authorised . . . The United States can't be a punching bag in the world anymore' (Wood-ward 1996: 262–3). With this robust policy in place, the United States took the necessary measures to enable a forceful military response to any attack on Gorazde. At the London Conference on 21 July the agreement of NATO allies France and the United Kingdom was secured. According to an inter-view by Blechman with Secretary of Defense William Perry, the defining moment with regard to the threat to use force came on 23 July when the chiefs of the US, British and French armed forces visited Belgrade to convey the new resoluteness of NATO in the aftermath of the Srebrenica massacres (Blechman and Wittes 1999: 21). On 26 July the North Atlantic Council met in Brussels to 'work out the command and control arrangements'[10] and ter-minated the dual key arrangement by handing military control from the UN over to NATO. By the end of July officials had 'presented Milosevic and Mladic with a list of targets that NATO would bomb the next time Bosnian

Serb nationalist forces struck in Bosnia' (Sharp 1997/98). The loss of the Srebrenica and Zepa 'safe areas' had been the final straw that broke the back of existing Western policy toward Bosnia. Out of the débâcle emerged US military and diplomatic leadership in Bosnia and willingness on the part of the European allies to accept this position. The question we turn to now is what effect did news media coverage have on US military intervention in Bosnia, specifically the initial decision to defend Gorazde? If we observe critical news media coverage and policy uncertainty preceding the decision to defend Gorazde, then the news media is likely to have been a factor in causing the policy outcome. Alternatively, if we observe policy certainty and news media coverage following the decision to defend Gorazde then media coverage is unlikely to have been a factor in causing the policy outcome. In order to assess these variables the policy–media interaction model was applied to the period between the fall of Srebrenica and the defence of Gorazde.

Media framing: empathising with refugees and criticising Western policy[11]

The fall of Srebrenica was treated by the news media as an event of pre-eminent importance and this was reflected in the quantity of coverage devoted to the story. The *Washington Post* and the *New York Times* ran 70 articles on Bosnia between 11 and 18 July, averaging over four articles each per day. Every day at least one of these articles was run on the front page. CBS treated the fall of Srebrenica as the key news story between 11 and 14 July, allocating it to the leading headline slot whilst CNN ran 84 news segments mentioning Bosnia over the eight-day period. Such extensive coverage secured the fall of Srebrenica as an event of both media and political importance. To understand more fully the potential political impact of the coverage, we need to understand how its content was framed.

Out of 35 newspaper articles selected for analysis, 12 contained significant reference to the refugees from Srebrenica whilst 22 contained significant reference to Western policy. In terms of subject matter, therefore, news media coverage tended to highlight the issue of refugees and Western policy. Emotive language was used when describing the plight of refugees and the use of descriptors such as 'mass of wailing humanity', 'dazed', 'weeping', 'trail of tears' and 'driven' indicated the presence of an empathy frame in the articles read. One notable CBS news bulletin was headlined 'Bosnia Bleeding'. A selection of empathy descriptors can be seen in Table 4.1. The following extract is an example of the empathy framing:

> The air was filled with anguished cries as the Bosnian Serbs loaded the first 3,000 women, children and elderly refugees on to buses at Potocari, the United Nations base overrun today outside Srebrenica, which was captured on Tuesday. The refugees were dropped off

Table 4.1 A selection of descriptors used in relation to the people of Srebrenica and the West* taken from *Washington Post* and *New York Times* articles

Failure descriptors	*Empathy descriptors*
Talking so nice and doing nothing	Feuding
Sickly	Human tragedy
Lack of authority	Bedraggled
Viability at issue	Hungry
Spinelessness	Scared
Presence at risk	Little food, water or medicine
Doing too little, too late	Rousted from their homes
Lacks the military means	Trail of tears/tears, sobbing
Inaction	Frantic
Absence of will	Desperately
Muddle through strategy	Prayed for their missing
Doing nothing	Dazed
Caught by surprise	Weeping
Impotence	Hysterical
Feckless	Carrying only the clothes on their backs
Collapsing	Trudged
One humiliation after another	Without shelter
Ineffectual	Huddling
Reluctance to use force	Driven out
At an end	Human suffering
Unless strengthened, it is doomed	Rape
	Mass killing
	Murder
	Throats cut
	About to give birth
	Mass of wailing humanity

Note
*'West' includes US, UN, NATO, UNPROFOR and EU.

outside Kladanj, about 25 miles away, where they were forced to walk the last six miles across the front lines to the Government-held town.[12]

References to Western policy included the use of critical descriptors such as 'doing too little too late', 'absence of will', 'impotence', 'one humiliation after another' and 'sickly' (see Table 4.1) and indicated the presence of a failure frame in the news articles read. The following extract is an example of the failure framing of Western policy:

With Srebrenica, one of the six safe havens the United Nations had pledged to protect, already fallen to the Serbs last week, and a second, Zepa, heading to that end, the allies and the Clinton administration displayed the same division they have shown over the past three years as the situation worsened. Clinton and his aides have been united in only one thing: that unless the UN mission to protect civilians can be strengthened, it is doomed.[13]

The keyword test of the empathy and failure frames supported the empathy and critical frame inferences.[14] Starting with the empathy/distance frames, the number of times the population of Srebrenica were referred to as 'refugees', 'people', 'women', 'elderly' and 'children' (empathy keywords) was quantified. Conversely, the number of times the labels 'Muslim', 'Bosnian', 'men', 'soldier' and 'fighter' (distance keywords) were used to refer to the population of Srebrenica was quantified. Examining Table 4.2 empathy keywords outnumbered distance keywords 517 to 195. Regarding the failure framing of the West, the number of times the words 'fail', 'withdraw' and 'end' were used in relation to the West was counted. One would expect these terms to dominate in news reports that focused upon the failure of the West to protect Srebrenica and the possibility of the UN mission collapsing. Conversely, the number of times the keywords 'success', 'protect' and 'continue' were used in relation to the West were counted. One would expect these success/non-failure framing terms to dominate in news media reports that focused upon the positive aspects of the 'safe area'[15] policy and the continuance of the UN presence in Bosnia. Again, the critical keywords outnumbered support keywords, 180 to 71 (see Table 4.2).

Overall both the interpretive and systematic framing analyses indicated that news media coverage tended to highlight the plight of the refugees from Srebrenica in a tone that empathised with their suffering and also served to emphasise the failure of Western policy in Bosnia.

Table 4.2(a) Media coverage of the UN and the West, 11–18 July 1995

Failure frame		Success/non-failure frame	
Keyword	Frequency	Keyword	Frequency
Fail	62	Succeed	5
Withdraw	107	Protect	56
End	11	Continue	10
Total	180	Total	71

Table 4.2(b) Media coverage of the expelled population of Srebrenica, 11–18 July 1995

Empathy frame		Distance/neutrality frame	
Keyword	Frequency	Keyword	Frequency
Refugees	236	Muslim	83
People	148	Bosnian	29
Women	68	Men	66
Children	52	Soldier	15
Elderly	13	Fighter	2
Total	517	Total	195

Sources: Washington Post, available online at http://www.washingtonpost.com; *New York Times* and CNN search available via Lexis-Nexis; and CBS evening news segments available via Vanderbilt TV News Archive.

'What do we do next?'[16]

Following the fall of Srebrenica the US executive was placed in a difficult position with regard to whether they would act to retake Srebrenica or move to ensure adequate defence of other 'safe areas'. For example, on 11 July Anthony Lake was asked by a journalist for an assessment on the situation in Bosnia. Lake replied bluntly 'let me give you a very brief answer: No!'[17] When asked to elaborate, Lake said 'because this is a fluid situation, is one reason. I'm leaving, and as you know is our practice, when we're in the middle of a situation like that, for a variety of reasons, we prefer not to comment.'[18] On the same day also, White House spokesperson Mike McCurry was placed in a difficult position when asked whether the US would intervene to save Srebrenica. McCurry initially attempted to deflect these questions by stating that the European-led RRF was set up to respond to crises such as the Bosnian Serb assault on Srebrenica. When it was pointed out that the US marines were available offshore and the RRF was not yet fully deployed, McCurry refused to be drawn to comment. At this point a frustrated journalist remarked:

> Well Michael, what is the point of the president going to Denver and making a public pledge to rescue peacekeepers in danger when the first and most prominent case of that comes up and no one in this administration can say whether or not this is what he was talking about?[19]

More specifically, analysis of press briefings across the White House, Department of Defense and State Department sub-systems indicated there was no policy line regarding whether or not greater force would be used to defend the threatened Gorazde 'safe area'. For example, on 13 July a State Department spokesperson stated:

> I think there are two factors at work. One is that the United Nations and the troop-contributing countries have got to make a fundamental decision – whether they will use military force or military strategy to try to either regain what has been lost or to protect what may be lost. That is a very important question, one that has not yet been fully answered.[20]

Again, on 18 July, McCurry stated: 'I'll say it's not useful at this point for me to speculate on any possible military action in connection with strengthening UNPROFOR because there's a lot of speculation out there that, frankly, right now is inaccurate.'[21] In short, official statements during this crisis period indicate that there was no policy regarding the use of force and therefore policy uncertainty existed during the period in question. The presence of policy uncertainty is also indicated by Richard Holbrooke (1992: 348), Warren Christopher (1998: 348) and Ivo H. Daalder (1999: 72–3), all of whom note that one of the key decisions during the days following Srebrenica was the decision to draw a line at Gorazde. Clearly this decision would have been under discussion in the days leading up to it. In addition to uncertainty over whether or not to defend Gorazde, US policy toward Bosnia was in a state of flux or transformation (i.e. undecided policy) during this period. As noted earlier, Lake had been working on his end-game strategy that involved a renewed diplomatic effort and a threat to bomb if required. This broader policy development was given the go ahead at the 17 July meeting (Daalder 1999: 101) and was finalised in early August.

Overall the presence of no policy with regard to a decision to defend Gorazde and the presence of undecided policy regarding Lake's end-game strategy indicate the presence of policy uncertainty in US executive sub-systems at a micro and macro level respectively.

Assessing media influence

By emphasising the failure of the West and empathising with the expelled population of Srebrenica, news media coverage was of a critical 'do some-thing' nature. This critical coverage took place alongside policy uncertainty when US policy-makers were unsure whether or not any further violations of UN 'safe areas', specifically an attack on the Gorazde 'safe area', should be responded to with the use of force. The theoretical insight provided by the policy–media interaction model is that under these conditions media cover-age is likely to have influenced the policy process, causing a strong CNN effect to occur and helping to produce a decision to intervene in order to defend Gorazde. Specifically the existence of no policy regarding the use of force meant that policy-makers would have been pressured to respond to the critical coverage or else face further negative publicity. With respect to the enabling effect, the presence of critical coverage and policy uncertainty indi-cates a strong CNN effect, as opposed to an enabling effect, having occurred (in which case we would have expected to observe policy certainty in favour of intervention with policy-makers exploiting empathy-framed coverage). The inference of a strong CNN effect is supported by Woodward's account of the 18 July meeting when it was decided to defend Gorazde. Vice President Gore declared:

> The worst solution would be to acquiesce to genocide . . . and allow the rape of another city [Gorazde] *and* more refugees. At the same time we can't be driven by images because there's plenty of other places that aren't being photographed where terrible things are going on. But we can't ignore the images either . . . My 21-year-old daugh-ter asked about that picture [in the *Washington Post* of a Muslim

woman who hung herself following the Serb assault] . . . What am I supposed to tell her? Why is this happening and we're not doing anything? . . . Acquiescence is not an option.

(Woodward 1996: 262–3)

Other policy-makers also recognised the importance of media coverage during this period. For example, although not wishing to over-emphasise media impact during this period, Anthony Lake noted the importance of media coverage in 'establishing a context' for policy deliberations and 'increasing the pressure more on the administration'.[22] Lake also referred to there being a 'cumulative effect' through three years of negative coverage. He noted that 'the inability of UNPROFOR . . . and the pictures of UNPROFOR hostages [following air strikes earlier in 1995] . . . and UNPROFOR failing' were an effect. 'There were few pictures of the humanitarian work UNPROFOR was doing . . . nearly all the pictures were of failures.'[23]

In addition to influencing the decision to defend Gorazde, evidence indicates that critical media coverage also provided additional bargaining power during a period of undecided policy when those in the administration sought the adoption of a more forceful and engaged stance toward Bosnia (as manifested in Lake's end-game strategy). For example during the 17 July meeting, when Lake presented his end-game strategy to the principals, Clinton drew upon the critical coverage to move forward Lake's policy. Clinton declared 'I don't like where we are now . . . This policy is doing enormous damage to the United States and to our standing in the world. We look weak . . . [it] can only get worse down the road . . . we have a war by CNN' (Woodward 1996: 261). In addition Alexander Vershbow and Anthony Lake both agreed that media coverage helped those within the administration who sought both a decision to defend Gorazde and a more forceful US stance toward Bosnia. Indeed a clear example of this phenomenon is Holbrooke's use of ABC's *Nightline* to describe the loss of Srebrenica as the West's 'greatest collective failure since the 1930s'.[24]

Outside the internal politics of the Clinton administration, Vershbow and Lake argued that the fall of Srebrenica and the ensuing press coverage provided the US with an 'opportunity to forge a consensus amongst allies' to take a more forceful stance in Bosnia.[25] Here, whilst a strong CNN effect had persuaded US policy-makers to defend Gorazde, an enabling effect then came into play when persuading its NATO allies of the need for action. In addition Holbrooke has also emphasised the importance of news media coverage with regard to US intervention in Bosnia in 1995, stating that 'the reason the West finally, belatedly intervened was heavily related to news media coverage' (Holbrooke 1999: 20).[26] Finally, and with respect to public opinion, Sobel, in a comprehensive review of opinion poll data notes that 'although support for allied air strikes against Serb military forces in Bosnia was initially low . . . approval grew over time and [by late 1993] most

Americans became willing to use US air power when either UN troops[27] or Bosnian civilians in safe havens were attacked'[28] (Sobel 2000: 114). So if policy-makers were considering the broader state of public opinion, as indicated by opinion polls, this would have served to reinforce the immediate pressure from the critical and empathy-framed media coverage. Overall, the theoretical model, secondary accounts and primary interview data support the inference of a strong CNN effect in this case. Before drawing final conclusions, however, it is necessary to consider other factors influencing the policy process during this period.

Recognising the importance of other factors

First and foremost Loza, Woodward and Holbrooke all emphasise the importance of the moves by Lake to develop a coherent and goal-orientated policy toward Bosnia, his so-called end-game strategy (Loza 1996: 38; Woodward 1996: 254–60; Holbrooke 1998: 68). This in turn was driven by the desire to avoid a humiliating UN withdrawal from Bosnia. The factor most often cited as threatening the continuing viability of the UN mission was the possibility that Britain and France might withdraw their peacekeeping troops (Loza 1996: 38; Woodward 1996: 257; Gow 1997: 274; Holbrooke 1998: 63–70). Gow (1996: 274) also argues that the moves in Congress to lift the arms embargo on Bosnia-Herzegovina with the Bosnian Self-Defence Act, coupled with the possibility that the Bosnian government might withdraw support for UNPROFOR in light of its general failure to fulfil its mandate, added to the likelihood of UNPROFOR collapsing. Clearly these factors would all have been important in moving the US to a more forceful stance in Bosnia. That is to say US military intervention could have been designed to avert the collapse of UNPROFOR, the continuation of which was threatened by these pressures.

At the same time, however, none of these factors were decisive or, in other words, can account for the decision alone. The Bosnian Self-Defence Act only allowed for the lifting of the arms embargo *after* a decision by either the Bosnian government or the troop-contributing countries had been made to terminate the UN mission.[29] Hence the passing of the legislation could not, in and of itself, have threatened the termination of UNPROFOR. In respect to British and French withdrawal, whilst London and Paris had signalled that 'withdrawal was contemplated' (Gow 1997: 276) after May 1995 there is little evidence that the matter was prominent during the decision period in July. Indeed both Loza (1996: 28) and Gow (1996: 274) point out that 'by this time [July 1995] Bosnia had gained a symbolic significance much greater than its real importance' (Loza 1996: 28) and that, consequently, neither France nor Britain were inclined to 'endure the humiliation of withdrawal' (Gow 1996: 274). Regarding the Bosnian government, whilst it had repeatedly expressed its dissatisfaction with the UN mission over the preceding years, there is again little evidence that this matter was a prominent issue during the decision period in question. In particular Bosnian President Izetbegovic is quoted as having stated that although he would probably not 'extend the UN peacekeepers' mandate when it expires in November', he would 'not ask them to leave before then' (Izetbegovic, cited in Power 1995). Hence, whilst these factors were clearly important in influencing US policy, they do not negate the importance of the strong CNN effect in this case.

A second way of explaining US military engagement is in terms of the image and credibility of both the UN mission and the Western alliance following the fall of Srebrenica. Most available accounts point to the impact of the fall of Srebrenica in moving US policy toward a more forceful stance. For Loza, Srebrenica was the final act to unite the West against the Bosnian Serb nationalists (Loza 1996: 38) and for Gow it left the UN mission threadbare (Gow 1997: 274). Woodward argues that it enabled Lake to move forward his end-game strategy (Woodward 1996: 261) whilst, for Holbrooke, the fall of the 'safe area' 'left no more energy . . . in the international system' (Holbrooke 1998: 70). Finally, Clinton himself cites the collapse of Srebrenica as a turning point for US policy:

> When that happened, and the threat of hostage-taking . . . caused Srebrenica to fall without a terrific response in terms of air punishment. That collapsed the support for the United Nations, and all of us, including the United States and NATO, who had supported it, suffered in prestige . . . not because we didn't win, but because the UN didn't do what it said it was going to do. You can't go about the world saying you're going to do something and then not do it.[30]

With the UN mission publicly discredited and in ruins, the US was faced with either aiding a humiliating UN withdrawal or, as was the case, taking a firm stand against any further Bosnian Serb nationalist aggression by taking a military lead in Bosnia and defending the Gorazde 'safe area'. Importantly, whilst concern over Western credibility would have been an important factor in its own right, it does not negate the importance of media influence at this point. Clearly the widespread and critical news media coverage detailed here inevitably played a part in elevating the political significance of the fall of Srebrenica. The claim that policy-makers were affected by the horrific footage coming back from Srebrenica is supported by the statements revealing Clinton and Gore discussing the damaging nature of news media coverage during this period (as detailed above). Introducing news media coverage as a factor also helps makes sense of Clinton's own reference to both Western prestige being damaged and the US looking weak during this period. The critical coverage identified in this study would have played an important part in both communicating the horror of Srebrenica to Western policy-makers and raising the political stakes. In short, the negative media coverage would have contributed to making Western credibility an issue at this point. Also, whilst the concern over credibility raises questions about the humanitarian intent of policy-makers during this decision process, it does not undermine the importance of the media in this case. Indeed, as noted in Chapter 1, whether or not there exists humanitarian intent on the part of policy-makers is, to an extent, distinct from whether or not the media motivated policy-makers to act. Indeed the intention of policy-makers in this case might have been to respond to critical coverage by intervening rather than a direct concern to save lives (with this being a by-product of their need to respond to the critical coverage).

Overall, the case study findings, primary interviewing and secondary accounts all point toward media coverage being a factor in producing the decision to defend Gorazde and in helping to move forward Lake's end-game strategy which represented broader US diplomatic involvement in Bosnia. Other factors, as noted, were also important but none are sufficient on their own (unlike the desire to stop refugee flows in the case of the Iraq case study) to explain the intervention and, therefore, they do not negate the importance of media influence in this case. At the same time it must be accepted that disentangling the relative significance of each factor is difficult to achieve from this case study alone. As such the extent to which media coverage was a minor as opposed to major factor in the decision to defend Gorazde is unclear. In order to test further the inference of media influence in this case it is therefore necessary to compare the findings with another instance of air power intervention in Bosnia. Putting this precisely, if policy uncertainty and critical and empathising coverage are found to be associated with another case of air power intervention in Bosnia, then our confidence in the thesis that media coverage was a factor in producing air power intervention regarding Gorazde will be increased. In fact, as we will soon see, the decision to defend Gorazde is consistent with another instance of media-influenced air power intervention in Bosnia.

The 1994 market-place massacre

The mortar bombing of a Sarajevo market place on 5 February 1994 is another instance when a combination of critical and empathy-framed media coverage, combined with policy uncertainty, preceded a decision to threaten air strikes against Bosnian Serb nationalist targets. The market bombing itself was one of the most horrific atrocities to have been 'caught on camera', involving the graphic depiction of the aftermath of a mortar bomb that had exploded in the middle of a crowded market place. Within four days the Clinton administration had issued an ultimatum to Bosnian Serb nationalists to stop the shelling of Sarajevo or else face air strikes. As we shall shortly see, patterns of policy certainty and media framing closely followed those observed during the decision to defend Gorazde.

Policy uncertainty

As in the Gorazde case, policy was in a state of flux, or evolution, when the market-place bombing occurred. Although the Clinton administration had briefly entertained the idea of greater involvement in Bosnia in early 1993, policy-makers had quickly decided to maintain a distance from the diplomatic and military response to the crisis. According to Warren Christopher (1998: 347) Clinton had been reading books on Balkan history that portrayed the region as trapped in an unbreakable circle of violence (for example, see Robert Kaplan's *Balkan Ghosts*). The siege of Sarajevo continued however and Bosnia, as a US political issue, never went away. In January 1994 NATO leaders met to try to thrash out a consensus on how to deal with the conflict. More than a week prior to the mortar bombing, French Foreign Minister Alain Juppé had pressurised Secretary of State Warren Christopher 'for a new US effort to bring pressure on the Muslims to settle' (Drew 1994: 410). The diplomacy also became public in a potentially embarrassing, at least for the Clinton administration, fashion. On 25 January the *New York Times* ran a front-page article, headlined 'US Rejects Plea to Act in Bosnia' (Sciolino 1994), detailing Juppé's criticisms of US policy. Juppé declared:

> If the Americans do not convince the Bosnian Muslims that they must stop fighting and that there is no chance that the United States would come to their rescue, then the United States will give them incentives to pursue the fighting on the ground. It would be a catastrophe. And we say to our American friends that they will be responsible for this.
>
> (Juppé, quoted in Sciolino 1994)

The French Foreign Minister then went on to make an even more provocative criticism of US policy: 'Warren Christopher told me today that there were six children killed in Sarajevo, and at the same time he told me everything was going well with the NATO initiative in New York . . . He said, just wait and see. Well, a wait-and-see policy is no longer possible for moral and political reasons' (Juppé quoted in Sciolino 1994).

According to an account by Elizabeth Drew (1994: 410), various sections of the US executive took advantage of these events and set about creating a new initiative for policy-makers. As Drew points out, the public nature of the disagreements with France played no small part in facilitating a change in policy: 'State Department officials had been already at work drawing up new proposals and saw Christopher's displeasure over his encounters with his counterparts, and the resulting bad publicity, as an opening for pushing a new initiative' (Drew 1994: 410). At the same time, the arrival of policy-makers more inclined to take forceful action, Secretary of Defense William Perry and General Shalikashvili, altered the balance of opinion within the administration on the issue of forcible intervention. By 4 February, one day before the mortar attack in Sarajevo, Warren Christopher had completed a position paper noting the difficulty for the US of remaining passive in response to Bosnia. He concluded 'It is increasingly clear that there will likely be no solution to the conflict if the United States does not take the lead in a new diplomatic effort' (Sciolino and Jehl 1994).

After news of the mortar bombing broke the administration, whilst adopting a low-key approach to avoid raising expectations over possible actions, moved to produce a response to the mortar bombing. Anthony Lake claims that '[w]e were thinking that first night, "we've got to do something"' (Lake cited in Sciolino and Jehl 1994) and the next day White House counselor David G. Gergen advised Clinton he had to 'put some steel' into policy and 'appear strong' (Gergen, cited in Sciolino and Jehl 1994) to the American public. The following day, in reply to the market-place bombing, Clinton publicly announced that deliberations were underway on how to respond to the attack:

> I have just completed a meeting with advisors discussing the terrible and outrageous incident in Sarajevo yesterday . . . And I have approved having the Secretary of State and Ambassador Albright continue their consultations with our allies about what next steps should be taken in response to this particular incident and to make an effort to try to reach a settlement, hoping that the shock of this incident will perhaps make all parties more willing to bring this matter to a close.[31]

One journalist, sceptical of Clinton's commitment to act, stated in response:

> Yesterday you said in your statement that you called the massacre a cowardly act. But some members of Congress are saying that the US is acting cowardly by repeatedly saying that they will consider air strikes without making good on those threats.[32]

Secretary of State Warren Christopher also confirmed that policy deliberations were underway on how to respond to the bombing:

> Over the weekend, John, I've been in touch more than once with most of my NATO colleagues. That whole range of issues is under discussion at the North Atlantic Council. It's under intense scrutiny and consideration. And, as I say, I think in the next few days the North Atlantic Council will be taking important decisions in this regard.[33]

At this point Sciolino also quotes an administration official who claimed policy-makers were divided over whether or not to use force: "'[t]here is a clear divide over whether or not to use force," a senior Administration official said' (Sciolino 1994).[34]

Finally though, and drawing upon a French proposal to create a demilitarised zone around Sarajevo, US policy-makers on Monday, 7 February formulated a tough response involving the setting up of an exclusion zone around Sarajevo and an ultimatum for Bosnian Serb nationalists to withdraw their weaponry or else face air strikes. Clinton agreed to this plan later that night (Sciolino and Jehl 1994). At this point, just over 48 hours since the market-place bombing had hit the news headlines, US policy had solidified around a decision to threaten to use force. In the following days US policy-makers sought to persuade key European allies, specifically those with ground troops already in Bosnia, to agree to the new policy to protect Sarajevo. Personal telephone lobbying of the British and Canadian Prime Ministers by President Clinton was necessary to create a consensus throughout NATO (Sciolino and Jehl 1994).[35] On 9 February, after a 14-hour meeting (Drew 1994: 411) of the North Atlantic Council (NAC), the NATO allies accepted the US policy. President Clinton, framing his announcement in terms of a shared and public experience of the Saturday mortar bombing, set out the justification and terms of the threat to use force:

> Like people everywhere, I was outraged by the brutal killing of innocent civilians in the Sarajevo market last Saturday. The events of the past year and the events of the past few days reinforce the belief that I have that more must be done to stop the shelling of Sarajevo and the murder of innocents. Therefore, the United States, working with our allies, has developed a series of proposals to address the situation in Sarajevo and to reinvigorate the negotiations to bring the bloodshed and the aggression in Bosnia to an end. As a result, just now in Brussels, NATO has decided that if any Bosnian Serb heavy weapons are found within 20 kilometers of Sarajevo within 10 days – or after 10 days – or if there is any further shelling of Sarajevo, NATO commanders stand ready to conduct air strikes against Serb artillery positions. NATO would carry out such strikes in accord with procedures it agreed on last August.[36]

In short, similar to the Gorazde case study, during the two days immediately following the market-place bombing, policy uncertainty existed at both the macro level and micro level. At the macro level some policy-makers were seeking a more forceful stance toward the Bosnian conflict, that is to say there existed undecided policy, and at the micro level no policy existed with regard to a military response to the market bombing.

News media coverage between 5 and 9 February 1994

Between the market-place bombing and the issuing of the ultimatum four days later, media coverage of Bosnia was intense. The *New York Times* ran 48 articles mentioning Bosnia (giving a daily article average of 12) whilst the *Washington Post* ran 21 articles mentioning Bosnia (average 5.25 articles per day).[37] The *New York Times* carried at least one front-page story on Bosnia every day (6–9 February) except on the day of the attack whilst the *Washington Post* ran at least one front-page story on Bosnia (7–9 February) except the day of the attack and the next day (a Sunday). In terms of the news networks, CNN ran 132 reports between 5 and 9 February, giving a daily average of 26.4 reports mentioning Bosnia.[38] ABC and CBS headlined (except the day of the attack when the story was second) each evening whilst Bosnia was 'the' headline news on NBC every day except 5 and 8 February when the story was the second headline and still run within the first ten minutes of the news starting.[39] In summary, the Sarajevo market-place bombing was, instantaneously, a major story commanding the full attention of both print and electronic media.

In terms of content and framing, the coverage, generally speaking, conformed to an empathy framing, at times containing explicit criticism of the Clinton administration's repeated failure to act in Bosnia and implicitly pushed for some kind of response to the market-place bombing.[40] For example, on the day of the bombing the three main news networks[41] carried horrific footage of the aftermath of the shelling containing images of mutilated bodies. For the next two days these same channels all opened their evening news programmes with follow-up stories detailing the aftermath of the market-place bombing. At the same time, ABC gave headline airtime to Bosnian Prime Minister Haris Silajdzic, who accused the UN of appeasement, and Fred Cuny (USAID), who accused Bosnian Serb nationalists of launching the attack. CNN coverage[42] was, if anything, even more dramatic, and was both empathising and implicitly pressuring for action to be taken. The following text is an extract from a CNN report by Roger Walters on the day of the shelling:

> Between 50 and 60 civilians were killed. The situation is so confused, no one is sure how many are wounded, but the estimates run above 150. These people were mangled by flying steel from what was thought to be a 120 millimeter mortar shell. They had no warning – walking among the market stalls, a tremendous explosion occurred. A moment later, the ground was littered with decapitated bodies as well as severed arms and legs. Eight bodies were so badly mangled they could not even tell if they were men or women. Sarajevo's hospitals are overwhelmed. The wounded lay moaning in the corridors waiting for medical attention. The dead lay among the dying. So

outrageous was the carnage, the Bosnian government is now characterizing this as a fight between good and evil.[43]

Also, a significant degree of airtime was given to members of the Bosnian government and critics of Western policy who used the opportunity to condemn the passivity of the international community; CNN headlines ran 'Civil War Between Good and Evil, Say Bosnian Officials',[44] 'Bosnian Vice President Pleads for International Support',[45] 'Congressman, Former Diplomat Slams US Policy in Bosnia',[46] 'Modern Medicine No Match for Recent Sarajevo Carnage',[47] and 'Muslim Genocide at Hands of Serbs, Asserts Bosnian VP'.[48]

In terms of the broadsheet newspapers, a similar pattern of empathy-framed coverage emerged. Moreover, the vast bulk of op-eds openly criticised the Clinton administration's past failures to act in Bosnia and, whilst often not making precise policy prescriptions, demanded that 'something be done' in response to the mortar bombing. For example, in the *New York Times*, four out of the five editorials run on Bosnia throughout the period demanded a response to the bombing.[49] *Washington Post* editorials were slightly less sympathetic toward air power intervention but still contained strong criticism of the Clinton administration's failings in Bosnia.[50] An example of such critical framing can be seen in the following extract in an op-ed by Anthony Lewis:

> In one bloody moment the hypocritical façade of President Clinton's empty policy on Bosnia crumbled. The mortar shell that killed 68 people as they shopped in Sarajevo's market on Saturday brought an end to the pretence that America had a meaningful policy. Mr Clinton inherited a Bosnian horror from European appeasers and President Bush. After a weak show of wanting to act he essentially withdrew from the problem, hoping Americans would forget it. From the lowest echelon of the State Department to near the highest, no one believed in the non-policy. How far the rot of official cynicism had gone was shown in a report given at the National War College last month by Richard Johnson, a department officer who formerly headed its Yugoslav desk. He titled the paper 'The Pinstripe Approach to Genocide'.[51]

Assessing the impact

As with the July 1995 decision to defend the Gorazde 'safe area', a combination of policy uncertainty, characterised by both a context of policy evolution (undecided policy) and the absence of specific policy on the use of force (no policy), and critical and empathising news media coverage was associated with a decision to threaten the use of air strikes in pursuit of a humanitarian objective. According to the policy–media model a strong CNN effect is likely to have occurred under these conditions. Anecdotal interview-based material, accounts of what policy-makers were saying at the time and in-depth accounts of policy deliberations all support the inference of a strong CNN effect in this case. For example Strobel (1997: 57), drawing upon his discussions with policy-makers, argues that the television images enabled Warren Christopher to 'make his case both publicly and within the administration' for more forceful action. Christopher himself acknowledged the influence of the media in an interview with NBC's *Today* programme stating that '[t]elevision images moved forward a policy we had clearly started on' (cited in Gowing 1994: 72). Although Christopher implies here that the intervention would have occurred anyway, Drew (1994: 411) suggests that the actual policy of protecting Sarajevo was a function, not of Christopher's new-found desire for the US to become more closely involved in the Bosnian War, but of the market-place massacre and its televising across the world:

> Whether the administration and its allies would have done anything militarily about Sarajevo if the attack, and the terrible television pictures, had not happened cannot be known. The administration had been moving toward a new policy of diplomacy that could have used military force, but this hadn't involved setting up the special protection for Sarajevo.

Also when interviewed in 2001, Anthony Lake recalled, without prompting, the dramatic impact of images from the Sarajevo market bombing on policy-makers.[52] Finally, CNN correspondent Ralph Begleiter at the time claimed that administration sources had confirmed that Clinton was heavily influenced by media coverage: 'Well, for the first time today I heard a US official use the phrase crisis in Bosnia', and I've been told by administration officials that President Clinton was deeply struck by the images from Sarajevo, particularly in the market place last Saturday, and that he basically told his aides 'we've got to do something, we've got to find a way to do something'.[53]

Conclusion

The further correlation found in the secondary case study increases our confidence in the inference of media influence in the Gorazde case. In both cases empathy-framed coverage of atrocities and policy uncertainty were associated with policy responses from the US and are indicative of the occurrence of a strong CNN effect (although other factors were present). In the case of the 1994 mortar bombing, as with the decision to defend Gorazde in July 1995, the response came in the form of a threat to use force. In particular both case studies highlight the role of critical and empathy-framed media coverage in enabling those policy-makers, during periods of undecided and no policy, who advocate intervention to sell their policy to other members of the policy-making elite.

5

THE LIMITS OF
THE CNN EFFECT

Overview

In this penultimate chapter the core case study analysed is the 1999 air campaign, Operation Allied Force, against Serbia and the failure of policy-makers to intervene directly in order to provide protection to the Albanian Kosovars. As detailed in Appendix D, despite terrible images of refugees fleeing Kosovo and much criticism throughout Washington and media as to the adequacy of the air campaign, at no point did the Clinton administration intervene, either with ground troops or close air support, to prevent attacks on Albanian Kosovars. As such the case represents one instance in which it appears that extensive news media coverage of a humanitarian crisis ran alongside policy-makers failing to respond to critical coverage. The secondary case study focuses upon the decision by the UN Security Council to withdraw UN forces from Rwanda during the 1994 genocide. The two cases highlight the limits of media influence when there exists a high level of policy certainty and allow us to examine whether the factors hypothesised to lead to media influence do actually vary in cases where media coverage was unable to influence policy-makers to intervene (non-intervention in the case of Rwanda and non-deployment of ground troops in the case of Kosovo) during a humanitarian crisis.

The layout mirrors the previous two case study chapters. First the background to events in Kosovo is detailed before reviewing recent debates regarding the role of the media in Kosovo. As well as the relationship between news coverage and US policy contrasting arguments regarding the media's role as a manufacturer of consent for Western policy and the adversarial role played by the press when criticising the air war campaign are also considered. Media coverage and policy certainty are then analysed and, in particular, close attention is given to whether a ground war decision was taken toward the end of the air campaign. The Rwanda case study is dealt with second, the results of which are then compared with those from the Kosovo case study.

Kosovo

The crisis in Kosovo developed from the dissolution of the Federal Republic of Yugoslavia. Although the conflict was late to flare up, compared with conflicts in Bosnia and Croatia, from the early 1980s ethnic tensions were apparent in Kosovo with elements of the Albanian Kosovar population seeking greater independence from Belgrade. During 1989, in the face of a growing Albanian Kosovar separatist movement, Milosevic exploited both the fears of the Serbian Kosovars[1] and the desires of nationalist Serbs, who perceived Kosovo as the heartland of the Serb people, by withdrawing the limited autonomy granted to Kosovo. Over the next seven years Milosevic continued to repress the Kosovar Albanian population. In response Albanian Kosovars supported a strategy of non-violent opposition to Belgrade.

When the war in Bosnia came to an end in 1995 the Dayton peace negotiations sought to secure peace throughout the region. However, Kosovo was left out of these negotiations and, therefore, a key opportunity to resolve the situation in that area was missed. In the following years increasing numbers of Albanian Kosovars became disillusioned with the lack of international support for the non-violent opposition and increasingly lent support to the Kosovo Liberation Army (KLA). By 1997 the situation in Kosovo was rapidly deteriorating as KLA attacks on Serbian paramilitary units were responded to with overwhelming force by Serb forces including retribution against civilians. By 1998 the international community, steered by the US, began to respond to the burgeoning crisis. In 1998 the UN Security Council passed Resolution 1160 condemning the excessive use of force by Serb forces whilst both Richard Holbrooke and Chris Hill (Special Envoy to Kosovo, formerly the Ambassador to Macedonia) sought a negotiated settlement between the KLA, the moderate Albanian Kosovar leader Rugova and Belgrade. By the summer of 1998 agreement had been reached on the deployment of observers throughout Kosovo in order to monitor ceasefire agreements and report on human rights violations. However, attempts to reach an actual ceasefire agreement failed and, against the backdrop of repeated fighting and the displacement of over 200,000 people, the US started to move toward a decision to use force against Serbia.

September 1998 to March 1999: the lead-up to US military intervention

The slide toward war started in September 1998 when NATO devised two contingency plans, one involving the deployment of troops to monitor a future peace deal, the second involving the use of air strikes. At first the threat of force, coupled with diplomacy, appeared to work and a ceasefire agreement was reached between all sides that allowed the deployment of 2,000 monitors, the Kosovo Verification Mission (KVM), throughout Kosovo. NATO also maintained a threat to use air strikes if Serbian forces engaged in further attacks on the Albanian population. However, fighting continued and, in January 1999, in what is widely considered to have been a turning point regarding the use of force, the Racak massacre occurred. Over 45 Albanian Kosovars were killed in an alleged assault by Serb government forces. According to Strobe Talbott:

> Racak was of course a very significant moment because of the horrific and much publicised nature of the crime but also because it seemed to be part of a pattern of escalation, of Serb repression and it had a galvanising effect for very understandable reasons on the Albanian community both in terms of fear and in terms of militant determination to resist.[2]

Echoing Talbott, Alexander Vershbow also noted a significant CNN effect at this time.[3] Also Christopher Hill (former Ambassador to Macedonia) claims that 'the press reinforced the pressure that we have to do something in Kosovo' (Hill, interviewed in Saberi 2000: 32). Although air strikes were not authorised, NATO officials were sent to Belgrade to threaten Milosevic with military action if further ceasefire violations and atrocities occurred. Against the backdrop of Serb defiance, highlighted by the Racak massacre, and the continuing conflict between the KLA and Serbia, the US cajoled both parties into attending peace talks at Rambouillet in France. Precisely what purpose these talks served is a matter of controversy. For some they represented a last ditch attempt by the US to forge an agreement between both sides. For others the talks involved a deal designed to be rejected by Milosevic, therefore clearing the way for NATO air strikes against Serbia (e.g. Chomsky 1999; Herring 2000). Either way, by mid-March the talks had collapsed and NATO was close to using force. The Kosovo Verification Mission was speedily withdrawn from Kosovo and, on 24 March, NATO commenced air operations against Serbia.

Operation Allied Force

The initial justifications for Operation Allied Force were both to send a signal to Milosevic not to escalate attacks on the Albanian Kosovars (arguably only a rhetorical justification as we shall see below) and to force him to comply with US demands. For example, in a press conference, Clinton explained the purpose of the bombing as follows:

> Our strikes have three objectives. First to demonstrate the seriousness of NATO's opposition to aggression, second to deter President Milosevic from continuing and escalating his attacks on helpless civilians, and third, if necessary, to damage Serbian capacity to wage war against Kosovo in the future.[4]

The hope of US policy-makers was that the air strikes would quickly succeed in persuading Milosevic to agree to whatever terms the US offered him. For example, on 24 March, Madeleine Albright stated 'I don't see this as a long-term operation . . . I think this is something to deter and damage [and] is achieved in a relatively short period of time.'[5] It was also known air strikes might well lead to a worsening of the humanitarian crisis in Kosovo, at least in the short term, and that their use could not protect Kosovar Albanians from attack. For example, as far back as February 1999, CIA director George Tennet briefed the US congressional leadership with regard to the planned military operations. In a BBC *Panorama* interview, Porter Goss (chairman of the House Intelligence Committee) was asked whether, in these briefings, Tennet had predicted that ethnic cleansing would follow the first air strikes. Goss replied: 'The short answer is yes, so I don't think the decision-makers, the policy-makers were misled by any analysis or any analytical picture.'[6] Also General Shelton, chairman of the Joint Chiefs of Staff, and General Klaus Naumann, chairman of NATO's Military Committee, claimed that it was widely known that bombing could not offer protection to the Kosovar Albanians. Shelton states: 'The one thing we knew we could not do upfront was that we could not stop the atrocities or the ethnic cleansing through the application of military power.'[7] Naumann claims: 'I said on one occasion in the council, we cannot stop this by using air power alone, it's impossible . . . but as soon as a statement [Clinton's statement of purpose detailed above] is done, it's there.'[8]

Unfortunately, soon after the air strikes began it became apparent that Milosevic was not willing to back down and that the worst predictions of the military and intelligence advisers were being realised as attacks on the Kosovar Albanians rapidly escalated. It was at this point that a massive refugee crisis occurred as Milosevic accelerated sharply the expulsion of Albanian Kosovars from the region. As increasingly desperate images were transmitted back from refugee camps, a substantial debate occurred in Washington over whether the bombing campaign was sufficient to reverse the expulsion of Albanian Kosovars and indeed whether it was only worsening their plight. An important element to this debate was the question of whether ground troops would be required in order to reverse the ethnic cleansing of Kosovo. The ground war debate was heightened by the involvement of high profile politicians such as Colin Powell (former chairman of the Joint Chiefs of Staff) who emphasised the inadequacy of air power alone. NATO commander Wesley Clark's own scepticism with regard to the air campaign was at best thinly veiled during this period. For example, when asked by CBS anchor Dan Rather if he believed air power was sufficient, Clark replied: 'I have my own military views and beliefs, as you might imagine. I'm looking very carefully at the mission that has been assigned, what the requirements are . . . and Dan I just have to leave it that way.'[9] Indeed Wesley Clark was persistent in his attempts to persuade policy-makers and NATO allies both to escalate the air campaign and plan for a ground invasion (Clark 2001: 221–92).

The debate over the adequacy of the air war and the need for a ground troop option was brought to a head in a failed attempt by Senator John McCain to force an escalation to a ground war via a congressional vote in late April. At around the same time, the bringing together of NATO leaders for the fiftieth NATO anniversary summit during late April enabled Western leaders to harden the resolve of the alliance to maintain the air campaign. At the same time, the sceptical NATO commander Wesley Clarke was removed from press briefings after a press conference was interpreted by journalists as 'undercutting support for the air campaign and feeding efforts to promote a ground attack' (Clark 2001: 273–4). General Shelton told Clark:

> Wes, at the White House meeting today there was a lot of discussion about your press conference . . . The Secretary of Defense asked me to give you some verbatim guidance, so here it is: 'Get your f—g face off the TV. No more briefings period. That's it.'
>
> (Clark 2001: 273)

By the beginning of May, elite criticism of the air war had dissipated and in the following weeks the air campaign intensified alongside vigorous diplomacy via Russia. The air campaign ended in early June with a peace deal involving the deployment of over 40,000 NATO troops in Kosovo and the complete withdrawal of Serbian forces from the province.

Kosovo and the media

NATO's eight-week air campaign against Serbia provoked widespread controversy. For those who had championed the cause of 'humanitarian' intervention throughout the 1990s, Operation Allied Force was confirmation of the increased willingness of Western governments to protect human rights, even if this meant violating state sovereignty. Other more sceptical commentators argued that NATO's humanitarianism was limited in that Western governments were willing to fight (i.e. deploy air power) but not to die (i.e. deploy ground troops) (Paul Robinson 1999; Ignatieff 2000). More critical commentators, both from the left and the right of the political spectrum, challenged the prevalent assumption that the air war could be described as humanitarian at all. These critics argued instead that the air strikes represented an exercise in power politics aimed at coercing Milosevic into complying with US demands and served only to worsen dramatically an ongoing humanitarian crisis (Chomsky 1999; Luttwak 1999; Hammond and Herman 2000a; Herring 2000). These controversies were reflected in a diversity of opinions on precisely what role news media played during the crisis. Broadly speaking, two perspectives on the role of news media have emerged. First, that the media manufactured consent for Western policy and, second, that the news media played an oppositional role critiquing US and NATO policy. I shall outline briefly each in turn.

For many of those opposed to the war the news media functioned primarily to manufacture consent for Western policy (Chomsky 1999; Hammond 2000; Hammond and Herman 2000b; Herring 2000). According to these critics NATO's 'pro-war narrative' (Herring 2000), amongst other things, rested upon the Rambouillet negotiations being presented as a genuine last ditch attempt by Western governments to secure peace in the region and the claim that the mass expulsion of Kosovar Albanians was planned and decided upon before NATO air strikes started. In support of this pro-war narrative, media coverage ignored moves by Serbia to compromise during the Rambouillet talks, the draconian requirement put forward during negotiations demanding that NATO be allowed to occupy *all* of Serbia and statements by policy-makers that suggested the Rambouillet talks were merely designed to clear the way for NATO to bomb Serbia.[10] In short, as Hammond and Herman describe (2000b: 202), 'the mainstream media portrayed the diplomatic process as one of a reasonable NATO interested in a negotiated settlement confronting an evasive and unreasonable enemy'. Again, regarding the debate whether the bombing was in retaliation to attacks on Kosovar Albanians or rather was actually precipitating their wholesale expulsion, Hammond and Herman (2000b: 204) argue that 'NATO's role in this humanitarian disaster was denied or played down, on the grounds that the Serbs were planning on doing this anyway, a claim of NATO officials and apologists which they had never mentioned prior to the bombing.' As result of such omissions and uncritical acceptance of official policy, Hammond and Herman (2000b: 207) conclude:

> The mainstream media of the leading NATO powers supported the war against Yugoslavia with almost uniform and uncritical enthusiasm. They accepted without question the justice of the NATO cause . . . In this fetid atmosphere of sanctimony, the hugely biased reporting which characterised the Kosovo conflict flourished.

The second interpretation of media–state relations is that the news media were often highly critical of the NATO air campaign, and functioned as a 'watchdog' of official policy. For example, US newspapers often criticised the air campaign, arguing that it could not achieve the objectives set. Particularly in the early stages of the war, headlines such as 'Despite Lessons, Clinton Seen Lacking Strategy'[11] and 'Allies Facing the Limits of Air Power: Pitfalls of a Clinton Policy Dubbed "Immaculate Coercion" Grow Evident'[12] portrayed the air war policy in a bad light. Also, toward the end of the air war, repeated errors by NATO, such as the bombing of refugees and the destruction of the Chinese embassy in Belgrade by cruise missiles, created brief but appalling coverage for NATO and Western governments became increasingly concerned that Milosevic might be winning the propaganda war. Indeed, one of the major developments *vis-à-vis* NATO's media campaign was the deployment of 'heavy weight' spin doctors such as Alastair Campbell from the British government during May in order to counter critical news media coverage (Brown 1999).

These two perspectives on media–state relations will be reviewed in light of the case study findings. The specific task in hand, however, is to determine the level of policy certainty and media framing during the air campaign. As this is a case of non-influence (and even 'non-intervention' in the sense that there was no direct intervention on the ground or via close air support to protect the Albanian Kosovars), we expect to observe policy certainty against escalation to a ground war combined with either distance framing (therefore implicitly supporting avoiding direct ground troop intervention) or critical and empathy framing in which case we would expect policy certainty to prevent any CNN effect from occurring. In order to evaluate these possibilities we need to apply the policy–media interaction model to the period between 1 April and 26 May 1999.

News media empathy and some criticism of official policy[13]

News media coverage of Operation Allied Force was vast. Between 1 April and 26 May over 1,000 articles in the *New York Times* and the *Washington Post* made reference to Kosovo. This equates to over nine articles per day on Kosovo in each paper. Coverage of Kosovo over the eight weeks rarely left the front pages of the broad sheets and topped CBS news bulletins almost every day, whilst CNN ran 1,406 news segments on Kosovo between 1 April and 26 May. By devoting substantial coverage, the media identified Operation Allied Force as an event of pre-eminent importance.

The interpretive aspect of the framing analysis proceeded along broadly similar lines to that conducted into media coverage of the fall of Srebrenica. Over the period 1 April to 26 May, 429 reports made significant reference to Western policy and the refugees. So, as with the fall of Srebrenica, news media coverage highlighted the topics of refugees and Western policy. Selected reports were then read in order to:

1   identify the extent to which reports referring to Western policy were critically mixed or supportively framed and
2   identify the extent to which reports referring to the refugees were empathy, mixed or distance framed.

Reference to Western policy in the *Washington Post* and the *New York Times* during April tended to be critical with many reports highlighting the failure of the bombing campaign to prevent ethnic cleansing. A list of critical descriptors can be found in Table 5.1. An example of the critical framing can be seen in the following *New York Times* report:

> NATO must now begin to assemble ground troops, ready to enter Kosovo as a fighting force if necessary or to be a protection force for returning refugees if and when the Serbian forces are gone. Ruling out ground forces at the start was a grievous political mistake, convincing Mr Milosevic that we were not serious. A majority of Americans, and a larger majority of Britons, now favor the use of ground troops.
>
> (Lewis 1999: section A, p. 15)

Interestingly, the bulk of critically framed reports appeared in April. Throughout May coverage became more supportive overall. This point will be returned to later. For CBS and CNN, the coverage was different. For CBS, no clear frame, either supportive or critical, could be discerned during the interpretive analysis. For CNN, whilst the ground war/air war debate was covered, most references, as indicated by the keyword test, regarding the air campaign were positive, indicating that coverage was supportive of the existing policy. In May attention to the air war/ground war debate in both CBS and CNN bulletins subsided in line with print media.

Reference to refugees was empathy framed throughout the eight-week period. A list of empathy descriptors can be found in Table 5.1. An example of empathy framing can be seen in the following extract:

> The new wave of Serbian attacks, growing food shortages and the latest Serbian policy of allowing Albanians to freely cross the border here has swollen the flood of refugees fleeing from Kosovo. More than 3,000 dishevelled and dispirited ethnic Albanians trudged across the border here today clutching their life possessions in tote bags and backpacks, tripling the number who entered the previous day.
>
> (Rohde 1999: section A, p. 14)

The keyword test supported these inferences.[14] Starting with the empathy/distance frames, the number of times the population of Kosovo were referred to as 'refugees',[15] 'people', 'women' and 'children' (empathy keywords) was quantified. Conversely, the number of times the 'distancing' keywords 'Muslim', 'Albanian/Kosova(r)', 'men' and 'soldier' were used to refer to the population of Kosovo was quantified.[16] Regarding the failure/success frames, the number of times the words 'fail', 'lose' and 'not work' were used in relation to the West were counted. Conversely, the number of times the success keywords 'success', 'win' and 'work' were used in relation to the West was counted. Generally the

Table 5.1 A selection of descriptors used in relation to the Kosovar Albanians and Western* policy taken from *Washington Post* and *New York Times* articles

Critical words	Empathy words
What have his [Clinton's] policies done?	Thousands of refugees
Created instability	Charred bodies
Bombing alone is not sufficient	Desperate people
Instead of weakening Milosevic, he [Clinton] has united the Serbian people around Milosevic	Rape, torture and executions
	Misery of the refugees
	Three nights sleeping outside
Minimise risks rather than maximise results	Flood of refugees
	Devoid of life
Sending mixed messages	Hundreds of people hunker down
Foreign policy is being driven by public opinion	Old and young suffering from exposure
	Mother died in childbirth
Stop making vague pronounce-ments	People sleeping in the open
	Helpless men, women and children
Kosovo policy jinx	Refugee limbo
Shameful miscalculation	Refugee misery
Totally unprepared	Hepatitis and pneumonia raging
No plan	Makeshift shelters
Grievous political mistake	Smoke rises from smouldering homes
Clinton badly needs bipartisanship to save his policy in Kosovo	Devastated mosque
	Homes reduced to rubble
Administration can be faulted on its execution	
Gamble so much on Milosevic's caving in as soon as the bombs started falling	
We are unprepared	
Failed to weaken Milosevic	
Without the troops, there can be no victory	

Note
*'Western' includes US, UN, NATO, UNPROFOR and EU.

keywords selected reflected the policy debate in April which centred on whether the West would fail or succeed in Kosovo, whether the West was winning or losing and whether the air campaign was working or not.

The results of the framing analysis are shown in Table 5.2. Keywords associated with the empathy frame outnumber those associated with the distance frame 1,696 to 586, therefore supporting the interpretive inference that news media coverage was framed so as to empathise with the Kosovar refugees throughout both April and May. Regarding the critical/support framing, for the *New York Times* and *Washington Post* keywords associated with critical framing outnumbered those associated with support framing eight to two in April indicating a failure framing in April. However CBS figures show a more mixed picture with two occurrences of support keywords and one occurrence

Table 5.2(a) Media coverage of the expelled population of Kosovo, April and May 1999

Empathy frame		Distance/neutrality frame	
Keyword	Frequency	Keyword	Frequency
Refugees	724	Muslim	25
People	877	Albanian or Kosova(r)	482
Women	45	Men	65
Children	50	Soldier/fighter	14
Total	1,696	Total	586

Table 5.2(b) Media coverage of the NATO air war, April 1999

Failure frame		Success/non-failure frame	
Keyword	Frequency	Keyword	Frequency
Fail	6 + (**0** + *2*)	Succeed	2 + (**0** + *22*)
Lose	0 + (**1** + *3*)	Win	0 + (**1** + *14*)
Not work	2 + (**0** + *8*)	Work	0 + (**1** + *9*)
Total CBS and CNN	14		47
Total NYT and WP	8		2

Table 5.2(c) Media coverage of the NATO air war, May 1999

Failure frame		Success/non-failure frame	
Keyword	Frequency	Keyword	Frequency
Fail	1 + (**0** + *1*)	Succeed	1 + (**0** + *7*)
Lose	0 + (**0** + *1*)	Win	0 + (**0** + *1*)
Not work	0 + (**0** + *1*)	Work	0 + (**0** + *6*)
Total CBS and CNN	3		14
Total NYT and WP	1		1

Note
New York Times and *Washington Post* totals are outside brackets. CNN (bold italic) and CBS (bold) totals are inside brackets.

Sources: Washington Post, available online at http://www.washingtonpost.com; *New York Times* and CNN search available via Lexis-Nexis; and CBS evening news segments available via Vanderbilt TV News Archive.

of a critical keyword. This supports the interpretive inference that CBS coverage was mixed in April. CNN coverage, conversely, was generally supportive of the air campaign. Although dissenting voices were given airtime, as noted earlier, success keywords outnumbered failure keywords 45 to 13 in April. Overall the results therefore indicate a split between TV news and the broadsheets with the newspapers adopting a critical line, whilst TV news remained either neutral (CBS) or supportive (CNN). In May, keywords associated with both the support and critical frames occurred less frequently supporting the interpretive inference that the air war/ground war debate, at least in the media, died down after April. CNN coverage remained clearly supportive in May with support keywords outnumbering failure keywords 14 to 3.

Overall, during both April and May, an empathy frame prevailed in news media reports that encouraged empathy with the Albanian Kosovars rather than emotional distance. A failure frame predominated in newspaper reports during April that highlighted debate over the failure of Western policy, whilst CBS remained neutral and CNN coverage was generally supportive of official policy. In May, media attention to the air war/ground war debate subsided across all media outlets examined. With the continuance of empathy-framed coverage during May (which would have had the effect of building support for the air war) and the supportive coverage from CNN, overall coverage during May can be described as supportive of NATO's air war against Serbia.

'No intention to use ground troops'

The policy line not to use ground troops in anything but a permissive environment was consistently and clearly articulated across all three sub-systems of the US executive. This policy line was often articulated alongside the assertion that the air campaign was working. For example, on 10 April, Major General Wald declared, 'There's no intention right now at all to employ ground troops. The air campaign is going as planned.'[17] Also, the 'no ground troop' policy line was often reiterated in response to critical comments and questions from journalists. For example, the following exchange occurred on 6 April between a journalist and White House briefer Joseph Lockhart:

> *Journalist:* Joe, a couple of weeks ago, the biggest criticism of the President seemed to be that he didn't have an exit strategy. Now, you're hearing more and more that he doesn't have an entry strategy for ground troops. You've got Congress, you've got the press, even the polls are saying that there's a growing consensus for ground troops. My question is, is it possible that President Clinton is waiting for consensus to reach a critical mass before he then goes for ground troops, saying that this is the way the public has moved him and he's not out there alone?

> *Lockhart:* No, I think the President has made his choice, as he told you yesterday, on the best option available. He has no intention of introducing ground troops, and he's made his decision with the best advice he has from his military and foreign policy advisors.[18]

On 13 April, James Foley of the State Department declared: 'we have confidence in the air campaign. What we have made clear is that we don't have any intention now to introduce ground forces in a combat situation.'[19] At times, a different emphasis was placed on this 'no ground troops' policy line. For example, in late April, White House briefer Lockhart dropped the 'no intention' line. He stated instead: 'let me say that we have said all along that we need to persist with this air campaign, that is the option that we believe to be best as we are highly confident that it will get us to our military objectives'.[20] And in late May there is a slight shift in emphasis when the caveat 'no option is off the table' was added to policy statements. For example Rubin from the State Department stated:

> We have confidence it [the air campaign] can achieve its objective of getting President Milosevic to accept NATO's five conditions, and thus deploy a force with NATO at its core, get the Serb forces out and bring the refugees home. The other two are in there, too. With respect to our view, we have confidence in the air campaign, we haven't taken other options off the table, but we have no intention of deploying ground troops in anything but a permissive environment.[21]

However, despite these subtle shifts, policy never deviated significantly from the line that the air war was working and that there were no plans to fight a ground war.

Overall, there were no indications of policy uncertainty (i.e. 'wavering', 'inconsistent/undecided' and 'no' policy line). Rather, the policy line that the air war was working and that there was no intention to launch a ground invasion was consistently articulated. As such the analysis of press briefings indicates that there was no decision to launch a ground invasion during the period examined.

Was there a secret decision to launch a ground invasion?

Some commentators, however, maintain that the Clinton administration had decided to authorise a ground invasion in late May/early June (e.g. Erlanger 1999; Wintour and Beaumont 1999). For example, Erlanger cites Ivo H. Daalder, a former National Security Council official: 'In the end, the President concluded that he could not risk losing the war, and he was therefore prepared to send ground forces into Kosovo to assure a NATO victory' (Erlanger 1999). If this was the case then the press briefing analysis might be incorrect and, moreover, media coverage might have been a cause of this change in policy. In fact direct evidence for a change in policy is limited. The indication of a subtle shift in policy after 18 May, when press briefers introduced the caveat 'no option is off the table', could be read as an indicator of future action that had already been decided upon but was being kept secret. Also in late May the US executive started plans to strengthen the force that was to be used to implement any peace deal and press briefers spoke of a large increase in the intended numbers of troops. For example, on 18 May, Pentagon press briefer Kenneth Bacon stated:

NATO is in the process of reviewing what that force [Kosovo Force (KFOR)] should be. The initial plan was for a force of 28,000 people, and that would go in to enforce a peace – not to invade, not to create peace, but to enforce peace. NATO is in the process of increasing the size of that force, because they've decided that given all the changes that have taken place in Kosovo it's likely we'll need a larger force. Those numbers aren't clear yet, but the numbers of 45,000 to 50,000 have been floated around.[22]

Again, such a troop build up could be taken as indicative of plans for a ground invasion.

Beyond these facts, however, little evidence has come to light to suggest that a ground invasion was anything but a distant possibility by the time the air war ended.[23] Indeed Strobe Talbott, US Deputy Secretary of State stated that, if Milosevic had not agreed to the terms set out by Russian and Finnish diplomats in late May, the policy was simply to continue bombing rather than escalate to a ground war.

What would have happened if he had not accepted the terms? We would have kept bombing and the strains in NATO's and Russia's relations would have been more difficult over time to manage. I think there would have been increasing difficulties within the alliance in preserving the solidarity and resolve of the alliance. I don't think that it was a matter of days by any means but I think that it was a good thing that the conflict ended when it did and on the terms that it did.[24]

Also the then NATO Supreme Allied Commander (Europe) General Wesley Clarke has stated that 'we just never got to it [deploying ground troops]. We would have been OK had we had to do it, but we didn't have to do it' (quoted in Saberi 2000: 90). In his memoirs, Clark states 'I heard that the ground option had been taken up at the White House [for discussion] . . . [but] no one "wanted" to use ground troops. It would be far preferable if we could do the job with air power, but having the ground option ready to go would apply great pressure against Milosevic' (Clark 2001: 236). He (2001: 450) concludes:

The United States sought to succeed without the use of ground troops. Despite the military leaders' recommendations to plan for ground operations, the civilian leadership resisted. The President's statement that 'he had no intent' provided the initial rationale, but strong political and organizational forces were at work throughout the campaign [against the ground troop option].

Moreover the claim that policy-makers did decide to launch a ground invasion is inconsistent with the resistance of the Clinton administration and

NATO to any escalation that would involve US forces being exposed to greater risk (e.g. Luttwak 1999; Rodmen 1999). For example Luttwak (1999: 41) makes a trenchant point when discussing the reluctance to authorise close air support in order to prevent ethnic cleansing:

> NATO already had aircraft deployed on Italian bases that could have done the job just as well: US A-10 'Warthogs' built around their powerful 30 mm antitank guns and British Royal Air Force Harriers ideal for low-altitude bombing at close range. Neither was employed, again because it could not be done in perfect safety. In the calculus of the NATO democracies, the immediate possibility of saving thousands of Albanians from massacre and hundreds of thousands from deportation was obviously not worth the lives of a few pilots.

A further example of resistance to casualties was the Clinton administration's reluctance to deploy the Apache gunship helicopters. These were initially deployed at the request of NATO commander Wesley Clarke in mid-April alongside the suggestion that they would be deployed rapidly. And yet it quickly became clear that they would not be deployed in the near future. By mid-May, with still no sign of the helicopters being used, Pentagon briefers were alluding to the reason why they were not being used; on 14 May a Pentagon briefer stated: 'I don't want to discuss the Apache operation, because it's a future operation, and training and rehearsals are underway with that. But yes, I consider the shoulder-fired SAM threat to be one that is significant.'[25] Clark (2001: 303) also notes the tendency of his political masters to defer to Pentagon resistance to the deployment of the Apaches stating: 'Their [Pentagon] view nicely suited the political climate in Washington, where it was feared that casualties might discredit the campaign.'[26]

All this evidence highlights the reluctance of the Clinton administration[27] to risk the lives of US combatants and indicates that it would have been unlikely, therefore, to launch a ground invasion that would have resulted in the almost inevitable loss of many US soldiers.

Overall, as the evidence stands, the more justifiable interpretation of events is that a ground war decision was not taken by Clinton and his advisers, although the option was being prepared for both as a precaution if the air campaign failed and as a way of increasing the pressure on Milosevic. The Clinton administration could, at any point, have opted to escalate the war by using Apache helicopters and mobilising troops to go into Kosovo either to take the whole territory or to create 'safe areas', but it did not. Instead the US executive and NATO opted to expand the air war and sought a negotiated settlement via the Russians from late April onwards. Accordingly the evidence on balance indicates the existence of a high degree of policy certainty within the US executive to pursue the air campaign and not escalate to the use of either close air support or ground troops.[28]

Media influence: enabling and impediment effects, but no strong CNN effect

Overall the research shows critical and empathy-framed press coverage set against policy certainty in the US executive against an escalation to a ground war whilst TV news remained empathising but less critical and, in the case of CNN, supportive of policy. In terms of assessing overall impact these findings suggest media pressure to escalate to a ground war was at best ambiguous. The print media pressured for action whilst TV news gave policy-makers far less of a hard time and, in the case of CNN, served, if anything, to support US policy. Overall the research indicates that media coverage, taking into account the difference between print media and TV news, was mixed in terms of placing pressure on policy-makers to move to a ground war during April. Media coverage might have covered the ground war debate but policy-makers did not give into pressure from newspaper coverage by escalating to a ground war and, indeed, the existing air war policy benefited from more positive coverage in TV news. Moreover the subsidence of critical coverage in May (and supportive coverage from CNN), combined with empathy framing throughout May, meant that at this point overall coverage became supportive of Western air power intervention in Kosovo. In terms of the policy–media interaction model, the presence of mixed coverage (April) and supportive coverage (May), coupled with policy certainty, indicates that a strong CNN effect is unlikely to have occurred in this case. This is consistent with the fact that at no time did policy-makers move to intervene directly, by deploying close air support or ground troops, in the humanitarian crisis in Kosovo. Indeed Alexander Vershbow notes that coverage of the air war/ground war debate might even have helped support the goals of Western policy-makers. He states that, during this period, the CNN effect was at best 'marginal' and that 'policy was driven by the dynamics of the conflict' whilst 'media coverage of some significant events [e.g. the deployment of Apache helicopters in Albania] inadvertently helped in racketing up the political pressure on Milosevic'.[29]

Rather, instead of driving policy, the presence of empathy framing had a powerful enabling effect for the air power intervention by helping policy-makers to justify the policy to the public. For example, Vershbow notes that coverage of the refugees 'helped solidify public support . . . the cause may not have been as clear to the general public' without the media coverage.[30] Clark (2001: 240) also notes this effect, stating 'Above all we had a sense from the press and public reaction that Milosevic had made a serious strategic blunder by pushing the Kosovar Albanians out of Pristina. It was a galvanising moment for public opinion, and the sight of such human misery was certain to bring additional support to NATO'. Similarly, British Defence Secretary George Robertson declared:

> So we went from one week when people were saying 'why are you bombing?' to the following week when people were saying 'you're not

bombing enough'. We did it with the knowledge that the blood was not pouring down the screens of CNN and *Newsnight* in the first week, but we knew what was going on and that pretty soon there would be visible proof that would consolidate public opinion.[31]

Finally, on 12 April, Clinton declared: 'It is obvious to me that the support in the US and Europe for our actions in Kosovo has increased because of what people see going on' (cited in Saberi 2000: 18).[32] An analysis by Livingston (2000) of public opinion during the war against Serbia also supports this inference regarding the enabling effect, noting that, despite some drop in support, the US public upheld its support for NATO's air campaign.

In this case we also need to consider the possibility of potential negative coverage influencing policy outcomes (specifically the potential impediment effect). In this instance of non-influence it might be that fear of negative coverage of US casualties informed US reluctance not to escalate to a ground war (i.e. potential media coverage of US casualties, as well as the fact of possible US casualties, had an impediment effect). It certainly seems likely that such concerns informed US policy-makers. According to a review of opinion polls, Saberi (2000: 82) notes that US public opinion remained firmly against risking anything more than a handful of US lives. Lawrence Freedman (2000) argues that the 'body-bag' effect played a significant role during the Kosovo campaign concerning the reluctance of US policy-makers to escalate beyond air strike. The examples of US reluctance to employ close air support or the Apache helicopters owing to fear of casualties, detailed earlier, both support a strong impediment effect. Overall the potential impediment effect, as well as the desire to avoid US casualties period, is likely to have played a powerful constraining role on US policy-makers' views on the war against Serbia.

Media performance: manufacturing consent or government watchdog?

Drawing these findings together we can now evaluate the arguments set out earlier regarding the media as manufacturing consent for Western policy and, in contrast, acting as an adversarial 'watchdog' by criticising government policy. With respect to the latter argument, there is some support for the claim that the news media played an oppositional role to official policy. This occurred most obviously during April and within the print media when criticism of the air war-only strategy reached its height. At the same time, however, elite manufacturing consent theory, in particular Bennett's indexing hypothesis, helps explains why this coverage occurred and indeed why it died down in May. During April, when there existed elite dissensus over policy, the news media reflected this debate whilst the print media actually took sides in that debate and was, overall, predominantly critical of official policy. However, at the end of April, with the failure of McCain's attempt to escalate the conflict via a congressional vote, the hardening of resolve amongst NATO leaders at the 50th anniversary summit in late April and the removal of sceptical officials from press briefings, the level of elite dissensus reduced. This in turn reflected a reinvigorated PR campaign by NATO in May in order to maintain public support for the policy of air power intervention. As predicted by the policy–media interaction model, critical press coverage also declined.

With respect to the claim that the news media manufactured consent for Western policy, the research findings offer some support to the argument that news media coverage manufactured consent for executive policy. Although print coverage during April was set against executive policy TV news, in particular CNN tended to be supportive of existing policy. In addition, as noted above, the empathy-framed coverage of refugees helped provide policy-makers with a visible and compelling justification for Western air power intervention in Kosovo. Moreover, even if we ignore those in the media who were supportive of the war (i.e. CNN), the manufacturing consent argument is still cogent at a broad level. Whilst some critical coverage did occur, this operated within a certain set of boundaries, primarily concerning whether the air war was working or whether there should be an escalation to the use of close air support and/or ground troops. As described above, although some of this coverage was critical of official policy, it merely reflected elite dissensus. Hallin's typology of spheres, consensus, legitimate controversy and deviance are particularly useful in further illuminating this point. Legitimate controversy existed over the question of the utility of air power (at least during April) and the news media functioned within this sphere by covering this controversy. However media coverage never shifted into the deviant sphere by asking the kind of questions outlined earlier, such as the purpose of the Rambouillet negotiations and the role of NATO air strikes in exacerbating the humanitarian crisis, which would have brought into question the underlying legitimacy of NATO's action.

Media–state relations during the Kosovo campaign

The media played a number of roles during the air war against Serbia. During elite dissensus, newspapers played an oppositional role by challenging the utility of the air campaign but, when elite dissensus subsided so did critical coverage. At no point did policy-makers, determined to pursue an air war, give in to critical newspaper coverage by escalating the air campaign to a direct intervention involving ground troops or close air support. Moreover, TV news coverage did not, on balance, criticise the air war and CNN coverage was supportive of it. As such, the case highlights the limited potential of the CNN effect during periods of policy certainty owing to both the tendency of policy-makers to ride out criticism (newspapers) and the tendency of the media (CNN and CBS) to remain deferential to executive policy. At the same time TV news and the emotive coverage of refugees helped build support for US involvement in Kosovo, enabling policy-makers to explain and justify the air campaign underway. Moreover, the underlying legitimacy of NATO's actions was rarely questioned. In addition the fear of casualties, which in turn is partly linked to concern over press coverage of such casualties, served as a constraining force on US policy-makers, determining the nature and extent of NATO's military action. To evaluate further the relationship between policy certainty, media framing and non-influence during humanitarian crises, we now turn to the case of non-intervention during the 1994 genocide in Rwanda.

Genocide in Rwanda[33]

During April and May of 1994 more than 500,000[34] Rwandan Tutsis and Hutus were murdered by Hutu extremists (the *Interahamwe*) as part of a genocidal campaign aimed at ridding Rwanda of its Tutsi minority. The genocide was initiated after President Habyarimana of Rwanda and President Ntaryamira of neighbouring Burundi were killed when their aircraft was shot down when approaching Kigali airport in Rwanda. The two presidents had been involved in seeking peaceful co-existence between the majority Hutu and minority Tutsi peoples in both their countries. With their deaths, on 6 April 1994 Hutu extremists initiated a planned campaign of genocide. Both moderate Hutus and Tutsis were targeted in a brutal campaign that involved the hacking to death of civilians by machete. As the genocide gathered speed, Tutsi rebels of the Rwandan Patriotic Front (RPF) advanced on Kigali although, by this point, the genocide had spread throughout the country with murders continuing throughout May. Up to a million Tutsi and Hutu moderates are believed to have been murdered during the genocide. It was not until July that the tide had fully turned against the Hutu extremists when they were driven out of Rwanda by the RPF. These events were made even more remarkable by the fact that a UN peacekeeping force (UNAMIR) had been in place when the genocide was initiated but was withdrawn[35] two weeks later. In terms of understanding media influence on responses to humanitarian crises, the case is useful because US media covered the horrendous events in Rwanda and yet no intervention occurred. It is important to note that the focus of this case study is the period between 6 April and 21 April when it was decided to withdraw UNAMIR. There was a later Security Council decision to intervene in May (not actually implemented), a French intervention (Operation Turquoise) in June and an aid relief intervention in Zaire (Goma) later that summer to cope with the exodus of Hutus following the RPF's military victory in Rwanda. These interventions reflect different stages of the West's response to the crisis in central Africa and as such are distinct from the initial non-intervention decision. As a case of non-intervention (or even de-intervention), the case of the initial decision to withdraw from Rwanda allows us to examine the variation of policy uncertainty and news media framing in cases of apparent non-influence and non-intervention.

Two other researchers have examined the relationship between media coverage and the decision to withdraw from Rwanda. Strobel (1997: 144) concludes that the case is indicative of the 'shallow and limited' nature of media power because media attention to Rwanda failed to trigger US intervention to stop the unfolding genocide. He also argues that the presence of a presidential decision directive (PDD 25), which indicated a new and more forceful policy stance against intervention during humanitarian crises, helped mitigate media influence (1997: 146).

An account by Livingston and Eachus (1999) is slightly at variance with that of Strobel. These researchers also note that PDD 25 produced a level of policy certainty within the Clinton administration against involvement but, in contrast, argue that media coverage framed the genocide as an example of 'ancient tribal hatreds'. In doing so the coverage was ineffectual in terms of promoting intervention (Livingston and Eachus 1999: 215–16). The implication of Livingston and Eachus' argument is that the case of Rwanda does not demonstrate the shallow impact of media coverage per se, but rather the shallow impact of a particular form of coverage. This contrast between Livingston and Eachus and Strobel will be re-evaluated in light of the case study conclusions. The case study here draws upon the work of Livingston and Eachus and Strobel and primary research in order to evaluate the degree of policy certainty and distance framing in this case.

PDD 25 and US policy certainty against intervention

As Livingston and Eachus (1999: 224–6) describe, the policy review that was to become PDD 25 was triggered by events in Somalia during 1993 when 18 US troops were killed in the capital Mogadishu. The perceived failure and subsequent withdrawal of US forces persuaded the Clinton administration to attempt to minimise US commitment to international peacekeeping operations. PDD 25, although only formally issued in May 1994 (Livingston and Eachus 1999: 224), was well developed at the time of the start of the genocide in April. Indeed, National Security advisor Anthony Lake had published the basics of the directive on 6 February 1994.[36] In essence, the directive imposed strict conditions with regard to US military involvement in multilateral interventions, including a requirement that there be a 'clear statement of American interests in the operation' (Livingston and Eachus 1999: 224). As such a powerful impediment effect, born out of the loss of US troops in Somalia, that constrained US policy-makers with regard to the deployment of ground troops, was dominating policy-making during this period. With this policy development underway, it was already unlikely that the crisis in the tiny African country of Rwanda was to meet the criteria for US involvement. Indeed, James Woods (Deputy Assistant Secretary, Department of Defense at the time) states that he was ordered to remove Rwanda from a confidential list of 'international hot spots'. He states: 'I put Rwanda/Burundi on the list, I won't go into personalities but I received guidance from higher authorities: "look if something happens in Rwanda/Burundi, we don't care, just take it off the list."[37] In short, the policy context indicates a high level of policy certainty against intervention during this period.

Consistent with this high level of policy certainty at a general level against intervention, when the crisis in Rwanda erupted on 6 April all the evidence points overwhelmingly to a high level of policy certainty against involvement and in favour of withdrawal. Few attempts were made to highlight events in Rwanda. Between 6 April and 21 April (when the UN Security Council voted to withdraw UNAMIR), the US State Department ran just five press briefings which made mention of events in Rwanda[38] and most of these concerned attempts to withdraw US citizens from the country. When confronted directly with the question of whether or not to withdraw, briefer Mike McCurry stated:

> It's very clear from the events of the last several days that the UN mission that was in Rwanda cannot operate effectively because it was under attack at various points in the last couple of days. But the status of that mission and what it might do and how it might proceed in the future is something that will be under discussion at the United Nations.[39]

UN Security Council reference to events was equally scant. Despite the fact that the Security Council was debating the future of the UN mission, the UN issued only three documents on Rwanda during this period, none of which were press releases.[40] In short, whilst it was unknown at this point that genocide was occurring, it would appear that few attempts were being made to inform the public as to the horrendous nature of the killings in Rwanda. Here it should be noted that, with respect to the period prior to the UN withdrawal on 21 April, most of those who were involved in policy decisions state that no one was aware that the killings were part of a planned genocide. For example, Iqbal Riza, Chief of Staff to the UN Security Council, states that in 'the first few days, neither the people on the ground . . . nor here knew this was a planned genocide . . . we all viewed it as a breakdown in the ceasefire'.[41] Michael Barnett (US mission to the UN) states that early on 'it was unclear [before 21 April] what the origins of the killings were. There was a sense that it was spontaneous . . . it just seemed there was a mass killing spree.'[42] However, the fact that large numbers of civilians were being murdered was known. For example, Barnett states 'we knew there were widespread killings . . . that was known in the first few days . . . clear within a week',[43] Captain Luc Lamaire of UMAMIR stated 'we realized immediately they were murdering people'[44] whilst, on 14 April, US briefer McCurry condemned 'the brutal killing of political figures and the slaughter of innocent civilians'.[45] The effect of this apparent absence of official commentary was that the available information detailing atrocities was less likely to find its way to journalists. To put it another way, the US and other Security Council members made few attempts to explain, at least via press briefings and public statements, the level of violence being perpetrated on innocent civilians. If policy-makers were determined to avoid involvement in the Rwandan crisis, this low profile with regard to publicising events served to reinforce this policy objective.

At the same time, those involved in policy testify to the desire of the Clinton administration to seek withdrawal. According to Barnett there was little mood to do anything but withdraw:

> I don't think anyone imagined there would be an intervention . . . by and large the assumption was to withdraw . . . the general mood was to reduce US and UN exposure . . . [the policy was] withdrawal from the start . . . It wasn't like Yugoslavia where there was heated debate over what to do . . . the issue never went to the principals.[46]

According to Tony Marley (political military advisor for the US State Department from 1992–5), US policy at this point was motivated by

1 the belief that because there was no longer a peace in Rwanda the peacekeeping force must be withdrawn
2 the desire to support its NATO ally, Belgium, in its attempts to withdraw its troops from Bosnia and
3 the desire to avoid any possible US troop deployment in Rwanda.

Marley states:

> The US was very concerned, especially Defense Department officials, that no US personnel or US resources be siphoned off into another peacekeeping operation in Africa. This was, remember, following the Somalia débâcle. The best way to ensure that this would not happen was to prevent there being a UN peacekeeping operation in Africa. If there were no peacekeeping operation, US support could not be required for it.[47]

Finally, according to Howard Adelman and Astri Suhrke (1996)[48] on 12 April during 'informal consultations . . . the American Ambassador [to the UN] expressed serious doubts about the viability of UNAMIR . . . [and] . . . the next day, he suggested withdrawing, leaving only a skeletal force'. On 14 April 'the US claimed the Security Council needed a resolution for orderly evacuation of the force . . . [and on 15 April] . . . the US delegation [to the UN] expressed firm opposition to keeping UNAMIR in place' (Adelman and Suhrke 1996).[49]

In short, there existed policy certainty against intervention in Rwanda and in favour of withdrawal. In this context, we would expect to observe either empathy-framed coverage pressuring for intervention, but failing to influence policy-makers, or distance framing which reflected the non-interventionist agenda of the Clinton administration. It is to the analysis of media coverage that we now turn.

Distance framing

As both Strobel (1997) and Livingston and Eachus (1999) argue, the US news media did pay some attention to the unfolding events in Rwanda. With respect to quantity of coverage, between 6 April and 21 April the *New York Times* ran 56 articles that mentioned Rwanda (an average of 3.5 per day) of which eight were on the front page (7–14 April). The *Washington Post* ran 31 articles (1.9 per day) of which seven were on the front page (7, 9, 10, 11, 13, 14, 17 April). CNN ran 43 news reports mentioning Rwanda (1.9 per day) whilst ABC, CBS and NBC[50] also covered Rwanda fairly consistently, at least between 7 April and 14 April after which, similar to the newspapers, attention started to fade. Between these same dates Rwanda was headline news on ABC for two days and on most other days was still run within the first ten minutes of the news starting. NBC coverage was slightly less focused, running Rwanda as the headline on only one day (9 April) between 7 and 14 April and with Rwanda normally falling out of the first ten minutes of the news starting. Finally, CBS paid little attention to Rwanda, never once running it as the headline story and running it during the first ten minutes of the news on only four occasions (8, 10, 13 and 15 April). Overall, in terms of quantity of coverage, Rwanda certainly did not receive headline blanket coverage in the news. However, as the above figures show, it did receive a significant degree of media attention.

The distance framing of the coverage, however, helped inhibit any potential political impact the above coverage might have had.[51] As Livingston and Eachus (1999) document, much of the coverage belied the true nature of the killings, in part by presenting the killing as a breakdown in a ceasefire and/or as part of a regular round of tribal bloodletting.[52] A good example of this kind of tribal framing can be seen in the following extract from a CNN bulletin:

> Behind them now, a week of butchery unleashed when the presidents of Rwanda and neighbouring Burundi died in a suspicious plane crash. That upset a hair-trigger balance between the ruling Hutu majority and their former overlords, the minority Tutsis. Rwanda, over-populated, over-farmed, underfed and wracked by tribal hatreds, 400 years in the making. The history of Rwanda is full of massacres like this – killings followed by counter killings.[53]

At the same time it was clear from much of the coverage that, whatever the cause of the killings, large numbers of innocent people were being killed. For example, the following extract from a *Washington Post* article is typical of the extent to which coverage did report the killing of civilians:

> The hospital, Kigali's largest, has two doctors left to aid the overflow of wounded men, women and children – some lying on dirty mattresses and floors next to corpses draped in blankets . . . Out back, about 40 bodies, most of them men, rotted in the drizzle. A young woman lay naked atop the pile, her limbs stiff with rigor mortis, and several dead children lay torn with gruesome knife wounds.[54]

Overall, however, there was little attempt to try to understand the basis of the killings as anything other than the inevitable result of innate tribal hostility therefore creating a distance framing of events. Editorial comment reflected this tendency. Out of eight editorials run in the *New York Times* and *Washington Post*,[55] none explicitly called for anything to be done to stop the killings.[56] That media coverage failed to generate pressure to act was also indicated by Michael Barnett who stated that 'At the time in the US . . . there was no coverage that suggested the US go in any other direction [than withdrawal] . . . there was a tendency to portray events as a "tribal" conflict . . . there was a sense that the coverage reinforced certain kinds of policy consideration [i.e. a policy of withdrawal].'[57] In short, distance framing dominated in almost all the media coverage that in turn inhibited serious attention to the crisis from both policy-makers and the broader public.

Assessment

The results of this case study are relatively unambiguous. The policy certainty analysis indicates a high degree of certainty against intervention and in favour of withdrawal. This was in part created via a powerful impediment effect owing to concern over US casualties that had developed following the deaths of US soldiers in Somalia and which was encapsulated in PDD 25. News media covered the events in Rwanda but the distance framing of coverage implicitly supported a policy of non-intervention. The dismissal of the killings as the consequence of a 'regular round of tribal bloodletting' reduced any sense of responsibility or desire to 'do something' whilst editorials made little or no mention of any potential intervention that might stop the killings. In short, media coverage had the effect of reinforcing the US executive's determination to avoid involvement in Rwanda. In turn, this consistency between media coverage and the policy objectives of the Clinton administration reflected a broader elite consensus on the issue. In the absence of elite dissensus, few dissenting voices were heard in the media that might have challenged or criticised the chosen policy of non-intervention.

With respect to Strobel's (1997: 144) claim that this case demonstrated the 'shallow and limited' nature of media impact, these findings challenge this interpretation. Consistent with Livingston and Eachus (1999), the research here suggests the actual framing of reports caused coverage to be ineffectual in terms of pressuring for intervention and rather helped support the desire not to intervene. Hence the case of non-intervention in Rwanda is not indicative of the shallow and minimal impact of the media, as suggested by Strobel, but rather is suggestive of the minimal impact of a particular form of coverage, that of distance framing. If coverage had been empathy framed the political effect might have been far greater, although influence on policy is still unlikely to have occurred owing to the high levels of policy certainty.

Media influence and performance during executive policy certainty

In conclusion, policy certainty (reflecting an impediment effect) against intervention, coupled with few attempts to publicise the killing of civilians by the UN Security Council and US executive, ran hand in hand with distance framing which implicitly supported a policy of withdrawal. As such, and similar to the Kosovo case study, the case of Rwanda highlights the unlikelihood of media influence on policy when the executive is decided upon a particular course of action. In contrast to the Kosovo case study, however, Rwanda also highlights the extent to which media coverage remains deferential to executive policy unless there exist alternative elite sources willing to challenge official policy (Hallin 1986; Bennett 1990; Zaller and Chui 1996; Mermin 1999). In Kosovo, elite criticism of the air war policy was reflected in a certain level of critical newspaper coverage. In Rwanda, elite silence meant that little criticism of official policy found its way into the media.

6

THE CNN EFFECT RECONSIDERED

Overview

This concluding chapter draws together the research findings of each case study and offers conclusions regarding both the conditions under which news media coverage influences policy-making (as indicated by the limited test of the policy–media interaction model) and the central research question, whether or not the news media influence decisions to intervene during humanitarian crises. In order to provide an assessment of the relationship between the CNN effect and a range of different types of policy response to humanitarian crises, the central research findings are also compared with a much broader set of cases that move beyond forcible intervention to include non-coercive operations such as government support of aid agency relief and military logistical support for relief work. The chapter concludes with a broader discussion that considers the implications of the research findings for post-Cold War media power, foreign policy-making and humanitarian action.

Determining the conditions under which the CNN effect occurs

As explained in Appendix C, whilst the policy–media interaction model is not being tested in this study, the overall case study research does allow us to assess, in a limited fashion, the validity of the model (see Table 6.1). Specifically we can examine the research as a whole in order to do three things. First, we can assess the validity of the theory that news media framing and policy certainty are key factors in determining media influence. Second, we can estimate the relative significance of each of these variables. Third, we can examine the validity of the insights provided by the model regarding the relationship between government and media during periods of policy certainty. I shall deal with each in turn.

With respect to the theory that news media framing and policy certainty are key determinants of media influence, the Kosovo, Rwanda, Bosnia and Iraq case studies support these hypotheses of the policy–media interaction model. The hypothesis that media influence occurs when policy is uncertain and

117

Table 6.1 Case study results

	Media framing	Level of policy certainty	Media–state relationship
Air power intervention in Bosnia (Gorazde 1995)	Critical and empathy	Uncertain	Strong CNN effect
Air power intervention in Bosnia (February 1994)	Critical and empathy	Uncertain	Strong CNN effect
Ground troop intervention in Somalia	Supportive and empathy	Certain	Manufacturing consent plus enabling effect and weak CNN effect
Ground troop intervention in Iraq	Critical and empathy	Certain	No strong CNN effect; enabling effect
Non-deployment of ground troops during air war against Serbia	April: mixed re. policy but empathy framing also May: supportive and empathy framed	Certain	No strong CNN effect; impediment effect dominated whilst empathy framing had enabling effect
Non-deployment of ground troops during the Rwandan genocide	Supportive and distance	Certain	Manufacturing consent; impediment effect dominated

framing is critical is supported by the two Bosnia case studies in which critical and empathy-framed news media coverage helped cause policy-makers, uncertain of whether or not to intervene, to move to defend threatened 'safe areas'. Of particular note in these cases was the type of policy uncertainty present. In both instances uncertainty was generated in part by policy-makers being *undecided* over what course of action and in part by *no* policy existing with regard to the use of force. In this context those policy-makers who sought intervention were able to draw upon the critical 'do something' coverage in order to achieve their objectives. This finding supports Strobel's (1997: 211) claim that media influence often occurs through helping policy-makers who are 'seeking to pursue new policies'. Conversely, the Kosovo, Rwanda and Iraq case studies support the hypothesis that media influence is unlikely when policy certainty exists. In the case of Kosovo, whilst newspaper coverage was critical during April, TV news ranged from mixed (CBS) to supportive (CNN) and at no point did policy-makers succumb to the critical newspaper

118

coverage and escalate to a ground war. During May coverage became more supportive of official policy. Media pressure was also further undermined via the enabling effect whereby empathy framing of Albanian Kosovars helped generate support for Western involvement in the crisis. In the case of non-intervention in Rwanda, distance framing of the genocide reinforced the high levels of policy certainty against involvement during the genocide whilst, in the case of Iraq, the Bush administration, with policy certainty against intervention, rode out critical 'do something' coverage and only acted when geo-strategic factors became critical. With respect to the framing variable and its importance in determining media influence, finding critical and empathy-framed news media coverage to be associated with two instances of influence and intervention (the Bosnia case studies) is indicative that it is a necessary factor in determining influence. This inference is further strengthened by the Rwanda case study in which distance framing was found to be associated with no influence and no intervention.

With respect to estimating the relative significance of each variable, the case study findings allow us to assess which variable is the stronger in terms of affecting policy outcomes. When setting out the policy–media interaction model in Chapter 2 it was theorised that when policy-makers are set on a particular course of action they are unlikely to be influenced by news media coverage. However it was also noted that we should remain open to the possibility that critical and empathy-framed media coverage might be able to force policy-makers, even when certain, to change course and intervene.

Two cases can be drawn upon in order to evaluate this question. In the case of Kosovo, although overall coverage was mixed during April, there did exist critical and empathy-framed *newspaper* coverage which was unable to alter executive policy. This suggests that policy certainty is the stronger of the two variables. This finding needs to be qualified for two reasons. First, because coverage was on one level supportive of the overall broad thrust of policy via empathy framing, therefore building support for intervention via the enabling effect, it is perhaps less surprising that the critical coverage did not influence policy. Second, the framing analysis indicated that, whilst newspaper coverage was critical and empathy framed, TV news remained mixed (CBS) and supportive (CNN) regarding the ground war/air war debate. The possibility therefore remains that, if TV news had also been critically framed, policy-makers would have been forced to change policy. Overall the findings *vis-à-vis* media impact during policy certainty in this case are somewhat ambiguous. On the one hand, the finding that policy-makers were able to ride out critical newspaper coverage can be argued to be indicative of policy-makers being able to do the same with critical TV news coverage. Research by Gowing (1994) suggests that policy-makers tend to have little time to watch TV news and are more likely to be influenced by the quality press, in particular the editorial opinion of a paper. On the other, it might be the case that TV news has a particularly powerful effect on policy-makers relative to newspaper coverage. For example it might be that policy-makers perceive, quite reasonably so, that TV news has a greater effect on public opinion than the opinion-editorials of elite newspapers. If this is the case then critical TV coverage might be a necessary condition for media coverage, overall, to influence policy outcomes. Fortunately the Iraq secondary case study allows us to evaluate further the impact of critical coverage during periods of policy certainty. In fact the case supports the thesis that policy certainty is the stronger variable. In this case, despite the presence of critical and empathy-framed coverage, the Bush administration avoided intervention until geo-strategic concerns surrounding NATO ally, Turkey, and its Kurdish 'problem' forced policy-makers to act. In short, comparing both cases, the indication is that policy-makers are able to ride out critical news media coverage when there exists policy certainty.

Finally, with regard to the relationship between the media and the state when there exists policy certainty within the executive, the Kosovo and Somalia case studies are consistent with the prediction of the policy–media interaction model which states that when policy-makers are set on a course of action, rather than be influenced by news media coverage, they are more likely to work harder to promote their chosen course of action through press briefings and public announcements. Recalling the details of the Kosovo case study, during April 1999 an elite debate occurred over the utility of the air war during which, as the framing analysis demonstrated, the US executive effectively lost 'spin' control with regard to newspaper coverage that became critical of policy. In response, the executive consistently articulated the policy line that the air war was working as revealed through the analysis of press briefings. By late April, the NATO summit enabled Western leaders to harden the collective resolve of NATO and present a united front concerning the air campaign. At the same time 'off message' officials (specifically NATO commander Wesley Clarke) were removed from press briefings whilst 'spin doctors' such as Alastair Campbell were brought in to strengthen the PR campaign. After this, the level of media criticism dropped with critical newspaper coverage subsiding and coverage becoming supportive of official policy. In short, rather than changing policy in response to the critical coverage, the executive, determined to stick with the air war policy, worked ever harder to promote their chosen policy and did so until elite and media criticism had dissipated in late April/early May.

The Somalia case study findings also support this theoretical insight of the policy–media interaction model. Recalling the details of the case study, when Bush initially decided to offer US ground troops to the UN (25 December) the executive staged major set-piece press briefings in order to promote the policy of intervention. Interestingly, not only did news media coverage substantially increase in response to these press briefings but also it was framed so as to be supportive of the intervention decision. Again, these findings support the claim of the policy–media interaction model that policy-makers, when decided on policy, utilise press briefings in order to sell policy and, more importantly, that the news media are highly responsive to, and influenced by, these PR campaigns.

The strong CNN effect: influencing air power intervention during humanitarian crises but not the deployment of ground troops

With respect to the central research question, whether the CNN effect influences intervention during humanitarian crises, the findings are mixed (see Table 6.2). In the apparently easy case of Somalia, because significant levels of news media coverage actually followed Bush's decision to intervene, it was found that media coverage could not have been a significant influence on the decision to deploy ground troops although both a weak and enabling effect existed in this case. Moreover, news media coverage not only followed the executive decision to intervene but also framed it in a way that was overwhelmingly supportive of that decision. Hence in this case the news media played a more familiar role in relation to US foreign policy by reflecting elite decisions and helping to build support for them. In short, in the cases in which we were most likely to find evidence of a strong CNN effect it actually turns out that media coverage manufactured consent for official policy. This finding of no influence with regard to ground troop deployment in Somalia was supported by the secondary case study. In the case of Iraq, although media coverage was intensely critical of Bush's non-intervention policy, the Bush administration maintained a policy of non-intervention until geo-strategic concerns propelled first air power, and then ground troop deployment, in order to resolve Turkey's refugee crisis. At this point empathy framing had an enabling effect by helping explain and justify US involvement in northern Iraq but at no point did a strong CNN effect occur. Because the core case was an easy one for finding media influence, actually not finding any evidence leads us to believe that the news media are far less influential than is widely held. As such these findings stand as a serious challenge to the claim that news media coverage is a factor in causing decisions to intervene during humanitarian crises and suggest that the CNN effect is somewhat of a myth.

Contrasting with these two cases is the investigation into two instances of intervention in Bosnia. In what at first appeared to be a hard case for the CNN effect (Gorazde in 1995), a combination of critical and empathy-framed media coverage and policy uncertainty prior to the threat to use force indicated that media coverage was likely to have been a factor in influencing the decision to intervene. In addition, the finding of a similar pattern of critical and empathy-framed media coverage, policy uncertainty and air power intervention in the February 1994 market-place bombing strengthens our confidence in the Gorazde case study findings. Because the core case was a

Table 6.2 Types of media effect and types of policy response to humanitarian crises

	Policy type	Strong CNN effect	Weak CNN effect	Enabling effect	Potential impediment effect i.e. body-bag effect	Manufacturing consent
Ethiopia 1984	Aid relief	Yes				
Zaire 1994	Non-coercive	Yes				
Bosnia 1994	Coercive air power	Yes				
Bosnia 1995	Coercive air power	Yes				
Somalia 1992–3	Coercive ground troops		Yes	Yes	Yes (although only with respect to potential CNN effect) and not sufficient to stop policy-makers deciding to intervene	Yes
Kosovo 1999	Coercive ground troops (not deployed)			Yes	Yes	Ambiguous (in April newspapers were critical but coverage became supportive overall in May)
Rwanda 1994	Coercive ground troops (not deployed)			Yes (in terms of distance framing supporting a policy of non-intervention)	Yes	Yes
Iraq 1991	Coercive ground troops			Yes		

hard case, the finding of news media influence is particularly significant for the claim that media coverage causes intervention and leads us to believe that media influence on intervention decisions is more significant than widely assumed.

Comparing all four cases, two suggest media influence is far greater than expected whilst the others that media influence is far less. As such the findings point in opposite directions with regard to media influence and therefore offer equivocal support for the claim that the CNN effect is a factor in influencing policy-makers to intervene during humanitarian crises. Is there any way we can further derive meaning from these ambiguous findings? It is useful here to introduce a distinction between types of forcible intervention.[1] In the Bosnia cases, media coverage was able to trigger the deployment of air power whereas, in the Somalia and Iraq case studies, the type of intervention at stake was the deployment of ground troops. In Somalia and Iraq a strong CNN effect did not occur (although the media had a weak effect in the case of Somalia and an enabling effect in both cases). Hence the research findings are suggestive of media influence being far greater *vis-à-vis* air power intervention than ground troop intervention during humanitarian crises. This finding is consistent with the claims of Wheeler (2000: 300) and Strobel (1997) that media influence on ground troop deployment is minimal.

Moreover, this finding is suggestive of a broader pattern of media effects being conditional on the type of policy in question and it is worth further evaluating this thesis with respect to Western responses to humanitarian crises. In his 1997 working paper, Livingston (1997: 2) speculates that media 'effects on policy are conditional and specific to policy types and objectives'. He then goes on to identify a variety of types of military intervention, ranging from consensual humanitarian operations through to *imposed* humanitarian operations (defined here as intervention) and conventional warfare. The crucial point that he makes is that each type of policy has 'different objectives, actual and potential costs, and operational requirements. As a result, the level of interest the news media have and the potential consequence [i.e. effect on policy] of that interest vary substantially' (Livingston 1997: 15). So, for example, consensual humanitarian operations have 'reduced potential costs resulting from failure, measured in money and lives, and, less precisely, political prestige' (Livingston 1997: 10) when compared with conventional warfare. Accordingly media influence is likely to be greater regarding consensual humanitarian operations than it is regarding conventional warfare. Relating this thesis to the research findings here, because air power intervention is less costly both in political terms and the risk of casualties amongst US forces than the deployment of ground troops, we would expect it, according to Livingston's argument, to be more susceptible to media influence. In the easy case of intervention in Somalia, little evidence of news media influence was found, therefore suggesting that media coverage is unlikely to be a significant factor with respect to the political and financially costly option of deploying ground troops during humanitarian crises. In the hard case of intervention in Bosnia, the finding of media influence suggests that news media coverage is likely to be a factor in the deployment of air power during humanitarian crises which is a far less costly form of intervention, both in political and economic terms. These findings are reinforced by the secondary case studies where ground troop deployment in Iraq was not influenced by media coverage and air power intervention in Bosnia was influenced by the CNN effect. In short, by introducing the thesis that media influence is contingent on the type of policy (Livingston 1997), we can go some way to resolving the contradictory research findings regarding news media and intervention.

We can now further evaluate this thesis through introducing a much broader range of cases analysed by other researchers, set out in Table 6.2, ranging from aid relief through to forcible intervention. It must be emphasised that this is a speculative exercise in that each of these cases requires further analysis through application of the model and the kind of in-depth analysis contained in this study. As such what follows should be taken as a speculative guide to the broader implications of the findings of this study which highlights the need for further systematic and theoretically informed research into these cases. With this qualification in mind, let us now examine research into other types of policy response.

In low-cost responses to humanitarian crises, such as government involvement in aid agency relief, we would expect the CNN effect to have a major impact on policy decisions. In row one of Table 6.2 there is what is perhaps the seminal instance of a Western response to a humanitarian crisis that occurred during the 1984 Ethiopian famine. In this case, when both Western civil society and governments responded with a major aid relief effort, we would expect the possibility of there having been a strong CNN effect because the policy response involved, at most, the allocation of additional funds, military logistical support and diplomatic engagement from Western governments (i.e. political risks and financial costs were relatively low). Otherwise the bulk of the response to this famine was by aid agencies that were in turn reinforced by public support and donations. The presence of a strong media effect on Western governments is suggested by Greg Philo's (1993) study 'From Buerk to Band Aid' in which he describes how the dramatic and emotive BBC news report by Michael Buerk and Mohammed Amin precipitated major international media attention to the famine. Following this, an increasing number of aid agencies and Western governments moved to provide a response to the famine. Philo cites a member of a TV film team who was working at the UN General Assembly in New York when the story broke: 'the effect of the NBC report was electrifying. Suddenly the *New York Times* and other newspapers were running front-page stories. From nowhere, the crisis in Africa became the lead agenda item at the General Assembly' (Philo 1993: 108).

Moving to non-coercive intervention involving the deployment of ground troops in non-hostile circumstance (see row two of Table 6.2) we would, as with aid relief, expect a large CNN effect given the low cost, at least in political terms, of deploying troops to help co-ordinate relief aid. One such case that is useful here, and which has been studied by Livingston and Eachus (1999), is that of the US response to the refugee crisis in Goma following the 1994 genocide in Rwanda. The crisis in Goma during the summer of 1994 developed following the defeat of the Rwandan genocists by the Tutsi-led RPF when around 1.2 million, mostly Hutu, refugees fled into eastern Zaire (now the Democratic Republic of Congo) and fell victim to 'dehydration, cholera and dysentery' (Livingston and Eachus 1999: 221). Unlike during the genocide in Rwanda, the news media highlighted the plight of the Hutu refugees (Livingston and Eachus 1999: 219–22) and preceded the deployment of US troops and a massive airlift of relief supplies as part of a straightforward 'feeding and watering' (Livingston and Eachus 1999: 227) operation. An official, cited by Strobel (1997: 144), details a strong CNN effect upon the decision to launch this consensual humanitarian operation:

> None of those [media reports of the Rwandan genocide] provoked or provided the kind of catalyst for a US military intervention . . . The [later scenes of refugee] camps were a different matter . . . The mind-numbingness of it all was almost a made-to-order operation for what the US can do and do very quickly. But it was into a basically benign environment.

Viewing Table 6.2, as we move through to coercive operations involving the use of air power, we continue to see evidence of a strong CNN effect in the two Bosnia cases detailed in this study. However, as we move on to much more costly and potentially risky operations involving the deployment of ground troops in a hostile environment, the likelihood of the strong CNN effect drops off. In the cases of ground troop deployment in Iraq and Somalia, policy decisions are not significantly shaped by media coverage and, instead, other factors take over as prime determinants of policy. Moreover in these cases, whilst media coverage might still play a role through the enabling effect (e.g. Somalia, northern Iraq), the potential impediment effect (i.e. body-bag effect or the Vietnam syndrome) can play an equally important role serving to constrain policy-makers fearful of taking casualties. In particular the cases of Kosovo and Rwanda highlight this broader constraint acting upon policy-makers. In Kosovo the Clinton administration sought, at all costs, to avoid US casualties as witnessed by the 'no ground war' line and the failure to deploy Apache gunship helicopters. Failure to intervene in Rwanda during the genocide was informed by PDD 25 that was itself the outcome of the loss of US troops in Somalia in 1993. Extrapolating from this finding, it seems likely that the potential impediment effect (or body-bag effect) is likely to overcome any immediate pressure that might exist to deploy ground troops during humanitarian crises. A similar point was argued in the chapter on

Somalia when arguing that it was unlikely that a potential CNN effect persuaded policy-makers to intervene in Somalia and that, instead, fear of potential future casualties would have negated a potential CNN effect in this case. In short, whilst policy-makers might feel pressured in the short term to respond to empathy-framed coverage, this does not cause them to pursue a policy that might lead to negative coverage and public reaction in future weeks when casualties are taken. This thesis, however, requires further analysis, in particular via an investigation of cases in which critical 'do something' coverage ran alongside policy debates over whether to deploy ground troops in a hostile environment.

In summary, combining the case studies conducted in this book with other research suggests that the type of media effect is contingent on the type of policy in question. The studies outlined here suggest evidence in support of the presence of a strong CNN effect in instances of aid relief and deployment of troops as part of a non-coercive operation, whilst this book suggests a strong CNN effect in relation to air power intervention during humanitarian crises. However, the research here into instances of ground troop intervention during humanitarian crises indicates that media coverage is not a major factor in producing these high cost, risky operations. The widespread assumption that these interventions were media driven is a myth. Moreover, in instances involving ground troop deployment, it seems likely that any immediate CNN effect is likely to be countered by a potential impediment effect whereby policy-makers fear the possibility of taking casualties and pursue less risky options instead.

Future research

Before concluding with a more general discussion of the issues underpinning this study, we can map out some possible directions for future research on the CNN effect. As well as the need for further research into non-coercive forms of intervention (including the cases outlined above), three issues stand out as critical to the further development of our understanding of the effect of the media during Western responses to humanitarian crises. The first is the need to search for cases that do not appear to fit the research findings of this study. The second and third concern the need to develop systematic and theoretically informed approaches to measuring both alternative routes of media influence, such as the potential and weak CNN effects, and the presence of other factors that might be necessary to cause intervention. Each are considered in turn.

First, with respect to further case study research, searching for hard cases that challenge the findings of this study can test the robustness of the conclusions reached here. For example, instances of ground troop deployment in which a strong CNN effect appears to have occurred, or instances of air power intervention during which a strong CNN effect has not occurred, would present hard case tests for this study. If such cases cannot be found or if, on further inspection, they appear to support the conclusions of this study, then our confidence in the findings here will be increased. At the same time cases might be examined which appear to challenge the theoretical claims of the policy–media interaction model. In particular, instances where a strong CNN effect occurred, despite the presence of policy certainty, should be searched for, as well as instances of critical and empathy-framed coverage and policy uncertainty when media influence was not present. Again, if such cases are not found, then the confidence in the interaction model will be increased. Overall, only by proceeding via hard case selection can we strengthen our confidence in the research findings here and there is little to be gained from simply seeking out cases that appear to fit the conclusions of this study.

Second, concerning other types of influence, as noted in Chapter 2, the policy–media interaction model is designed to capture instances of the strong CNN effect rather than other types of possible media effect such as the weak, potential (including the impediment effect) and enabling effects. In this study, assessments of these other types of effect have been based on anecdotal evidence and logical inference. However, a contribution is to be made by establishing the criteria by which these other types of effect can be systematically measured. In particular, and with regard to the weak CNN effect, interview-based research will suffer the problems discussed in Chapter 1 and is therefore unlikely to be a reliable indicator at least on its own. Given, however, that the researcher is trying to provide evidence of perhaps only one TV news bulletin having a weak effect on a policy-maker, interviews would have to be relied upon in order to attempt to reconstruct the precise sequence of events. Close analysis of news media coverage would help to identify the crucial news bulletin or report that influenced a policy-maker. With respect to the potential CNN effect, reliance on interviews is, again, unlikely to yield stable research findings. This said, the absence of any obvious indicators (e.g. media coverage) would perhaps force the researcher to fall back on interviews as a way of assessing this effect. Because this would involve policy-makers remembering their speculations as to the possible consequences of a particular policy option, the findings are likely to possess a relatively high level of uncertainty. Perhaps the most that can be done to measure this route of influence is to infer its presence when there exists no other alternative and empirically supported explanation for a particular policy outcome. Either way, measuring this type of influence provides a challenging puzzle for the researcher. Overall, systematic and theoretically informed approaches to measuring these types of effect are necessary if we are to further our understanding of their significance regarding intervention during humanitarian crises.

Third and finally, regarding multiple factor explanations for intervention during humanitarian crises, this book has focused upon assessing the importance of one factor – the media – in influencing intervention decisions.

Yet, as we have seen in each case analysed, a number of factors are likely to combine to produce an intervention decision, ranging from geo-strategic concerns over refugee flows to concern of credibility. Further research should focus upon untangling the explanatory weighting of the various factors that might come to influence intervention decisions. First and foremost, a useful contribution can be made by specifying the theory and method by which we can measure the impact of factors, such as concern over US credibility in determining intervention decisions. In particular, in the case of the US decision to defend the Gorazde 'safe area', it was argued that critical media coverage was a factor in part due to it helping bring into question Western credibility and prestige. Whilst concern over credibility might exist without the media being present, it is also the case that media coverage of significant events, for example the hostage-taking of UNPROFOR troops televised around the world or the fall of Srebrenica, are also capable of causing policy-makers to be concerned about national credibility and prestige. A significant contribution can be made here by theorising the ways in which media coverage might become linked to notions of credibility and prestige and, in turn, influence foreign policy outcomes. More generally, once a systematic and theoretically informed approach to measuring alternative factors, or a combination of factors, has been established, cases can be examined in order to establish whether or not any given factor is present during the decision-making process. Across a series of cases patterns can then be detected and an attempt made to set out a multiple factor explanation of why intervention decisions come to be made.

Concluding comments: media power in the post-Cold War era

This study has found that, under conditions of policy uncertainty and critical and empathy-framed media coverage, the news media can be a factor in influencing policy-makers to use air power in pursuit of humanitarian objectives. No evidence was found that media coverage could cause policy-makers to pursue the more risky option of deploying ground troops during humanitarian crises. The idea of the media driving this kind of intervention is a myth. In these final pages I want to relate these findings back to the various policy and academic communities outlined in Chapter 1.

For those interested in the scope of media power in the post-Cold War, real-time environment, the findings offer support to the claim of a more powerful media and, at the same time, caution against the over-estimation of media power. In particular finding that the news media functioned to mobilise support for US policy in the Somalia, Rwanda and (to a lesser extent) Kosovo case studies is a salient reminder of the continued tendency of news media coverage to follow a more familiar and traditional pattern of behaviour with respect to US foreign policy by being indexed to official policy and arguably helping to manufacture consent for that policy. Accordingly, claims by communication theorists such as Volkmer (1999: 3) that there now exists 'a worldwide homogeneously time-zoned *bios politikon*, instantaneously affecting worldwide political action or interaction via press conferences or public resolutions transmitted around the world by CNNI [CNN International]' appear substantially overstated. Despite the radical claims of some, new communication technologies have not transformed world politics and media–state relations.

At the same time, producing evidence of a pattern of media-driven air power intervention in Bosnia provides at least some support to the claim that news media coverage, under specific circumstances, has the power to influence policy outcomes. Whilst the predominant tendency of the news media might well be to follow elite cues, this should not be confused with an inability to influence elite and official opinion, as we saw in Chapters 1 and 2, with the dichotomous effect/non-effect debates regarding media–state relations, when there exist elite divisions over policy. Overall, the findings of this study indicate that post-Cold War claims regarding news media power do possess substance. At the same time, it suggests both change and continuity regarding the media–state relationship. In particular, in all of the cases examined the media, whilst at times influencing policy, still reflected policy preferences of parts of the US elite foreign-policy-making community. Elite, as opposed to executive, manufacturing consent theory is born out by this study, although further research into non-elite groups (for example the KLA in Kosovo) might be worthwhile in order to assess their influence on parts of the US government. Here Wolfsfeld's political contest model discussed in Chapter 2, which theorises the link between non-elite groups and the media agenda, could be usefully employed in order to assess the extent to which non-elite groups such as aid agencies might have played a part in setting the media agenda. More generally, the policy–media interaction model employed in this study, alongside Wolfsfeld's model, provides the basis for a more nuanced understanding of the media–state relationship that can help explain instances of both change and continuity.

For those in foreign policy circles concerned at the loss of policy control, the findings raise a number of important questions. Decision-makers are clearly not at the mercy of an oppositional and all-powerful news media as suggested by some commentators (e.g. Kennan 1993). Here an interesting point is made by Carruthers (2000: 205). She points out that the CNN effect debate resembles the 'post-Vietnam controversy over the media's alleged role in "losing" that war' in that both debates have been set against the proliferation of new communication technologies, TV in the case of Vietnam and CNN, in the case of recent interventions. The central point here is that the more extreme claims of some realist commentators such as George Kennan appear to be driven as much by a deep seated unease, or 'outright hostility toward' (Carruthers 2000: 205) the arrival of new technologies as they are by a calm assessment of actual media impact. Another interpretation might be, of course, that foreign policy elites, when faced with failure in Vietnam, and then in Somalia, have sought to shift the blame on to the news media. Journalists and editors provide an easy, and popular, target for frustrated politicians and this in turn might have led to the over-estimation of media power. Overall, instead of confirming the dire predictions of realists, this study supports the assertions of other researchers (Gowing 1996: 85–6; Shaw 1996: 219; Minear *et al.* 1997: 73; Strobel 1997: 219) that policy certainty and political leadership can do much to control the news media agenda and how journalists frame events. At the same time, the conditions that cause policy uncertainty, and therefore threaten to wrestle media control from policy-makers, are unlikely to go away. Unexpected events or effective lobbying by non-government groups (e.g. aid agencies) are likely to be a continual source of policy uncertainty. And in these situations, as the Bosnia case studies indicated, news media coverage enters and affects the decision-making process. Moreover, the proliferation of new communication technologies, in particular the Internet, potentially increases the flow of information, opening up greater possibilities for inconvenient stories to emerge and unsettle policy-makers. At the same time, it might be the case that governments have become increasingly adept at counteracting negative spin in the area of foreign policy (Preston 1996). Here research is necessary in order to assess the extent to which any radical potential of new communications technologies is counteracted by increased information management by government. More generally, an analysis of the conditions under which policy uncertainty occurs (i.e. what causes variation in the level of policy certainty) would be of help to those who seek to manage the news media.

For those in humanitarian circles who assume a degree of humanitarian intent and benefit from Western humanitarianism, and therefore seek to harness the power of the news media, the findings here are a mixed blessing. Finding that the media can trigger intervention is welcome to those who seek to use the media to facilitate humanitarian action by government. Certainly, if we accept the idea that media impact is dependent on the type of policy-finding that news media coverage can influence the deployment of air power, as I argued earlier in this chapter, suggests that less costly policies such as non-forcible intervention, development aid and so on are likely to be even more susceptible to media influence (although further research into such cases is required). For humanitarians this finding affirms the importance of the news media with regard to facilitating humanitarian action. Also, the identification of the precise conditions under which the media can influence policy is useful knowledge for those seeking to influence the policy process.

At the same time finding that, with respect to forcible intervention, media influence might be limited to the deployment of air power arguably supports a widespread criticism that media coverage is a fickle and inadequate creator of humanitarian action (e.g. Rosenblatt 1996; Gowing 1997; Jakobsen 2000). For example, Michael C. Barnett develops a substantial critique of the inadequacy of the Western response to the war in Bosnia. He argues that governments, perceiving no vital interest in the former Yugoslavia, but unable to disregard totally the ethnic cleansing, sought to find 'a middle road between disengagement and involvement' (Barnett 1996: 150). Hence, from Barnett's perspective, Western governments were forced to provide some kind of response to the war but sought to avoid substantive involvement. According to Barnett (1996: 151) the real threat unleashed by attacks on UN 'safe areas' (e.g. cases such as Gorazde and Sarajevo analysed in this study) was to the integrity of the mission, suggesting that the military engagements detailed in this study were designed to 'rescue reputation and not to protect civilians' (Barnett 1996: 155). Here military intervention in Bosnia represented a kind of image management, or 'presentational . . . policy' (Minear *et al.* 1997: 73) designed only to 'retrieve . . . [the] reputation' (Barnett 1996: 155) of Western governments. Peter Jakobsen has also made a critique of the role of the news media with regard to humanitarian action (2000: 132). He argues that:

> By ignoring conflicts during the pre- and post-violence phases and by being highly selective in its coverage of conflicts in the violence phase, the media helps to shift focus and funds from more cost-effective long-term efforts, directed at preventing violent conflict and rebuilding war-torn societies, to short-term emergency relief. It also creates a situation where the provision of emergency relief to a large extent is determined by factors that have nothing to do with humanitarian need.

Overall, Jakobsen (2000: 141) concludes that the CNN effect is 'probably more of a hindrance than a help for Western conflict management at the general level' (Jakobsen 2000: 141). The overall implication of criticisms such as those of Barnett (1996) and Jakobsen (2000) is that humanitarian action would be better off without the news media being present.

The problem here for humanitarians seeking to use the media to facilitate humanitarian action is two-fold. First, Western governments are generally reluctant to become involved in conflicts where there is no perceived national interest. The associated doctrine of non-intervention in the internal affairs of states is a powerful realist belief that inhibits Western policy-makers from embarking upon what has been dismissed as the 'foreign policy of Mother Teresa'. Policy-makers are therefore unlikely to act of their own volition during 'distant' crises. Rather some kind of external pressure is required for them to act. When policy-makers are forced to respond, the desire is often to minimise the extent of involvement. As we have seen in the case of the Western response to the war in Bosnia, instances of forceful intervention were often in response to widely publicised atrocities whilst the resulting intervention was limited to that of air power. In short, policy-makers seek to adopt policies that, whilst responding to the demand of media coverage, do not draw them into costly and unwanted engagements. Second, at the same time, media coverage itself is often inadequate. The news values that inform editorial and journalistic practice mean that substantive media reporting tends to be confined to dramatic incidents that in turn hold press attention for short periods. By focusing upon the dramatic, reporting often ignores the underlying political and social complexities of a war. The limited attention span of media reporting does little to encourage the kind of long-term response required to facilitate both ideal humanitarian action and conflict prevention/resolution discussed by Jakobsen (2000). Perhaps more importantly, the entire humanitarian framework for reporting, epitomised by the empathy framing highlighted in this study, fails to relay the political and military context of a crisis. The image of suffering people pressures only for a humanitarian response, not concerted and long-term attempts to resolve the broader political and military situation.

Accepting these points, there is undoubtedly scope for improving the quality of humanitarian reporting.[2] Perhaps the most important improvement would be to improve the content of such reporting so as to create political pressure, not simply to respond with short-term ad-hoc policies but rather pressure for policy-makers to develop clearly thought-out long-term strategies. At the very least, finding that news media coverage can affect policy decisions should lead those in humanitarian circles not to reject the utility of the news media but rather to explore ways of facilitating the kind of media coverage that creates useful political pressure and beneficial humanitarian outcomes.

APPENDIX A:
POLICY UNCERTAINTY

Theoretical development of policy uncertainty

In terms of theorising policy uncertainty, I concentrated upon an area of the policy studies literature that focuses upon how policy is formulated and the role of policy *sub-systems*. Early rational actor theories of decision-making focused upon an idealised conception of the foreign policy process whereby policy-makers rationally selected the most appropriate course of action in order to protect or further the perceived national interest. In terms of explaining policy outcomes, a frequent charge against this model was that it tended to exaggerate both the degree of control and information that was available to policy-makers. In particular the model tended to ignore the internal dynamics of the institution (i.e. the foreign policy-making establishment) which actually generated foreign policy. In the seminal work *Essence of Decision*, Allison (1971) reassessed US policy-making during the Cuban Missile Crisis and presented a sophisticated challenge to the rational actor model. The bureaucratic model sought to explain foreign policy formulation in terms of the internal dynamics of institutions. Specifically Allison considered the impact of both organisational routines (standard operating procedures) and the particular interests of sub-systems, such as the Pentagon and State Department, in affecting policy formulation. As Welch (1992) explains, 'Allison highlighted how both '*organizational routines* constrain the formation of options and . . . affect implementation' and how 'political gamesmanship . . . operate[d] during the moment of decision itself as well as in the option-formation stage or during implementation'. In short, the bureaucratic model highlighted how various power centres or sub-systems act to promote their own vested interests and, as a result, policy outcomes become the result of a trade-off between these various interests. Whilst more recent literature has focused upon the policy implications of the broader social and political environment that foreign policy-making establishments exist in (e.g. Farrell 1996; Katzenstein 1996), the general thesis that sub-systems are important in terms of understanding policy formulation remains cogent. More recent analyses that fit within the bureaucratic paradigm (Smith and Clarke (1985),

Hilsman (1987) and (George (1989)) have advanced our understanding through a greater sensitivity to the power imbalances, or hierarchies of power, that exist between policy sub-systems. In particular, the work of Hilsman (1987) and George (1989) provides a useful conceptualisation of the policy process upon which we can build a definition of policy certainty.

Hilsman develops a political process model which 'sees a number of different individuals and organisations involved in the policy-making process. Each of these has power. Some have more power than others, and the power of each varies with the subject matter' (Hilsman 1987: 820). In terms of policy creation, the different power centres 'attempt to build coalitions among like-minded power centres . . . Sometimes they succeed in getting their ideal solution adopted; sometimes they succeed in getting the half . . . they estimated was the best they could do' (Hilsman 1987: 82–3). Importantly, Hilsman (1987: 82–3) notes that sometimes the outcome of this bargaining process is 'a policy that none of the power centres really wanted but a compromise that achieves something less than half a loaf for all'. He also notes that not always is 'policy always completely logical or internally consistent'. Similarly George (1989: 11) argues that:

> Efforts at rational calculation of policy take place in three inter-related contexts or subsystems within the policy-making system: *the individual context* (e.g. the chief executive, secretary of state); the *small group context* of the face-to-face relationships into which the executive enters with a relatively small number of advisors; and the *organisational context* of hierarchically organised and co-ordinated processes involving the various departments and agencies . . . in the executive branch.

George also notes, however, that the central danger for 'rational' decision-making is that policies emerging from the 'play of intra-governmental politics within the executive . . . may be more responsive to the internal dynamics of such a policy-making process than to the requirements of the foreign-policy problem itself' (George 1989: 114). Drawing upon a typology of distorted policy developed by Schilling (1962), he specifies the types of faulty policy that might emerge from intra-governmental politics. These include:

1 *no policy at all*
2 *compromised policy* – when the direction that policy should take is left unclear, or the means for achieving a well enough defined objective are left unclarified or unfocused
3 *unstable* or *blind policy* – when the internal struggle over policy is not really resolved once and for all with the result that there may be continuing shifts in the power and influence of rival policy coalitions, with similar shifts in the direction and content of the policy

4   *contradictory or leaderless policy* – when different parts of the executive branch pursue conflicting courses

5   *paper policy* – when a policy is officially promulgated but lacks support within the executive branch needed for effective implementation and

6   *slow policy* – when continuing competition and conflict among the policy actors delay the development of sufficient consensus and co-operation among them (George 1989: 114).

Clearly, these writers, although not intentionally, provide us with an idea of what we might mean by policy uncertainty. Hilsman's (1987: 11) reference to illogical or internally inconsistent policy being created from the internal dynamics of the policy process and George's (1989: 114) reference to policy emerging from the 'play of intra-governmental forces' (especially the list of 'faulty' policies), all allude to the possibility that policy is often not agreed upon. It is precisely in these situations that we can talk of policy uncertainty existing within government.[1] From this literature the definition of policy uncertainty, outlined in Chapter 2, was developed.

Measuring levels of policy uncertainty

A number of complementary approaches were employed to assess levels of policy certainty. Specifically, the observable implications of policy uncertainty (no policy, inconsistent or undecided policy and wavering policy) were searched for in executive press briefings and press conferences, secondary sources including memoirs and primary interviewing. The primary approach involved analysing officially released documents, such as press briefings and press statements issued by the three central policy sub-systems of the US executive: the White House, the Pentagon and the State Department. The use of this data source allowed a relatively systematic tracking of the state of policy on a day-to-day basis. Of course, what is said in press briefings cannot be taken at face value. Studied ambiguity is often the very objective of a press briefing as public pronouncements of a definite and unequivocal nature limit the manoeuvrability of policy-makers at a later date. At the same time, press briefings will also often be used in order to misinform adversaries in which case declarations of official policy might disguise true policy intentions. Also, press briefings might be used to present an image of steadfastness and resolve when, in fact, no policy has been agreed upon. Clearly, in any of these cases, reliance on what is said in press briefings might lead to invalid inferences with regard to levels of policy certainty. At the same time, such problems should not be exaggerated, particularly in the context of this study. Press briefings are perhaps the crucial arena in which the executive attempts both to set news agendas and to sell policy to the wider public. With respect to crisis situations, maintenance of public support is considered vital and policy-makers are unlikely willingly to display indications of uncertainty in such situations.

Evidence of *wavering, no* or *inconsistent/undecided* policy in these situations is therefore a strong indication of uncertainty within the executive. Conversely, when the executive is already intent on taking military action, press briefings play a key role in justifying and promoting policy to both journalists and the broader public. In such situations one would expect policy-makers to promote the policy of intervention actively, in which case we would observe high levels of policy certainty in press briefings. As such, press briefings are a useful indication of the presence, or absence, of policy certainty in the run up to a military intervention. These points notwithstanding, the potential problems outlined above require caution on the part of the researcher. In order, therefore, to strengthen inferences made via the press briefing analysis, I drew upon a variety of secondary sources and primary interviewing in order to assess levels of policy certainty.

Only when indications from these alternative sources and the press briefing analysis were consistent with each other were inferences regarding levels of policy uncertainty stated with confidence. White House press briefings (WHPBs) back to 1992 were downloaded from the White House website at http://www.whitehouse.gov, State Department press briefings (SDPBs) back to 1992 from the State Department website at http://secretary.state.gov/www-/briefings and Department of Defense press briefings (DDPBs) back to 1994 were downloaded from the Pentagon website at http://www/defenselink.mil/-news. All press briefings prior to these dates were obtained from the Federal News Service via Lexis-Nexis at http://www.Lexis-Nexis.com. It should be noted, however, that, with the transition from the Clinton to the Bush administration, press briefings relating to the Clinton administration have been removed. This might also occur with State Department and Department of Defense briefings. Briefings now unavailable from the White House, or any other part of the US government, can be obtained from the Federal News Service (via Lexis-Nexis if necessary).

APPENDIX B:

FRAMING

The concept of framing refers to the 'specific properties of . . . [a] narrative that encourage those perceiving and thinking about events to develop particular understandings of them' (Entman 1991: 7). As 'mentally stored principles for information processing' (Entman 1991: 7), frames offer ways of explaining, understanding and making sense of events. Slant, bias or frame of reference are other terms used to refer to framing. In abstract terms then, the concept of framing offers us a way to understand how information contained within any given text is mediated so as to privilege a particular reading of that text. Identifying frames serve to reveal the text author's frame of reference and is suggestive of the likely audience response to the text. In this respect, whilst a framed text may be read in different ways by different people, it is reasonable to assume that audiences will, by and large, adopt the frame of reference suggested by the text. As Entman (1993: 56) points out '[i]f the text frame emphasises in a variety of mutually reinforcing ways that the glass is half full, the evidence of social science suggests that relatively few in the audience will conclude it is half empty'. The work of Kahneman and Tversky (1984), Iyengar (1991), Zaller (1992) and Nelson *et al.* (1997) supports the working assumption that framing affects the attitudes and beliefs of receivers.

Measuring framing

In order to identify the empathy/distance and support/critical frames I employed a combination of approaches. First, news reports were read in order to both identify their subject matter and develop a sense of the overall tone of reports. This aspect of the framing analysis is unsystematic and interpretative but does possess a high degree of validity, requiring the researcher to read complete news texts and develop a sense of the overall tone and emphasis of media reports. The next method employed, by contrast, is more systematic and reliable, involving the quantification of keywords used in reports. The approach involved first predicting a set of keyword labels one would expect to be associated with each frame. With respect to empathy/distance framing, an important issue is how news reports label the population involved in the humanitarian crisis. Were they labelled as refugees, therefore emphasising their status as victims, or were they labelled, for example, as 'Africans', therefore defining them as an 'other' and maintaining emotional distance for the majority US non-African audience? Another useful labelling device to look for is whether suffering people were referred to as 'people' or members of a state (e.g. 'Iraqi')? These two terms are similar in audience effect to the 'African' and 'refugee' labels. The use of 'people' reminds the reader of his or her essential similarity with the victims of the humanitarian crisis whereas the use of 'Iraqi' reminds the reader of the difference. Finally a conjunction of three keywords – 'women', 'children' and 'elderly' – versus the three keywords – 'fighters', 'soldiers' and 'men' – are both possible ways in which populations associated with a humanitarian crisis could be described. In empathy framing one would expect a preponderant use of the keywords 'women', 'children' and 'elderly'. In a distance frame one would expect to see 'fighters,' 'soldiers' and 'men' repeatedly used. The first string of words carries connotations of innocence and vulnerability in Western culture, therefore encouraging sympathy; the latter carries connotations of responsibility and power, therefore tending to minimise sympathy. The aforementioned keywords are only a guide as to the keywords actually searched for in each case as the precise keyword formulations varied slightly across cases. Precise details of the keywords are provided in each case study.

Regarding critical/support framing the keyword choices are largely conditional on the case being examined. In particular it is necessary to establish precisely what aspects of a policy might have been open to criticism and the actual policy debates that might have been occurring in each case. For example, the debate over intervention in Iraq in 1991 revolved around the responsibility of Western leaders for the failed Kurdish uprising versus the perceived illegality of intervention in the 'internal affairs' of another state. Alternatively, debate over Bosnia, where peacekeeping forces were already on the ground, concerned the need to use greater force in order to maintain Western and NATO credibility versus the absence of a 'perceived' national interest that could justify greater involvement. Because keywords are conditional on the policy debate in question, it is not possible to devise a general set of keywords that can be searched for in order to gauge where the news media stood in relation to the official policy line. Accordingly, keywords used for establishing critical/support framing are detailed in the case study chapters after the relevant policy context is discussed.

The approach to measuring framing employed in this study, which combined interpretive analysis with a systematic keyword test, was preferred over the commonly used approach of using two researchers to code media reports separately and then testing the researchers' findings via inter-coder reliability tests. This was for two reasons. First, during the early stages of the research, several approaches were tried when testing the presence of frames and it was found that a keyword analysis provided the toughest test with regard to the presence of a given frame. As such the keyword test was a robust and reliable indicator of the validity of frame inferences. Second, whilst the dual coder approach does provide a measure of statistical confidence via the inter-coder reliability figure it still leaves opaque the precise criteria by which both coders reach their final decision. For example coders might be asked to decide whether an article was critical of policy or supportive of policy. Even if both agree that the article was, say, critically framed, this still leaves the precise criteria by which each coder decided that the article was critical undisclosed to outside observers. Alternatively, with a keyword search, the exact criteria (i.e. the specified keywords) by which the coder is gauging a frame is clearly stated and as such is subject to the scrutiny of observers outside the research process. Therefore the keyword approach is more 'explicit, codified and public' (King *et al.* 1994: 8) than that of the dual coder approach.

Counting keywords

When searching for keywords the method employed was not simply to count all the occurrences of keywords in the news report. This would have led to unnecessary contamination of the results by, for example, including the counting of keywords when they were used in relation to something other than the focus of interest. For example, in the coverage of a refugee crisis the keyword 'people' might be present in a news media text but which refers, not to the refugees, but to the aid workers. Rather the method employed was to count keywords only if they were used in relation to the subject of enquiry. In particular a keyword was counted only if it was used in the sense implied by the frame with which it was associated. For example, the keyword 'fail' might be used in relation to US policy (thereby indicating failure framing) but only in the context of an interviewee asserting the success of US policy against critics. In this instance it would not be appropriate to count the keyword fail as indicative of failure framing. Also, reading the context of the keywords is necessary to prevent the inadvertent counting of keywords preceded by a negative. For example, in terms of support/distance framing the keyword 'fail' might be used to indicate the presence of critical framing toward official policy. However if the keyword 'fail' was preceded by 'not' it makes little sense to count it as an indicator of failure framing. Finally, any formulation of the keyword e.g. 'fail', 'failed' and 'failing', was counted. Inevitably a degree of interpretation and judgement is involved in deciding whether the occurrence in a news text of a particular keyword should be understood as indicative of the associated frame. Wherever there was uncertainty over the meaning (in relation to a specified frame) of the use of a particular keyword, the method adopted was to count or discard the keyword so that it would count against the frame that had been indicated in the interpretive section of the framing analysis. This ensured that the keyword search remained a hard test of the interpretive analysis. The counts were then repeated in order to check that there was no significant variation (i.e. that affected overall results) between counts.

Overall, the approach to measuring framing in this study meets stringent methodological standards. First, because keywords associated with both the empathy and critical framing and the opposite distance and support framing are searched for, selection bias is avoided whereby the researcher considers only the evidence that supports the 'expected' frame. Second, I make clear the textual elements (i.e. keywords) that I understand as being indicative of a particular frame and then search for them in media reports. This ensured the process was 'explicit, codified and public' (King *et al.* 1994: 8) and allows other researchers to replicate the work and check the reliability of the findings. Third, juxtaposing both the frame and its opposite provides a robust reference point against which to reveal the frame. For example, by highlighting how empathy keywords outnumber distance keywords in a news report the approach demonstrates how, for one reason or another, one interpretation of events was preferred over another, equally possible, interpretation. Finally, as noted above, the keyword test was found to provide the toughest possible test of interpretive inferences regarding frames. If interpretive inferences agreed with the keyword test we therefore have high confidence in the validity of the framing inferences.

Data source

In order to develop a measure of overall news media framing, I analysed a selection of *New York Times* and *Washington Post* articles alongside CBS evening news segments and CNN transcripts. CNN was used for obvious reasons whilst CBS is regarded as representative of the other two key networks (ABC and NBC) (Entman 1991: 9) whilst the *New York Times* and the *Washington Post* are the two most influential of the dailies (Entman 1991: 9). For example, former Secretary of State Henry Kissinger stated 'the one thing that is read by everybody in Washington is the editorial and op-ed page of the *Washington Post*' (Kissinger cited in Linsky 1986: 70). In terms of 'foreign' news, most other broadsheets across the US follow the agenda and reference frames (broadly speaking) of these two key papers. *Washington Post* articles were obtained online at http://www.washingtonpost.com; *New York Times* articles and CNN transcripts were obtained via Lexis-Nexis at http://www.lexis-nexis.com; CBS evening news segments were obtained from the TV News Archive, Vanderbilt University, Tennessee, see http://www.vanderbilt.edu.

APPENDIX C:

TESTING THE POLICY–MEDIA INTERACTION MODEL

The extent to which the case study results can be used to confirm or discon-firm the validity of the policy–media model is limited and needs to be briefly discussed. It must be remembered here that this study aims to test the claim that news media coverage is a cause of intervention. As such the policy–media interaction model is not under test in this study. Rather, the model serves as our principal measure of news media power. For example, when researching the case of US intervention in Somalia in 1992, I might find that policy was uncertain and that news media framing was critical. Accord-ing to the policy–media model these findings would indicate that news media coverage was a factor in the decision to intervene. However, the finding of news media influence in Somalia, based on the presence of policy uncertainty and critical framing, cannot then be used to confirm the validity of the policy–media interaction model because the logic here would be circular. To spell this out more clearly, let us take the logic step by step:

- *Step one*: In the case of Somalia we find policy uncertainty and critical framing. These findings, according to the policy–media interaction model, indicate media influence. It is concluded that intervention in Somalia is a case of media influence.
- *Step two*: At this point it would be easy to then make the claim that by revealing the existence of news media influence in Somalia we have also, in some way, demonstrated the utility/validity/truth of the policy–media model which claims that policy uncertainty and critical framing causes media influence.

However, this is not a valid step to make as it involves circular reasoning:

- *Step one*: The policy–media interaction model helps 'prove' Somalia is a case of news media influence.
- *Step two*: Somalia, as a now proven case of news media influence, in turn helps to 'prove' the validity of the policy–media model.

Here, step two is tautological. The case of news media influence in Somalia is being used to help prove the validity of the policy–media model. But we only know Somalia is a case of news media influence because it has been defined as such by the policy–media model. If we were to test the validity of the model, we would have to select cases of known news media influence, and non-influence, and then observe the variation of the model's variables across these cases. However it is precisely because we do not have 'known' cases of news media influence (at least in the context of intervention during humanitarian crises) that we are embarking upon this study. Moreover, as argued when discussing the importance of theory in Chapter 1, instances of news media influence are not knowable in any straightforward fashion and this is why the model is employed in the first place.

This notwithstanding, the case study results will facilitate a limited test of the policy–media interaction model. How? Because each study involves additional research strategies over and above the measuring of the model's variables (framing and policy certainty), evidence for news media influence will not rest entirely upon the model. To the extent that these additional research strategies reveal news media influence, the model can be tested. For example if all the additional research strategies point to the presence of news media influence, and there existed critical framing and policy uncertainty as well, we can increase our confidence in the validity of the model. In effect, what is occurring here is that alternative evidence for news media influence is being used to identify first a case of news media influence. The case of news media influence identified a priori is then used to test the policy–media model. Alternatively, of course, in a given case we might find that all the additional research strategies point toward news media influence but the model indicates otherwise; for example, that there existed supportively framed news media coverage whilst high levels of policy certainty existed within government. This finding would clearly challenge the validity of the policy–media interaction model.

In short, whilst this study will provide a limited assessment of the model it must be remembered that the model is not the focus of analysis. As such in the first instance we must accept the theoretical insights of the model as a set of assumptions about how and why news media influence occurs.

APPENDIX D:

CASE SELECTION

Selecting an easy case

The five major forcible interventions of the 1990s by the US were Operation Provide Comfort in northern Iraq in 1991, Operation Restore Hope in Somalia in 1992, air power intervention during the 1992–5 war in Bosnia in 1995 (one example of which was Operation Deliberate Force in 1995), Operation Restore Democracy in Haiti in 1994 and Operation Allied Force in Kosovo in 1999. Each of these interventions involved the use/or threat of use of force during a humanitarian crisis. But which of these cases, on initial inspection, appears to have been the most obvious case of news media driven intervention? One way of answering this question is to consider the likelihood of other factors having influenced these interventions. Two factors stand out as alternative explanations for intervention: US national interest and geo-strategic concerns over regional peace and stability. Let us consider each in turn. Whilst the suffering of, for example, Kurds and Bosnians does not constitute a threat to US national interests in the traditional sense, humanitarian crises can still be interpreted in terms of a challenge to US interests. Here a useful typology is provided by Joseph Nye (1999: 26). He argues that there are three categories of threat to US interests.[1] These are 'A' list threats where the survival of the US is threatened (Nye places the Cold War Soviet threat in this category), 'B' list threats which feature 'imminent threats to US interests – but not [its] survival – such as North Korea or Iraq' and, finally 'C' list threats which include 'important contingencies that indirectly affect US security but do not directly threaten US interests' (Nye 1999: 26). Nye includes the crises in Bosnia, Kosovo and Somalia in this last list. Whilst assuming that 'C' list crises only present themselves to US policy-makers when the news media covers them, Nye (1999: 30) justifies their inclusion within a definition of what constitutes the national interest by arguing:

> In today's world the United States has a general interest in developing and maintaining the international laws and institutions that deal not

just with trade and the environment, but with arms proliferation, peacekeeping, human rights, and other concerns. Those who denigrate the importance of law and institutions forget that the United States is a status quo power. They also ignore the extent to which legitimacy is a power reality. True realists would not make such a mistake.

With respect to geo-strategic concerns, Nye (1999: 33) argues that, in cases such as Kosovo and Bosnia, US interests have combined with both 'humanitarian values and the strategic concerns of European allies and NATO'. The key concern here was the threat of war spreading and creating more general regional instability and the associated problem of vast cross-border refugee flows destabilising surrounding states (Adelman 1992: 74). In these cases 'C' list crises can 'migrate to the 'B' list' (Nye 1999: 34) and even the 'A' list if NATO credibility is brought into question by an on-going crisis.

Returning to the issue of case selection, if neither of these alternative factors are present, the likelihood of news media having been the cause of the intervention is greater, therefore making the case an easy one for the CNN effect. Are either or both of these two factors present in the case list? In four of the cases there existed strong geo-strategic factors that might have motivated intervention. The crisis in northern Iraq in 1991 was precipitated when the government of Turkey refused to allow over half a million Kurds, fleeing from Iraqi government forces, to cross the border into Turkey. As such geostrategic concerns over refugee flows clearly existed in this case. In addition, US national interests were present as Turkey, which sought help from Western governments to deal with the Kurdish refugees, was both a member of NATO and a valued ally following its support for Operation Desert Storm against Iraq. The 1992–5 war in Bosnia was also accompanied by vast refugee flows, over 3 million, which consisted both of people who had been subjected to 'ethnic cleansing' and those who sought refuge from the war throughout Western Europe. In addition, as the war proceeded, concern grew over the credibility of the Western alliance in the face of repeated Bosnian Serb nationalist attacks on 'safe areas' and the taking hostage of UNPROFOR personnel. With respect to Haiti, as Minear *et al.* (1997: 59) point out, its 'location within the traditional US sphere of influence elevated its geopolitical importance' whilst 'the threat of refugees continuing to flow into the United States kept the crisis high on the national political agenda'. Moreover, in the actual run up to the decision to intervene in Haiti, Strobel (1997: 186) argues that media coverage actually took the side of those opposed to military intervention, indicating that intervention in Haiti was quite the reverse of the CNN effect with media coverage pressuring against intervention.

Finally, the crisis between 1998 and 1999 in Kosovo was accompanied by the displacement of over 300,000 refugees prior to the NATO action (Herring 2000: 229). In addition, even as far back as the Bush administration, the idea that war in Kosovo might lead to a wider regional conflagration including key NATO countries such as Greece and Turkey was prominent within US policy-making circles (Gellman 1999).

In the remaining case of Somalia, however, refugee outflows from the country were, by contrast, limited and the crisis remained largely confined within the borders of Somalia. Indeed, the crisis was primarily created by civil war leading to famine and, at the point of US intervention in 1992, the key concern was delivering food aid to remote parts of the country. Also there was no clear strategic interest that might have motivated intervention in Somalia, the US having lost interest in Africa with the ending of the Cold War. At the same time, Somalia still fits within Nye's broad definition of national interest as a 'C' list crisis. Hence it is still plausible that policy-makers might have been motivated by a broader sense of the importance of human rights, legitimacy and so on. However, of all the cases available, the absence of US national interest and geo-strategic concerns means that Somalia is the most likely candidate for a case of news media driven intervention and therefore serves well as the easy core case for this study. In addition the intervention in northern Iraq will be analysed as a secondary case study. As noted before, this is a less easy case for the CNN effect. However, because the case also involved deployment of ground troops during a humanitarian crisis, as did Somalia, the case serves as a useful comparison and check on the Somalia findings.

Selecting a hard case

In terms of selecting a hard case, we need to select the case in which news media coverage seems unlikely to have been a factor. Both US intervention during the Bosnian War (1992–5) and the 1999 Kosovo air campaign appear strong candidates for hard cases. In Kosovo, regional and security issues at stake in Kosovo suggest there is little evidence that media coverage was a major factor in moving policy-makers to act. As Alexander Vershbow notes: 'I don't think it [media] made a big difference . . . I think from the outset . . . my government was seized by the political and regional consequences [of the crisis] . . . and with protecting our investment in Bosnia.'[2] However this case is to be selected as the control case (to be discussed shortly). With respect to US air power intervention during the 1992–5 war in Bosnia, the Western response was characterised by a determined stance by Western governments (up until the very latest stages of the war) to avoid forcible intervention (e.g. Barnett 1996; Gow 1997; Herring 1997; Campbell 1998). Also, news media coverage of the war was often criticised for the extent to which it was distance framed. For example, Campbell (1998: 53–4) describes how news reports on Bosnia repeatedly spoke of the 'way in which *Serbs savor ancient hatreds*, how *Balkan hatreds defy centuries of outside meddling*, the way the end of the Cold War has seen a *conflict born of old grievances* such that *the contagion of Europe's new tribalism could infect us all*'. As noted in Chapter 2, this kind of coverage is not expected to produce political pressure to intervene.

In addition, as noted above, the war in Bosnia was also characterised by substantial refugee flows and concern over the credibility of NATO and the Western alliance. In short, given all these points, Bosnia presents itself as an unlikely case in which to find news media influence and as such serves as a suitable hard case for this study. One further case of US intervention with air power was selected as the secondary case study.

Selecting cases of non-intervention

These final cases must allow us to observe how the two factors – policy uncertainty and news media framing – vary in cases of apparent non-influence. This requires, ideally, the selection of a case in which extensive news media coverage failed to influence policy so that we can test if news media framing was distancing, as hypothesised by the model. The first prominent case of non-intervention in the 1990s involved the civil war, and associated humanitarian crises, in Liberia. However, as Minear *et al.* (1997: 48) note, news media coverage was generally sporadic and produced little pressure on policy-makers to act:

> visits by foreign television crews were infrequent, with headlines reserved for the most extreme violence . . . The Liberian conflict 'was reported as a weird, lower-order war', said an NGO press officer, reflecting on his unsuccessful efforts to call greater attention to the mayhem.

The utility of the case for this study is further compromised by the fact that the West African force, Economic Community Monitoring Group (ECOMOG), did intervene. Hence any question of whether the US would intervene would have been made irrelevant by the fact that intervention had already occurred. For these reasons Liberia can be rejected. Non-intervention during the 1994 genocide in Rwanda[3] is more useful. During April 1994, when the genocide of the Tutsi minority and Hutu moderates started, there was a crucial period when the Security Council could have decided to maintain and reinforce the UN force stationed in Rwanda. This period was accompanied by a degree of news media attention to the unfolding events. For example, between 6 and 15 April the three main networks devoted over 25 news bulletins to Rwanda, which equates to 30 minutes of airtime. The average ranking of these bulletins was fifth. At the same time the *Washington Post* ran eight articles on Rwanda of which four were front page and two were editorials. However, even with this fairly significant level of coverage, it is still plausible to argue that coverage was simply not sufficient to make news media coverage a potential factor. Accordingly, the usefulness of this case for testing distancing framing is limited. This case of non-intervention will, however, be analysed for the secondary case study.

A more useful case, in which extremely high levels of news media coverage were associated with apparent non-influence, is that of Operation Allied Force in 1999. The focus of concern is not the initial decision to start air strikes. Rather the period of apparent non-media influence occurred after the air campaign had begun when a massive refugee crisis developed as Milosevic accelerated sharply the expulsion of Albanian Kosovars from the region. It was during this period that desperate images were transmitted back from refugee camps and a debate occurred in Washington over whether ground troops (and close air support) were required both to offer immediate protection to the Albanian Kosovars and, in the long term, to ensure their return. At no point did the US intervene directly on the ground in order to prevent attacks on the Albanian Kosovars. Hence it was during the period, following the launching of air strikes, that the question of news media impact on policy became most relevant to our concerns here. As such the case represents one instance where it appears that extensive news media coverage of a humanitarian crisis ran alongside policy-makers failing to intervene *directly* to alleviate the suffering. Of course, this case is slightly ambiguous in the context of this study because in all the other cases we are trying to assess whether the media influenced or failed to influence intervention whereas, in this case, the aim is to assess why US policy, already at the stage of air power intervention, did not escalate to a ground war. This ambiguity does not decisively undermine the utility of this case study for two reasons.

First, the initial decision to initiate air strikes was not designed primarily to alleviate the humanitarian crisis within Kosovo but rather as an act of coercive diplomacy aimed at securing Milosevic's compliance with US demands (WHPB, 24 March 1999). Indeed, as detailed in Chapter 5 it was well known that the air strikes might lead to a worsening of the humanitarian situation, at least in the short term. Hence the humanitarian credentials of the initial decision to launch air strikes are ambiguous at best and, as outlined above, the question of direct intervention to protect Kosovar Albanians did not occur until after the air strikes had begun when the refugee crisis occurred. As such this case is sufficiently similar in key respects (i.e. it contains the question of whether to intervene during a humanitarian crisis with the use of force, in this case ground troops/close air support, and media coverage of that humanitarian crisis) to the other cases analysed in this study.

Second, the primary purpose of this case is to assess levels of policy certainty and framing in situations where the media did not appear to influence policy. Accordingly, owing to its combination of high levels of news media coverage and apparent non-influence, the case will be useful for observing levels of policy certainty and framing in a case of apparent non-influence on policy. The justification for the selection of this case aside, the research findings of this case are ambiguous, in part because media coverage was found to have built support for the air war through the empathy framing of refugees. The implications of this ambiguity for the overall research results are discussed in Chapter 5 and the conclusion.

NOTES

INTRODUCTION

1 See Pew Research Center for the People and the Press, 'Public Appetite for Government Misjudged: Washington Leaders Wary of Public Opinion'. Available online at http://www.people-press.org/leadrpt.htm. Source Entman (2000).

1 THE CNN EFFECT CONSIDERED

1 See Wheeler (1992: 2000) and Ramsbotham and Woodhouse (1996).

2 It should be noted that the UNPROFOR mission did become increasingly co-ercive as the conflict continued with mandates to provide armed protection for food convoys. This particular development represented a greying of the bound-aries between non-coercive, semi-coercive and coercive UN operations. Western governments, however, were rarely willing to back these resolutions with the actual use of force, at least until toward the end of the conflict (e.g. Operation Deliberate Force in 1995).

3 Ramsbotham and Woodhouse (1996) do make a convincing case for expanding the definition of intervention to include non-coercive operations. In the context of this study, as will become clear, I wish to retain a clear delineation between non-coercive operations (peacekeeping, aid delivery etc.) and the use, or threat of use, of force during a humanitarian crisis.

4 For further discussion of these issues see Chopra and Weiss (1992), Wheeler (1992 and 2000), Linklater (1993), Roberts (1993), Vincent and Wilson (1993), Rams-botham and Woodhouse (1996).

5 For example see Raymond R. Coffey (1992) 'Don't Let TV Cameras Shape Policy', James Hoge (1994), 'Media Pervasiveness', Michael Mandelbaum (1994), 'The Reluctance to Intervene', Jessica Mathews (1994), 'Policy vs TV'.

6 Interview with author, 22 January 2001.

7 Most notably Paul Harrison and Robin Palmer (1986), *News Out of Africa*, and Jonathan Benthall (1993), *Disasters, Relief and the Media*.

8 See also Richard Holbrooke's (1999) article titled 'No Media – No War'.

9 This notion of a *potential* CNN effect will be considered in Chapter 2 when dis-cussing various routes of media influence.

10 Both of Wheeler's insights will be evaluated in this study.

11 I use the term commentary because neither work contains primary research into media effects on policy (nor are they intended to) but rather represent insightful speculation.

12 See Sigal (1973), Hallin (1986), Bennett (1990), Entman (1991), Zaller and Chui (1996), Mermin (1999).

13 These charges are regularly levelled against the work of Herman and Chomsky (1988).

14 See Paletz and Entman (1981), Glasgow University Media Group (1985), Hallin (1986), Herman and Chomsky (1988), Bennett (1990), Entman (1991), Eldridge (1993), Herman (1993), Parenti (1993), Philo and McLaughlin (1993), Williams (1993), Zaller and Chui (1996).

15 It should be noted that the distinction introduced here, developed jointly with Eric Herring, serves as a conceptual device to delineate two possible aspects of the manufacturing consent paradigm. It is not suggested that the work of the authors cited as examples either (1) fits neatly into either category or (2) explicitly describes itself as belonging to one or other version of the manufacturing consent paradigm.

16 For example see Glasgow University Media Group (1985), Herman and Chomsky (1988), Entman (1991), Herman (1993), Philo and McLaughlin (1993).

17 Hallin updates his work on the media and Vietnam in *We Keep America on Top of the World* (1994) and attributes greater influence to the media in terms of strengthening 'prevailing political trends' and 'accelerating expansion of the bounds of political debate' (Hallin 1994: 55). At the same time he notes that 'media impact [on policy] is beyond the scope of [his] study' and concludes the media are 'intervening' and not 'independent variables' during political processes. Whether or not the media impacted upon policy decisions is left to one side.

18 Unlike Hallin (1986) and Bennett (1990) Herman and Chomsky (1988) analyse in some detail the policy–media interface and as such cannot be accused of black boxing this dimension of media–state relations. They do not, however, consider in detail instances when media coverage might influence and change policy but rather focus on media coverage as a reinforcement of government policy.

19 In the book *Media, Power, Politics*, Paletz and Entman (1981: 20) do note that elites can utilise the news media in order to redistribute power amongst themselves although this remains a relatively undeveloped hypothesis in their work which, as with Hallin (1986), Bennett (1990) and Mermin (1999), tends to deemphasise the possibility of independent news media influence.

20 For example Gowing (1994), Minear *et al.* (1997), Strobel (1997).

21 Peter Jakobsen (1996) has also published an analysis of post-Cold War UN peace enforcement operations. This paper is not reviewed here because, whilst presented as a 'structured focused comparison' (George 1979) of five variables across five cases, there is in fact no clear operationalisation of any of the key variables and, connected with this, there is no primary research presented.

22 For a full critique of Gowing's research design, methodology and claims see Robinson (2000a).

23 For the seminal discussion on the issue of policy-makers' perceptions during international crises see Jervis (1976).

24 Wheeler (2000: 165) has recently challenged Shaw's claim by arguing that the media did not cause Western policy-makers to intervene but rather enabled policy-makers to intervene. His central point is that, if they so wished, policy-makers could have ignored the media pressure. This critique is underpinned by Wheeler understanding *causation* as synonymous with policy-makers being *forced* to act. This is an incorrect understanding of causation. Causation does not mean 'A' forces 'B' to occur but that 'A' is a necessary condition for 'B' to have occurred. A more reasonable reading of Shaw's work is that, whilst media coverage did not force policy-makers to act, the presence of media pressure was a decisive factor in persuading policy-makers to intervene.

25 Indeed the research design, methodology and conceptualisation of the CNN effect are, to all intents and purposes, identical across both these studies although Mermin appears to be unaware of the earlier study by Livingston and Eachus (1995).

2 DEVELOPING A THEORY OF MEDIA INFLUENCE

1 For a full discussion of the concept of framing, see Appendix B.
2 White House press briefing (WHPB), 4 December 1992.
3 Interview with author, 22 January 2001.
4 Patrick O'Heffernan's (1994) 'Mutual Exploitation Model of Media Influence' does not theorise media influence on policy process but rather the exploitative relationship between officials and the media with respect to information. For example he argues that 'the mass media and foreign policy institutions around the world have grown up together, each utilising the other and learning how to better utilise the other in a dynamic, unending process. This model does not see the co-operative symbiosis of a "subtly composite unity" but a dynamic of two very desegregated, aggressive ecosystems constantly bargaining over a series of "wants" whilst they manipulate both the structure and output for their own advantage. Sometimes the result is mutually beneficial and sometimes it is not' (O'Heffernan 1994: 233). The issue of media impact on policy itself, rather than media impact on information management strategies employed by governments, is assumed.
5 Whilst Wolfsfeld does consider the broader structural conditions that determine whether the media are able to influence government, his analysis does not theorise or focus upon the conditions under which media directly affects and alters government policy. For example, Wolfsfeld posits six factors that determine the degree of influence the media might have over government. These are size and status of the media organisation, the political power of the media organisation's audience, the degree of official control over the environment, the extent to which journalists are dependent on the government for information and the resources of a news organisation. If a news organisation is large, possesses status, has a politically powerful audience and if government control over the information environment is weak with the media possessing sufficient resources to look elsewhere for information, then media influence is likely to occur. None of these factors, however, help explain the precise policy conditions under which the media can shape and change actual policy processes.
6 Linsky (1986: 87) also argues that the media speed up the policy process.
7 Interview with author, 11 April 2001.
8 Although air power intervention was underway, the case of Kosovo was chosen because of the apparent reluctance of US policy-makers to intervene directly, either with close air support or ground troops, in the face of widespread criticism of the inadequacy of the air war. As such the case serves as one instance of the apparent inability of the media to force policy-makers to intervene through escalation to a ground war and is useful in order to observe if the variables hypothesised to lead to media influence (policy uncertainty and framing) do indeed vary in instances of non-influence. See Appendix D for further details about the selection of this case.

3 THE CNN EFFECT MYTH

1 Interview with author, 16 January 2001.
2 Interview with author, 11 April 2001.

3 See also Mandelbaum (1994) and Kennan (1993).
4 Data selection for the period 5 to 25 November 1991: for the *Washington Post* a keyword search was conducted online using the search term 'Somalia'. This computerised search returned summaries of all stories containing the word 'Somalia'. *New York Times* articles referring to Somalia were identified via Lexis-Nexis researchers using a computerised search of articles containing the keyword 'Somalia'. Those searched returned 26 *New York Times* articles and 20 *Washington Post* articles. Only those articles that were primarily about Somalia were counted (news summaries mentioning Somalia were also ignored). CBS evening news bulletins were downloaded from the Vanderbilt TV News archive abstracts. Abstracts were then read to identify how many news segments referred to Somalia. Because news attention was so brief I decided not to order the actual segments of news for analysis, but rather relied on the brief content guide available online. CNN transcripts were obtained via Lexis-Nexis using the search term 'Somalia'. For the dates 9 November to 25 November 1992, 20 news segments were returned. Of these 13 made only passing reference to Somalia whilst two were run after Bush's decision was leaked on 25 November 1992.
5 Courtland Milloy, 'Amid Food, They Hunger In Despair', *Washington Post*, 25 November 1992, section B, p. 1; 'UN under Gun in Somalia', *Washington Post*, 24 November 1992, section A, p. 17; 'Somalis Land in Yemen', *Washington Post*, 19 November 1992, section A, p. 38; 'UN's Man in Somalia' *Washington Post*, 9 November 1992, section A, p. 15; 'Ways to Help Africa' letter to editor, *Washington Post*, 7 November 1992, section A, p. 22; 'Food Flights Resume to Somali Town', *Washington Post*, 6 November 1992, section A, p. 23.
6 See for example 'Amid Food They Hunger in Despair' and 'Ways to Help Africa', letter to editor, *Washington Post*, 7 November 1992, section A, p. 22.
7 'Shelling Damages a Relief Ship off Somalia', *New York Times*, 25 November 1992, section A, p. 8; 'UN Urges Warlords to Open Somali Port', *New York Times*, section 1, p. 18; Anthony Lewis, 'Abroad at Home; Action or Death', editorial, *New York Times*, 20 November 1992, section A, p. 31; Leslie Gelb, 'Foreign Affairs: Shoot to Feed Somalia', editorial, *New York Times*, 19 November 1992, section A, p. 27; 'Yemen Feeds Somali Boat People', *New York Times*, 16 November 1992, section A, p. 12; Jane Perlez, 'How One Somali Family, Some of It, Survives', *New York Times*, 16 November 1992, section A, p. 1; 'A French Vessel Goes to Aid Ship Bearing Somalis', *New York Times*, 16 November 1992, section A, p. 6; 'The Tragedy in Somalia Can't Wait for Clinton', *New York Times*, letter to editor, 14 November 1992, section 1, p. 18; Jane Perlez, 'UN Somalia Envoy Dismayed over Aid', *New York Times*, 13 November 1992, section A, p. 5; Jane Perlez, 'A Somali Place That Even the Alms Givers Fear', *New York Times*, section A, p. 3.
8 See CNN transcripts: 12 November 1992: 479–2; 15 November: 220–1; 22 November 1992: 242–3; 24 November 1992: 168–71; and 24 November 1992: 222–4.
9 State Department press briefings (SDPBs), 9, 10, 12, 13, 16, 17, 19, 20, 23 and 24 November 1992. SDPBs obtained from Federal News Service via Lexis-Nexis.
10 SDPB, 10 November 1992.
11 See SDPBs, 9, 13, 17, 19, 20, 23 and 24 November 1992.
12 SDPBs, 12 and 16 November 1992.
13 Data selection for the quantification of coverage for the period 26 November to 4 December: in order to obtain a sample of *Washington Post* and *New York Times* articles a keyword search was conducted online using the search term 'Somalia'. This returned summaries of all stories containing the word 'Somalia'. The brief story summary and headline were then used to judge which articles were primarily about Somalia and which only briefly mentioned Somalia. Only those articles that

were primarily about Somalia were selected and counted. The total number of articles returned by this method was 128. CBS evening news bulletins were downloaded from the Vanderbilt TV News archive abstracts, whilst CNN transcripts were obtained via a keyword search ('Somalia') of Lexis-Nexis (all returns were counted).

14 WHPB, 4 December 1992 (Bush's address to the nation).
15 Department of Defense background briefing (DDBB), 4 December 1992.
16 Department of Defense press briefing (DDPB), 7 December 1992.
17 Data selection for interpretive analysis: the selection of articles was obtained by listing all the articles selected for the period 26 November to 9 December from the *Washington Post* and *New York Times* that were primarily about Somalia (i.e. the same articles selected when quantifying overall coverage). The total number of articles returned was 128. These were listed chronologically and alternate articles selected for analysis. This gave a sample of 62 articles (two articles were missing from the *New York Times* selection). For CBS, between 26 November and 9 December, alternate days were selected for analysis (except both 4 December and 5 December were analysed) and only the first ten minutes of bulletins were analysed for each day owing to time constraints.
18 Michael Gordon, 'UN Backs a Somalia Force as Bush Vows a Swift Exit', *New York Times*, 4 December 1992, section A, p. 1.
19 Don Oberdorfer and Trevor Rowe, 'UN Moves toward Sending Armed Force to Deliver Food', *Washington Post*, 26 November 1992, section A, p. 1.
20 Jane Perlez, 'Thievery and Extortion Halt Flow of UN Food to Somalis', *New York Times*, 4 December 1992, section A, p. 1.
21 Raymond Bonner, 'Buy up the Somalis Guns', *New York Times*, 2 December 1992, section A, p. 23.
22 For the keyword test the same *New York Times* and *Washington Post* articles and CBS bulletins as those selected for the interpretative analysis were analysed. In addition CNN transcripts were retrieved from Lexis-Nexis using the search term 'Somalia'. This returned 407 news segments of which every tenth was selected for analysis. This gave a sample of 41 news segments.
23 Interview with author, 11 April 2001.
24 Although he does recall having in his mind 'images of 14-year-old kids [reference to clan gun men]' and that these might have come from television. His clearest recollection of media coverage was of when the marines landed ashore at Mogadishu. Interview with author, 16 January 2001.
25 Interview with author, 16 February 2001.
26 Interview with author, 16 January 2001.
27 Interview with author, 11 April 2001.
28 Interview with author, 16 February 2001.
29 Cited by Ann Devroy and Kenneth J. Cooper in 'Bush Calls Foreign Leaders for Support on Somali Force', *Washington Post*, 3 December 1992, section A, p. 32.
30 For a detailed account of Western policy toward Iraq over the last ten years, see Sarah Graham-Brown (1999).
31 For an examination of the significance of Resolution 688 and the intervention in northern Iraq see Chopra and Weiss (1992), Wheeler (1992 and 2000) and Ramsbotham and Woodhouse (1996).
32 See 'The President's News Conference with President Turgut Ozal of Turkey', 23 March 1991, *Public Papers of the Presidents of the United States, George Bush: 1989–1993*, available online at http://www.csdl.tamu.edu/bushlib/papers.
33 'Question-and-Answer Session with Reporters in Hobe Sound, Florida', 3 April 1991, *Public Papers of the Presidents of the United States, George Bush: 1989–1993*.

34 See, for example, 'Remarks at a Meeting with Hispanic Business Leaders and an Exchange with Reporters in Newport Beach, California', 3 April 1992, *Public Papers of the Presidents of the United States, George Bush: 1989–1993.*

35 'Statement on Aid to Iraqi Refugees', 5 April 1992, *Public Papers of the Presidents of the United States, George Bush: 1989–1993.*

36 'The President's News Conference with Secretary of State James A. Baker III in Houston, Texas', April 6, *Public Papers of the Presidents of the United States, George Bush: 1989–1993.*

37 There was a degree of dispute at the time over whether these 'safe areas' should be labelled enclaves (implying an erosion of Iraq sovereignty and the de facto legitimating of a Kurdish region) or simply safe havens. For clarity I refer to these areas as 'safe areas', a label that is now commonly used to denote such protected refugee areas.

38 *Keesing's Record of World Events*, April 1991, 38127.

39 Boucher quoted in John E. Yang, 'Bush: US Allies Concur on Refugee Zones in Iraq; Accord Stressed after Meeting with EC Leaders', *Washington Post*, 12 April 1991, section A, p. 32.

40 Williams quoted in John E. Yang, 'Bush: US Allies Concur on Refugee Zones in Iraq; Accord Stressed after Meeting with EC Leaders', *Washington Post*, 12 April 1991, section A, p. 32.

41 'Remarks and an Exchange with Reporters Prior to Discussions with President Jacques Delors', 11 April 1991, *Public Papers of the Presidents of the United States, George Bush: 1989–1993.*

42 Clyde Haberman, 'After the War; US Military Takes over Relief for Kurdish Refugees in Iraq', *New York Times*, 13 April 1991, section 1, p. 1.

43 John E. Yang, 'Military Mobilized for Refugee Relief; US Doubles Its Forces Aiding Kurds', *Washington Post*, 13 April 1991, section A, p. 1.

44 'Remarks on Assistance for Iraqi Refugees and a News Conference', 16 April 1991, *Public Papers of the Presidents of the United States, George Bush: 1989–1993.*

45 *NBC Evening News*, 17 April 1991, Vanderbilt TV News Archive Summary.

46 These findings are based on a straightforward Lexis-Nexis database search using the keyword 'Kurds' and returned articles were not filtered in order to remove those which made only passing reference to the Kurdish crisis. All the articles were read and, as one would expect, the majority concerned the Kurdish crisis.

47 Source: Vanderbilt TV News Archive. A complete set of transcripts is currently unavailable for CNN coverage this far back, hence accurate figures could not be established regarding the level of CNN attention to the crisis. However, from the transcripts available, and the fact that the crisis was headline news across all other major media outlets, it is safe to assume CNN also covered the crisis extensively.

48 It is important to note that the framing analysis here is largely interpretive and involves no formal systematic check as with the core case study. The frame inferences made here are, however, consistent with other researchers (Gowing 1994; Shaw 1996; Strobel 1997; Minear *et al.* 1997) who have analysed this case.

49 CNN, *Crossfire*, 3 April 1991: transcript 281.

50 See William Safire, 'Duty to Intervene', 15 April 1991, section A, p. 17; Anthony Lewis, 'Abroad at Home: Politics and Decency', 15 April 1991, section A, p. 17; Leslie H. Gelb, 'Foreign Affairs: White House Guilt?', 14 April 1991, section 4, p. 19; Danielle Mitterrand, 'Victory, Elation; Refugees, Despair', 14 April 1991, section 4, p. 19; 'The Law Learns from the Kurds', 14 April 1991, section 4, p. 18; Orrin G. Hatch, 'Safe Havens Aren't Enough', 13 April 1991, section 1, p. 23; A. M. Rosenthal, 'On My Mind: The War Goes On', 12 April 1991, section A, p. 29; Column 1; 'A Leader for Some Seasons', 9 April 1991, section A, p. 24;

Russell Baker, 'Observer: The Manly Joy of Anguish', 9 April 1991, section A, p. 25; A. M. Rosenthal, 'On My Mind; America at the Vistula', 9 April 1991, section A, p. 25; Anthony Lewis, 'Abroad at Home: The New World Order', 5 April 1991, section A, p. 25; A. M. Rosenthal, 'On My Mind: The Jews of Iraq', 5 April 1991, section A, p. 25; William Safire, 'Bush's Bay of Pigs', 4 April 1991, section A, p. 23; Flora Lewis, 'America Deserts the Rebels Cynically', 3 April 1991, section A, p. 21; A. M. Rosenthal, 'On My Mind: Why the Betrayal?', 2 April 1991, section A, p. 19; William Saffire, 'Bush's Moral Crisis', 1 April, 1991, section A, p. 17.

51 See Jim Hoagland, 'Here's a New One: The Beirut Syndrome', 14 April 1991, section B, p. 7; Mario Bettati· 'The Right to Interfere', 14 April 1991, section B, p. 7; 'Saving Endangered Iraqis', 10 April 1991, section A, p. 22; Jim Hoagland, 'Neither Moral Nor Smart', 9 April 1991, section A, p. 21; 'Ceasefire: Tough Terms', 5 April 1991, section A, p. 18; William Raspberry, 'Tempting to Insurrection', 5 April 1991, section A, p. 18; Richard Cohen, 'A Moral Failure', 5 April 1991, section A, p. 19; Charles Krauthammer, 'Tiananmen II', 5 April 1991, section A, p. 19; Jim Hoagland, 'Too Cautious in Iraq', 2 April 1991, section A, p. 21.

52 William Safire, 'Duty to Intervene', 15 April 1991, section A, p. 17.

53 Prepared statement on 'Impact of Television on US Foreign Policy', hearing before the Committee on Foreign Affairs of the House of Representatives, 103rd Congress, 26 April 1994, cited in Minear *et al.* (1996: 50).

54 'The President's News Conference with President Turgut Ozal of Turkey', 23 March 1991, *Public Papers of the Presidents of the United States, George Bush: 1989–1993.*

55 US Public Broadcasting System, *The Gulf War: Oral History Interviews.* Available online at http://www.pbs.org/wgbh/p.s/frontline/gulf/oral (accessed 26 May 2001).

56 'Mission of Mercy', *Time*, 19 April 1991, and 'Haven from the Hell Holes', *Sunday Times*, 21 April 1991.

4 THE CNN EFFECT IN ACTION

1 For further analysis regarding US intervention in Bosnia, see Robinson (2001c).

2 White House press conference (WHPC), 10 August 1995.

3 SDPB, 14 September 1995, and DDBB, 18 September 1995.

4 DDPB, 18 September 1995.

5 For an excellent account of US and NATO policy toward Bosnia, see Ripley (1999).

6 Interview with author, 1 March 2001.

7 According to the International Committee of the Red Cross (ICRC) more than 7,500 males went missing when Srebrenica was overrun (source ICRC news 01/31, 9 August 2001, available online at http://www.icrc.org). To date around 350 bodies have been exhumed (source ICRC).

8 Holbrooke on ABC's *Nightline* cited in Antony Lewis, 'Weakness as Policy', *New York Times*, 14 July 1995, section A, p. 25.

9 Chirac, cited in Ann Devroy and William Drozdiak, 'Clinton Agrees to Plan Defense of Safe Areas, French Seek Help in Shoring up UN Effort', *Washington Post*, 14 July 1995, section A, p. 17.

10 WHPB, 26 July 1995.

11 Data selection for the interpretive analysis: using the search term 'Bosnia', 41 articles were returned from the *Washington Post* online archive of which 30 were directly related to Bosnia. For the *New York Times* 58 articles were returned from the Lexis-Nexis database of which 40 were directly relevant to Bosnia. This gave a total of 70 articles. Half of these articles (35) were selected for analysis by selecting alternate articles. A total of eight CBS evening news segments from the

Vanderbilt archives relating to Bosnia were analysed for the period 11 to 18 July. CNN transcripts were retrieved from Lexis-Nexis using the search term 'Bosnia' (84 returns) all of which were included in the analysis.

12 Chris Hedges, 'Serbs Start Moving Muslims out of Captured Territory', *New York Times*, 13 July 1995, section A, p. 1.

13 Ann Devroy and Michael Dobbs, 'Unity Must Precede Balkan Action: White House Still Divided, Allies Feuding on Safe Area Defense', *Washington Post*, 18 July 1995, section A, p. 17.

14 Data selection for the keyword analysis: for the keyword analysis the sample was identical to that used during the interpretive analysis (see note 11).

15 Some articles, believe it or not, did! For example see Richard N. Haass, 'Bosnia Can Still Be Saved', *Washington Post*, 13 July 1995, section A, p. 25.

16 Clinton, quoted in Woodward (1996: 259).

17 WHPB, 11 July 1995.

18 WHPB, 11 July 1995.

19 WHPB, 11 July 1995.

20 SDPB, 13 July 1995.

21 WHPB, 18 July 1995.

22 Interview with author, 22 January 2001.

23 Interview with author, 22 January 2001.

24 ABC's *Nightline*, cited in Anthony Lewis, 'Weakness as Policy', *New York Times*, 14 July 1995, section A, p. 25.

25 Interview with author, 1 March 2001. Anthony Lake made the point that policy was largely set by this point. However, whatever the state of his end-game strategy, most accounts detailed here point to the period following the fall of Srebrenica as the period when policy was finally decided upon.

26 It is important to note that Holbrooke does not specify media coverage of any particular event. However, given that the fall of Srebrenica was a turning point for US policy regarding the use of force in Bosnia (see also Blechman and Wittes 1999), it is reasonable to assume that the media coverage of the 'safe area' crisis was part of that media coverage to which Holbrooke referred.

27 A CBS poll (2 August 1993) showed 61 per cent of those polled supported this policy option. Source: Sobel (2000: 114).

28 A CBS poll (21 April 1994) showed 54 per cent of those polled supported this policy option. Source: Sobel (2000: 114).

29 *Congressional Record*, 18 July 1995, S10179. Congressional record available online at http://www.senate.gov.

30 WHPC, 27 July 1995.

31 'Remarks by the President', White House press release (WHPR), 6 February 1994.

32 'Remarks by the President', WHPR, 6 February 1994.

33 SDPB, 7 February 1994.

34 Sciolino, 'Clinton Rules Out a Quick Response to Bosnia Attack', *New York Times*, 7 February 1994, section A, p. 1.

35 See also State Department briefing by Mike McCurry on 9 February 1994 during which he refers to telephone lobby by President Clinton.

36 Statement by President Clinton, 9 February 1994.

37 These findings are based on a straightforward Lexis-Nexis database search using the keyword 'Bosnia' and returned articles were not filtered in order to remove those which made only passing reference to Bosnia. All the articles were read and, as one would expect, the majority were primarily about Bosnia.

38 These findings are based on a straightforward Lexis-Nexis database search using the keyword 'Bosnia' and returned news transcripts were not filtered in order to

remove those which made only passing reference to Bosnia. All the articles were read and, as one would expect, the vast majority were primarily about Bosnia.

39 Source: Vanderbilt TV News Archive.

40 It is important to note that the framing analysis here is largely interpretive and involves no formal systematic check as with the core case studies. The frame inferences made here are, however, consistent with other studies (e.g. Strobel 1997) that analysed this case.

41 The analysis of ABC, NBC and CBS coverage is based on the story summaries contained in the Vanderbilt TV News Archive.

42 The analysis of CNN coverage is based on full text transcripts available from the Lexis-Nexis database.

43 CNN, 5 February 1994: transcript 604–1.

44 CNN, 5 February 1994: transcript 604–1.

45 CNN, 5 February 1994: transcript 301–1.

46 CNN, 5 February 1994: transcript 280–9.

47 CNN, 5 February 1994: transcript 280–8.

48 CNN, 5 February 1994: transcript 280–4.

49 See Anthony Lewis, 'The End of Pretending', *New York Times*, 7 February 1994, section A, p. 17; 'Bosnia: Lift the Embargo Now', *New York Times*, 6 February 1994, section 4, p. 16; Sadruddin Aga Khan, 'War Crimes Without Punishment', *New York Times*, 8 February 1994, section A, p. 23; 'Sarajevo: The Right Response', *New York Times*, 8 February 8 1994, section A, p. 22.

50 See Kemal Kurspahic, 'The Saddest City', *Washington Post*, 9 February 1994, section A, p. 23; 'Bosnia', *Washington Post*, 8 February 1994, section A, p. 18; Jim Hoagland, 'Sarajevo: The Rush to Posture', *Washington Post*, 8 February 1994, section A, p. 19.

51 Anthony Lewis, 'The End of Pretending', *New York Times*, 7 February 1994, section A, p. 17.

52 Interview with author, 22 January 2001. Lake was unsure of the exact date suggesting the event he recalled might have occurred in late 1993, but that he was unsure. Because of the extensive coverage of the market-place bombing, it seems likely this is the event he remembers.

53 CNN, 8 February 1994, transcript: 670–4.

5 THE LIMITS OF THE CNN EFFECT

1 Serbian Kosovars at this point made up approximately 20 per cent of the population in Kosovo.

2 'NATO's 'War Against Milosevic: The Untold Story', *Newsnight Special*, BBC 2, 20 August 1999.

3 Interview with author, 1 March 2001.

4 Cited in 'NATO's War Against Milosevic: The Untold Story', *Newsnight Special*, BBC 2, 20 August 1999.

5 PBS, *News Hour*, 24 March 1999 cited in 'NATO's War Against Milosevic'.

6 'War Room', *Panorama*, BBC 1, 19 April 1999.

7 'Moral Combat: NATO at War', BBC 2, 12 March 2000.

8 'Moral Combat: NATO at War', BBC 2, 12 March 2000.

9 CBS evening news, 9 April 1999.

10 See Herring 2000 for a detailed account of the negotiations at Rambouillet.

11 *Washington Post*, 27 March 1999, section A, p. 15.

12 *Washington Post*, 28 March 1999, section A, p. 1.

13 Data selection for the interpretive analysis: owing to the vast number of articles relevant to Kosovo over the eight-week period it was decided to select articles

making significant reference to Western policy and the refugees by a keyword search. This differs from the Somalia and Bosnia case studies in which articles were first selected via a keyword search and then those containing significant reference to policy or refugees were identified via headline/first paragraph analysis. The keywords 'Kosovo' and ('policy', 'refugee' or 'Muslim') were used and the search restricted to the first paragraph of a news story. Lexis-Nexis was used to search both the *New York Times* and the *Washington Post*. This was designed to retrieve articles that made significant reference to Western policy and the Albanian Kosovars. This search returned 429 articles. This sample had to be cut to a more manageable number for reading. The articles were listed chronologically and every eighth article was selected for analysis. This gave a sample size of 53 articles. CBS coverage was selected by analysing the first five minutes of every fourth day during the sample period in order to produce an affordable sample. In addition CNN transcripts were obtained from Lexis-Nexis using the search term 'Kosovo'. This returned 974 articles for April and 432 articles for May. For April every 20th article was selected whilst, for May, every tenth article was selected for analysis.

14 Data selection for the keyword test: the same *New York Times*, *Washington Post* and CBS sample as used for the interpretive analysis was subjected to the keyword analysis. In addition CNN transcripts were obtained from Lexis-Nexis using the search term Kosovo. This returned 974 articles for April and 432 articles for May. For April every twentieth article was selected whilst for May every tenth article was selected for analysis.

15 The term 'refugee' was not counted in order to avoid picking up references to refugee camps.

16 The keywords 'refugees', 'Muslim', 'people' and 'Albanian' were counted by the computer because the number of returns was simply too large to count manually (i.e. too time consuming). By getting the computer to do the counting, we would have picked up uses of the keywords that were not being applied to the Kosovar Albanians. Because this computerised counting method is applied to both the empathy frame and distance frame keywords, we should not be biasing the results either way however. Moreover, it is a reasonable assumption that most uses of the words 'Muslim', 'refugee', 'people' and 'Albanian/Kosova(r)' will be in relation to the people from Kosovo. Regarding the success/failure frame keywords, any formulation (i.e. 'success', 'successful', 'succeed' and 'succeeded') was counted whether describing policy in the past, present or future tense or hypothetical references such as 'if we succeed'. These criteria excluded the counting of occurrences such as 'we must win', 'how do we measure success' and 'what is a win' which I interpreted as neutral concerning the success versus failure frames. Words were only counted if used in the appropriate context. For example if 'we will win' was used in the context of advocating a ground war this was not, obviously, counted as favouring the existing policy.

17 DDPB, 10 April 1999.

18 WHPB, 6 April 1999.

19 SDPB, 19 May 1999.

20 WHPB, 21 April 1999.

21 SDPB, 19 May 1999.

22 DDPB, 18 May 1999.

23 Freedman (2000: 354) also notes that the issue of a forced entry into Kosovo had got no further than speculative planning for a semi-permissive entry (whereby ground troops would be expected to engage with a significantly weakened Serb army) by the time the war came to an end.

24 'NATO's War Against Milosevic: The Untold Story', *Newsnight Special*, BBC, 20 August 1999.

25 DDPB, 14 May 1999.
26 See also pages 319–20 of Clark's memoirs that detail further Clinton's resistance to the use of the Apaches owing to concerns over casualties.
27 Wesley Clark (Supreme Allied Commander, Europe) emphasises Pentagon resistance to the use of the Apaches but also notes that 'Defense Secretary Cohen was influenced by the objection of the services' (Clark 2001: 232).
28 Clark's (2001: 268–374) memoirs detail his extensive efforts to persuade his political masters of the need to prepare, plan and move toward a ground option. At no point, however, does he indicate that an actual decision was taken by Clinton and his advisers to launch a ground invasion.
29 Interview with author, 1 March 2001.
30 Interview with author, 1 March 2001.
31 'NATO's War Against Milosevic: the Untold Story', *Newsnight Special*, BBC, 20 August 1999.
32 Saberi's interviews with NATO spokesperson Jamie Shea and General Wesley Clark all indicate the benefit policy-makers felt from media coverage of the refugee crisis in terms of justifying NATO's actions.
33 For more detailed context and background, see Prunier (1995) and Gourevitch (1998).
34 Source: 'The International Criminal Tribunal for Rwanda: Bringing the Killers to Book' by Chris Maina Peter, *International Review of the Red Cross*, 321: 695–704.
35 In reality the force was 'scaled down', rather than withdrawn, from 2,500 troops to a token 250. The effect, of course, was the same signalling to the killers that they would remain unopposed by the international community.
36 'The Limits of Peacekeeping' by Anthony Lake, *New York Times*, 6 February 1994, section 4, p. 17.
37 'When Good Men Do Nothing', *Panorama*, BBC, 7 December 1998.
38 This figure was arrived at by conducting a search of SDPBs using the keyword 'Rwanda'.
39 SDPB, 14 April 1994.
40 This figure was arrived at by using a keyword search of the UN website at http://www.un.org which contains press briefings and statements issued by the Security Council.
41 'When Good Men Do Nothing', *Panorama*, BBC, 7 December 1998.
42 Interview with author, 26 February 2001.
43 Interview with author, 26 February 2001.
44 'When Good Men Do Nothing', *Panorama*, BBC, 7 December 1998.
45 SDPB, 14 April 1994.
46 Interview with author, 26 February 2001.
47 Interview with Tony Marley (Political Military Advisor for the US State Department from 1992–5), US Public Broadcasting System (PBS). Available online at http//www.pbs.org/wgbh/p.s/frontline/show/evil (accessed 8 March 2001).
48 'Study 2: Early Warning and Conflict Management' by Howard Adelman and Astri Suhrke in *The International Response to Conflict and Genocide: Lessons From the Rwanda Experience* (Steering Committee of the Joint Evaluation of Emergency Assistance to Rwanda). Available online without pagination at http://www.reliefweb.int/library/nordic/index.html (accessed 3 March 2001).
49 'Study 2: Early Warning and Conflict Management' by Howard Adelman and Astri Suhrke in *The International Response to Conflict and Genocide: Lessons From the Rwanda Experience* (Steering Committee of the Joint Evaluation of Emergency Assistance to Rwanda). Available online without pagination at http://www.reliefweb.int/library/nordic/index.html (accessed 3 March 2001).

50 This search was based on the news summaries available at the Vanderbilt TV News Archive.

51 As with the other non-core case studies, the framing analysis here is largely inter- pretive and involves no formal systematic check. The inferences made here, however, are broadly consistent with other research such as that by Livingston and Eachus (1999).

52 See also Beattie *et al.* (1999) for a useful discussion of the media's tribal framing of Africa.

53 CNN, 13 April 1994: transcript 588–3.

54 Peter Smerdon, 'At a Hospital, Soldiers Kill Casually: The Wounded are Piled Amid the Dead', *Washington Post*, 12 April 1994, section A, p. 13.

55 'Take Care of My Children', *Washington Post*, 8 April 1994, section A, p. 21; 'Not Two of a Kind', *Washington Post*, 9 April 1994, section A, p. 20; 'One, Two, Many Rwandas?', *Washington Post*, 17 April 1994, section C, p. 6; Richard Cohen 'Global Tribalism', *Washington Post*, 19 April 1994, section A, p. 15; Alison Des Forges, 'A Life Saved', *Washington Post*, 19 April 1994, section A, p. 15; Frank Smyth, 'French Guns, Rwandan Blood', *New York Times*, 14 April 1994, section A, p. 21; 'Double Tragedy in Africa', *New York Times*, 10 April 1994, section 4, p. 18; Clifton R. Wharton, 'The Nightmare in Central Africa', *New York Times*, 9 April 1994, section 1, p. 2.

56 It should be noted that one editorial, 'Take Care of My Children', which revealed the details of a telephone conversation between a Rwandan and a US Human Rights Watch contact, was extremely shocking and powerful. However it did not advocate any kind of action, but merely relayed the intense danger faced by Rwandans during this period. Other editorials were either clearly distancing or else in no way advocated intervention.

57 Interview with author, 26 February 2001.

6 THE CNN EFFECT RECONSIDERED

1 See Blechman and Kaplan (1978) regarding the distinction between types of forcible intervention.

2 See Edward Girardet (1996) 'Reporting Humanitarianism: Are the New Elec- tronic Media Making a Difference?' in Rotberg and Weiss (eds) (1996), for a detailed discussion of the problems with media coverage of humanitarian crises.

APPENDIX A: POLICY UNCERTAINTY

1 Cox (1995: 13) makes a similar point with respect to US post-Cold War foreign policy: 'in the absence of strong leadership, policy-making became detectably less coherent as different sections of the foreign policy community vied with one another to impose their own particular views'.

APPENDIX D: CASE SELECTION

1 Nye's analysis is based upon comments made by William Perry and Ashton Carter.

2 Interview with author, 1 March 2001.

3 Whilst France did intervene between May and June 1994, and the US much later during the refugee crisis in Goma, the early phases of the Rwandan genocide (April through mid-May) were characterised by non-intervention and, in fact, de- intervention by the international community as UN troops were withdrawn.

BIBLIOGRAPHY AND
FURTHER READING

Adelman, H. (1992) 'The Ethics of Humanitarian Intervention', *Public Affairs Quarterly*, 6(1): 61–87.

Adelman, H. and Suhrke, A. (1996) 'Early Warning and Conflict Management' in *The International Response to Conflict and Genocide: Lessons from the Rwanda Experience*, Copenhagen: Steering Committee of the Joint Evaluation of Emergency Assistance to Rwanda, http: www.reliefweb.int/library/nordic/index.html (accessed 8 March 2001).

Allen, T. and Seaton, J. (eds) (1999) *The Media of Conflict: War Reporting and Representations of Ethnic Violence*, London and New York, NY: Zed Books.

Allison, G. T. (1971) *Essence of Decision: Explaining the Cuban Missile Crisis*, Boston, MA: Little, Brown.

Badsey, S. (1994) *Modern Military Operations and the Media*, Camberley: Strategic Studies Institute.

Barnett, M. C. (1996) 'The Politics of Indifference' in T. Cushman and S. G. Mestovic (eds) *This Time We Knew*, New York, NY: New York University Press: 148–62.

Barrett, S. and Fudge, C. (eds) (1981) *Policy and Action*, London and New York, NY: Methuen.

Baudrillard, J. (1991) 'La Guerre du Golfe n'a pas eu lieu', *Libération*, 29 March 1991. For an English translation, see Baudrillard (2000) *The Gulf War Did Not Take Place*, translated and with an introduction by P. Patton, Sydney: Power Publications.

Baumgartner, F. and Jones, B. (1993) *Agendas and Instability in American Politics*, Chicago, IL: University of Chicago Press.

Beattie, L., Miller, D., Miller, E. and Philo, G. (1999) 'The Media and Africa: Images of Disaster and Rebellion' in G. Philo (ed.) *Message Received*, Harlow: Longman: 229–67.

Bennett, Lance (1990) 'Toward a Theory of Press State Relations in the United States', *Journal of Communication*, 40(2): 103–25.

Bennett, W. Lance and Paletz, D. L. (eds) (1994) *Taken by Storm: The Media, Public Opinion and US Foreign Policy in the Gulf War*, Chicago, IL: University of Chicago Press.

Benthall, J. (1993) *Disasters, Relief and the Media*, London: I. B. Tauris.

Beschloss, M. R. (1993) *Presidents, Television and Foreign Crisis*, Washington DC, WA: The Annenberg Washington Program in Communications Policy Studies of North Western University. Available online at http://www.annenberg.nwu.edu/pubs/pres (accessed 8 March 2001).

161

Blair, A. (1999) speech by UK Prime Minister, Tony Blair, to the Economic Club of Chicago. Hilton Hotel, Chicago, USA, Thursday, 22 April 1999. Available online at http://www/fco.gov.uk/news (accessed 21 May 1999).

Blechman, B. and Kaplan, M. (1978) *Force Without War*, Washington DC, WA: Brookings Institution.

Blechman, B. and Wittes, T. M. (1999) 'Defining Moment: The Threat and Use of Force in American Foreign Policy', *Political Science Quarterly*, 114(1): 1–30.

Brown, R. (1998) 'It's Got to Make Some Difference, Hasn't It?: Communication Technology and Practice in World Politics', paper presented at the British International Studies Association Annual Conference, University of Sussex, 14–16 December 1998.

Brown, R. (1999) 'Campbell over Kosovo: Mobilization and Media Management in British Foreign Policy', paper presented at the British International Studies Association Annual Conference, University of Manchester, 21–3 December 1999.

Campbell, A. (1997) 'Media Reporting of Humanitarian Crises', *Crosslines Global Report: The Independent News Journal of Humanitarian Reporting*, issue 28, 5(2): 11–12.

Campbell, D. (1998) *National Deconstruction: Violence, Identity and Justice in Bosnia*, London and Minneapolis, MN: University of Minnesota Press.

Carruthers, S. L. (2000) *The Media at War: Communication and Conflict in the Twentieth Century*, London: Macmillan.

Chomsky, N. (1999) *The New Military Humanism: Lessons from Kosovo*, Monroe, ME: Common Courage Press.

Chopra, J. and Weiss, T. (1992) 'Sovereignty Is No Longer Sacrosanct: Codifying Humanitarian Intervention', *Ethics and International Affairs*, 6: 95–117.

Christopher, W. (1998) *In the Stream of History*, Stanford, CA: Stanford University Press.

Clark, W. (2001) *Waging Modern War*, New York, NY: Public Affairs.

Coffey, R. (1992) 'Don't Let TV Cameras Shape Policy', *Chicago Sunday Times*, 10 December.

Cohen, B. (1963) *The Press and Foreign Policy*, New Jersey, NJ: Princeton University Press.

Cohen, B. (1994) 'The View from the Academy' in W. L. Bennett and D. L. Paletz (eds) *Taken by Storm: The Media, Public Opinion and US Foreign Policy in the Gulf War*, Chicago, IL: University of Chicago Press: 8–11.

Cook, T. E. (1998) *Governing with the News*, London and Chicago, IL: University of Chicago Press.

Cox, M. (1995), 'US Foreign Policy after the Cold War', Chatham House paper, Royal Institute of International Affairs (RIIA), London: Pinter.

Culbert, D. (1987) 'Johnson and the Media' in R. A. Divine (ed.) *The Johnson Years, Volume One: Foreign Policy, the Great Society, and the White House*, Lawrence, KS: 224–7.

Culbert, D. (1988) 'Television's Visual Impact on Decision-Making in the USA, 1968: The Tet Offensive and Chicago's Democratic National Convention', *Journal of Contemporary History*, 33(3): 419–49.

Cusimano, M. K. (1995) *Operation Restore Hope: The Bush Administration's Decision to Intervene in Somalia*, Pew Case Studies in International Affairs, Washington DC, WA: The Institute for the Study of Diplomacy.

Daalder, I. H. (1999) *Getting to Dayton: The Making of America's Bosnia Policy*, Washington DC, WA: Brookings Institution Press.

Devroy, A. and Cooper, K. J. (1992) 'Bush Calls Foreign Leaders for Support on Somali Force', *Washington Post*, 3 December.

Devroy, A. and Cooper, K. J. (1995) 'Clinton Agrees to Plan Defense of Safe Areas, French Seek Help in Shoring up UN Effort', *Washington Post*, 15 July.

Drew, E. (1994) *On the Edge*, New York, NY: Simon and Schuster.

Durch, W. (1996) 'Introduction to Anarchy: Humanitarian Intervention and "State-Building"' in W. Durch (ed.) *Somalia in UN Peacekeeping, American Politics, and the Uncivil Wars of the 1990s*, New York, NY: St Martin's Press: 224–60.

Eldridge, J. (ed.) (1993) *Getting the Message: News Truth and Power*, London: Routledge.

Entman, R. (1991) 'Framing US Coverage of International News: Contrasts in Narratives of the KAL and Iran Air Incidents', *Journal of Communication*, 41(4): 6–27.

Entman, R. (1993) 'Framing: Toward Clarification of a Fractured Paradigm', *Journal of Communication*, 43(4): 51–8.

Entman, R. (2000) 'Declarations of Independence' in B. L. Nacos, R. Y. Shapiro and P. Isernia (eds) *Decision-making in a Glass House: Mass Media, Public Opinion and American and European Foreign Policy in the 21st Century*, London: Rowman and Littlefield Publishers: 11–26.

Erlanger, S. (1999) 'NATO Was Closer to Ground War in Kosovo than Is Widely Realized', *New York Times*, 7 November.

Farrell, T. (1996) 'Figuring Out Fighting Organisations: The New Organisational Analysis in Strategic Studies', *The Journal of Strategic Studies*, 19(1): 22–35.

Freedman, L. (2000) 'Victims and Victors: Reflections on the Kosovo War', *Review of International Studies*, 26(3): 335–58.

Freedman, L. and Boren, D. (1992) '"Safe Havens" for Kurds' in N. S. Rodley (ed.) *To Loose the Bands of Wickedness*, London: Brassey's: 155–90.

Gamson, W. A. and Lasch, K. (1983) 'The Political Culture of Social Welfare Policy' in S. E. Spiro and E. Yuchtman-Yaar (eds) *Evaluating the Welfare State: Social and Political Perspectives*, New York, NY: Academic: 397–415.

Gamson, W. A. and Modigliani, A. (1989) 'Media Discourse and Public Opinion: A Constructivist Approach', *American Journal of Sociology*, 95: 1–37.

Gelb, L. (1992) 'Shoot to Feed Somalia', *New York Times*, 19 November.

Gellman, B. (1999) 'The Path to Crisis: How the United States and Its Allies Went to War', *Washington Post*, 18 April.

George, A. L. (1979) 'Case Studies and Theory Development: The Theory of Structured, Focused Comparison' in P. Gordan (ed.) *Diplomacy: New Approaches in History, Theory and Policy*, New York, NY: Free Press: 43–68.

George, A. (1989) *Presidential Decision-making in Foreign Policy: The Effective Use of Information*, Boulder, CO: Westview Press.

Girardet, E. (ed.) (1995) *Somalia, Rwanda and Beyond: The Role of the International Media in Wars and Humanitarian Crises*, Geneva: Crosslines Global Report.

Glasgow University Media Group (1980) *More Bad News*, London: Routledge and Kegan Paul.

Glasgow University Media Group (1985) *War and Peace News*, Buckingham: Open University Press.

Gourevitch, P. (1998) *We Wish to Inform You that Tomorrow We Will Be Killed with Our Families*, London: Farrar, Straus and Giroux.

Gow, J. (1997) *Triumph of the Lack of Will*, London: Hurst and Company.

Gowing, N. (1994) *Real-time Television Coverage of Armed Conflicts and Diplomatic Crises: Does It Pressure or Distort Foreign Policy Decisions?*, Harvard working paper, Cambridge, MA: The Joan Shorenstein Barone Center on the Press, Politics and Public Policy at Harvard University.

Gowing, N. (1996) 'Real-time TV Coverage from War' in J. Gow, R. Paterson and A. Preston (eds) *Bosnia by Television*, London: British Film Institute: 81–91.

Gowing, N. (1997) 'Conflict Reporting: No Room for Shoddy Journalism', *Crosslines Global Report: The Independent News Journal of Humanitarian Reporting*, 28 (5)2: 9–10.

Graham-Brown, S. (1999) *Sanctioning Saddam: The Politics of Intervention in Iraq*, New York, NY, and London: I. B. Tauris.

Hallin, D. (1986) *The Uncensored War*, Berkeley, CA: University of California Press.

Hallin, D. (1994) *We Keep America on Top of the World: Television Journalism and the Public Sphere*, London and New York, NY: Routledge.

Hammond, P. (2000) 'Reporting "Humanitarian" Warfare: Propaganda, Moralism and NATO's Kosovo War', *Journalism Studies*, 1(3): 365–86.

Hammond, P. and Herman, E. (eds) (2000a) *Degraded Capability: The Media and the Kosovo Crisis*, London: Pluto Press.

Hammond, P. and Herman, E. (eds) (2000b) 'Conclusions: First Casualty and Beyond' in *Degraded Capability: The Media and the Kosovo Crisis*, London: Pluto Press: 200–8.

Harrison, P. and Palmer, R. (1986) *News Out of Africa: Biafra to Band Aid*, London: Hilary Shipman.

Herman, E. (1993) 'The Media's Role in US Foreign Policy', *Journal of International Affairs*, 47(1): 23–45.

Herman, E. and. Chomsky, N. (1988) *Manufacturing Consent*, New York, NY: Pantheon.

Herring, E. (1997) 'An Uneven Killing Field: The Manufacture of Consent for the Arms Embargo on Bosnia-Herzegovina' in M. Evans (ed.) *Aspects of Statehood and Institutionalism in Contemporary Europe*, Aldershot: Dartmouth: 159–82.

Herring, E. (2000) 'From Rambouillett to Kosovo Accords: NATO's War against Serbia and its Aftermath', *International Journal of Human Rights*, 4(3 and 4): 225–45.

Hilsman, R. (1987) *The Politics of Policy-making in Defense and Foreign Affairs*, Englewood Cliffs, NJ: Prentice Hall.

Hines, C. (1999) 'Pity, Not US Security, Motivated Use of GIs in Somalia, Bush Says', *The Houston Chronicle*, 24 October.

Hoge, J. (1994) 'Media Pervasiveness', *Foreign Affairs*, 73: 136–44.

Holbrooke, R. (1998) *To End A War*, New York, NY: Random House.

Holbrooke, R. (1999) 'No Media – No War', *Index on Censorship*, 28(3): 20–1.

Hooker, G. A. (1987) *A Realistic Theory of Science*, Albany, NY: State University of New York Press.

Hurst, S. (1999) *The Foreign Policy of the Bush Administration*, London and New York, NY: Cassell.

Ignatieff, M. (2000) *Virtual War*, London: Chatto and Windus.

Iyenger, S. (1991) *Is Anyone Responsible?* Chicago, IL: University of Chicago Press.

Jakobsen, P. V. (1996) 'National Interest, Humanitarianism or CNN: What Triggers UN Peace Enforcement after the Cold War?', *Journal of Peace Research*, 33(2): 205–15.

Jakobsen, P. V. (2000) 'Counter Point: Focus on the CNN Effect Misses the Point: The Real Media Impact on Conflict Management Is Invisible and Indirect', *Journal of Peace Research*, 37(2): 131–43.

Jervis, R. (1976) *Perception and Misperception in International Politics*, Princeton, NJ: Princeton University Press.

Kahneman, D. and Tversky, A. (1984) 'Choices, Values and Frames', *American Psychologist*, 39(4): 314–50.

Kaplan, R. (1993) *Balkan Ghosts: A Journey Through History*, New York, NY: Vintage Books.

Katzenstein, P. (1996) *Norms, Identity and Culture in National Security*, New York, NY: Columbia University Press.

Kennan, G. F. (1993) 'Somalia, Through a Glass Darkly,' *New York Times*, 30 September.

Kimball, J. (1988) 'The Stab-in-the-back Legend and the Vietnam War', *Armed Forces and Society*, 14(3): 433–58.

Kirisci, K. (1995) 'Provide Comfort and Turkey: Decision-making for Humanitarian Intervention'. Available online at http://snipe.ukc.ac.uk/international/papers.dic/-hirisci.html (accessed 20 July 1995).

King, G., Keohane, R. and Verba, S. (1994) *Designing Social Inquiry*, Princeton, NJ: Princeton University Press.

Kramer, M. (1990) 'Remembering the Cuban Missile Crisis: Should We Swallow Oral History?', *International Security*, 15(1): 212–18.

Kull, S. and Ramsey, C. (2000) 'Elite Misperceptions of US Public Opinion and Foreign Policy' in B. L. Nacos, R. Y. Shapiro and P. Isernia (eds) *Decision-making in a Glass House: Mass Media, Public Opinion and American and European Foreign Policy in the 21st Century*, London: Rowman and Littlefield Publishers: 95–110.

Lewis, A. (1999) 'At Home Abroad: Ends and Means', *New York Times*, 10 April.

Linklater, A. (1993) 'Liberal Democracy, Constitutionalism and The New World Order' in R. Leaver and J. L. Richardson (eds) *Charting the Post Cold War Order*, Oxford: Westview Press.

Linsky, M. (1986) *Impact: How the Federal Press Affects Policy-making*, New York, NY, and London: W. W. Norton and Company.

Livingston, S. (1997) 'Clarifying the CNN effect: An Examination of Media Effects According to Type of Military Intervention', research paper R-18, June, Cambridge, MA: The Joan Shorenstein Barone Center on the Press, Politics and Public Policy at Harvard University.

Livingston, S. (2000) 'Media Coverage and Public Opinion Dynamics during the 1999 War in Yugoslavia' in A. Schnabel and R. Thakur (eds) *Kosovo and the Challenge of Humanitarian Intervention*.

Livingston, S. and Eachus, T. (1995) 'Humanitarian Crises and US Foreign Policy', *Political Communication*, 12: 413–29.

Livingston, S. and Eachus, T. (1999) 'US Coverage of Rwanda' in H. Adelman and A. Suhrke (eds) *The Path of a Genocide*, London, UK, and New Brunswick, NJ: Transaction Publishers: 210–46.

Livingston, S. and Riley, J. (1999) 'Television Pictures in Multilateral Policy Decision-making: An Examination of the Decision to Intervene in Eastern Zaire in 1996', paper presented at the British International Studies Annual Conference, University of Manchester, 21–3 December 1999.

Loza, T. (1996) 'From Hostages to Hostiles', *War Report*, 43(July): 28–39.

Luttwak, E. (1999) 'Letting Wars Burn', *Foreign Affairs*, 78(4): 36–44.

McLuhan, M. (1964) *Understanding Media: The Extensions of Man*, London: Routledge and Kegan Paul.

McNulty, T. J. (1993) 'Television's Impact on Executive Decision-Making and Diplomacy', *The Fletcher Forum of World Affairs*, 17(Winter): 67–83.

Malcolm, N. (1996) *Bosnia: A Short History*, London: Macmillan.

Mandelbaum, M. (1994) 'The Reluctance to Intervene', *Foreign Policy*, 95: 3–8.

Mathews, J. (1994) 'Policy vs TV', *Washington Post*, 8 March.

Mehan, J. A. (1995) 'Entering a New Age' in E. Girardet (ed.) *Somalia, Rwanda and Beyond: The Role of the International Media in Wars and Humanitarian Crises*, Geneva: Crosslines Global Report: 222–70.

Mermin, J. (1997) 'Television News and American Intervention in Somalia', *Political Science Quarterly*, 112(3): 385–403.

Mermin, J. (1999) *Debating War and Peace*, Princeton, NJ: Princeton University Press.

Minear, L., Scott, C. and Weiss, R. (1996) *The News Media, Civil Wars and Humanitarian Action*, Boulder, CO, and London: Lynne Rienner.

Myers, G., Klak, T. and Koehl, T. (1996) 'The Inscription of Difference: News Coverage of the Conflicts in Rwanda and Bosnia', *Political Geography*, 15(1): 21–46.

Natsios, A. (1996) 'Illusions of Influence: The CNN Effect in Complex Emergencies' in R. I. Rotberg and T. G. Weiss (eds) *From Massacres to Genocide: The Media, Public Policy, and Humanitarian Crises*, The Brookings Institution, Washington DC, WA, and The World Peace Foundation, Cambridge, MA: 149–68.

Nelson, T. E., Clawson, R. A. and Oxley, Z. M. (1997) 'Media Framing of a Civil Liberties Conflict and its Effect on Tolerance', *American Political Science Review*, 91(3): 567–83.

Neuman, J. (1996) *Lights, Camera, War: Is Media Technology Driving International Politics?*, New York, NY: St Martin's Press.

Norchi, C. (1995) 'From Stage to Stagehand: The Media in the Post-Cold War International System' in E. Girardet (ed.) *Somalia, Rwanda and Beyond: The Role of the International Media in Wars and Humanitarian Crises*, Geneva: Crosslines Global Report: 140–98.

Nye, J. (1999) 'Redefining the National Interest', *Foreign Affairs*, 78(4): 22–35.

Oberdorfer, D. (1992) 'The Path to Intervention', *Washington Post*, 6 December.

O'Heffernan, P. (1994) 'A Mutual Exploitation Model of Media Influence in US Foreign Policy', in W. L. Bennett and D. L. Paletz (eds) *Taken by Storm: The Media, Public Opinion and US Foreign Policy in the Gulf War*, Chicago, IL: University of Chicago Press: 231–49.

Paletz, D. L. and Entman, R. (1981) *Media, Power, Politics*, New York, NY, and London: The Free Press.

Pan, Z. and Kosicki, G. M. (1993) 'Framing Analysis: An Approach to News Discourse', *Political Communication*, 10(1): 55–75.

Parenti, M. (1993) *Inventing Reality: The Politics of News Media*, New York, NY: St Martin's Press.

Philo, G. (1993) 'From Buerk to Band Aid' in J. Eldridge (ed.) *Getting the Message: News Truth and Power*, London: Routledge: 104–25.

Philo, G. and McLaughlin, G. (1993) *The British Media and the Gulf War*, Glasgow: Glasgow University Media Group.

Philo, G., Hilsum, L., Beattie, L. and Holliman, R. (1999) 'The Media and the Rwanda Crisis: Effects on Audiences and Public Policy' in G. Philo (ed.) *Message Received*, Harlow: Longman: 214–28.

Power, S. (1995) 'Bosnia Presses UN to Oust Serbs', *Washington Post*, 13 July.

Preston, A. (1996) 'Television News and the Bosnian Conflict, Distance, Proximity, Impact' in J. Gow, R. Paterson and A. Preston (eds) *Bosnia by Television*, London: British Film Institute: 112–16.

Prunier, G. (1995) *The Rwandan Crisis, History of a Genocide, 1959–1994*, London: Hurst and Company.

Ramsbotham, O. and Woodhouse, T. (1996) *Humanitarian Intervention in Contemporary Conflict*, Cambridge: Polity Press and Blackwell.

Ripley, T. (1999) *Operation Deliberate Force: The UN and NATO Campaign in Bosnia 1995*, Lancaster: Centre for Defence and International Security Studies (CDISS).

Roberts, A. (1993) 'Humanitarian War: Military Intervention and Human Rights', *International Affairs*, 69: 429–49.

Robinson, Paul (1999) 'Ready to Kill but Not to Die' – NATO Strategy in Kosovo', *International Journal*, 4(4): 671–82.

Robinson, P. (1999) 'The CNN Effect: Can the News Media Drive Foreign Policy?', *Review of International Studies*, 25(2): 301–9.

Robinson, P. (2000a) 'World Politics and Media Power: Problems of Research Design', *Media, Culture and Society*, 22(2): 227–32.

Robinson, P. (2000b) 'The Policy–Media Interaction Model: Measuring Media Power during Humanitarian Crisis', *Journal of Peace Research*, 37(5): 625–45.

Robinson, P. (2000c) 'The News Media and Intervention: Triggering the Use of Air Power during Humanitarian Crisis', *European Journal of Communication*, 15(3): 405–14.

Robinson, P. (2001a) 'Theorizing the Influence of Media on World Politics: Models of Media Influence on Foreign Policy', *European Journal of Communication*, 16(4): 523–44.

Robinson, P. (2001b) 'Operation Restore Hope and the Illusion of a News Media Driven Intervention', *Political Studies*, 49(5): 941–56.

Robinson, P. (2001c) 'Misperception in Foreign Policy-making and the Ending of War in Bosnia', *Civil Wars*, 4(4): 115–26.

Rodmen, P. (1999) 'The Imperiled Alliance', *Foreign Affairs*, 78(4): 45–51.

Rogers, P. (1999) 'Lessons to Learn', *World Today*, 55(8/9): 4–6.

Rohde, D. (1999) 'Crisis in the Balkans: The Villages: Serbs Step up Expulsions in Kosovo Area', *New York Times*, April 15.

Rosenblatt, L. (1996) 'The Media and the Refugee' in R. I. Rotberg and T. G. Weiss (eds) *From Massacres to Genocide*, Washington DE, WA: Brookings Institution: 136–46.

Rotberg, R. I. and Weiss, T. G. (eds) (1996) *From Massacres to Genocide: The Media, Public Policy and Humanitarian Crisis*, Washington DC, WA: Brookings Institution.

Sabato, L. (1991) *Feeding Frenzy: How Attack Journalism Has Transformed American Politics*, New York, NY: The Free Press.

Saberi, R. (2000) 'The Relationship between US Foreign Policy on Kosovo and CNN's Coverage of the Crisis', unpublished MPhil. thesis, University of Cambridge.

Schilling, W. (1962) 'Politics of National Defense: Fiscal 1950' in W. Shilling, P. Hammond and G. Snyder (eds) *Strategy, Politics and Defense Budgets*, New York, NY: Columbia Press.

Schraeder, P. J. (1994) *United States Policy Toward Africa: Incrementalism, Crisis and Change*, Cambridge: Cambridge University Press.

Sciolino, E. (1991) 'After the War: US Warns against Attack by Iraq on Kurdish Refugees', *New York Times*, 10 April.

Sciolino, E. (1994) 'US Rejects Plea to Act in Bosnia', *New York Times*, 24 January.

Sciolino, E. and Jehl, D. (1994) 'From Indecision to Ultimatum: A Special Report; as US Sought a Bosnia Policy, the French Offered a Good Idea', *New York Times*, 14 February.

Seaver, B. (1998) 'The Public Dimension of Foreign Policy', *The Harvard International Journal of Press/Politics*, Winter 3(1): 65–91.

Sharp, J. M. O. (1997/98) 'Dayton Report Card', *International Security*, 22(3): 101–37.

Shaw, M. (1996) *Civil Society and Media in Global Crises*, London: St Martin's Press.

Shawcross, W. (2000) *Deliver Us from Evil: Warlords and Peacekeepers in a World of Endless Conflict*, London: Bloomsbury.

Sigal, L. (1973) *Reporters and Officials*, Lexington, MA: D. C. Heath.

Smith, S. and Clarke, M. (1985) *Foreign Policy Implementation*, London: George Allen and Unwin.

Sobel, R. (2000) 'To Intervene or Not to in Bosnia: That Was the Question for the United States and Europe' in B. L. Nacos, R. Y. Shapiro and P. Isernia (eds) *Decision-making in a Glass House: Mass Media, Public Opinion and American and European Foreign Policy in the 21st Century*, London: Rowman and Littlefield Publishers: 111–31.

Strategic Survey (1995–6) 'A Fragile Peace for Bosnia', International Institute for Strategic Studies, London: Oxford University Press.

Strobel, W. (1997) *Late Breaking Foreign Policy*, Washington DC, WA: United States Institute of Peace.

Taylor, P. M. (1992) *War and the Media: Propaganda and Persuasion in the Gulf War*, Manchester: Manchester University Press. See also 2nd edition (1998).

Taylor, P. M. (1997) *Global Communications, International Affairs and the Media since 1945*, London: Routledge.

van der Gaag, N. and Nash, C. (1987) *Images of Africa: The UK Report*, Oxford: Oxfam.

Vincent, R. J. and Wilson, P. (1993) 'Beyond Intervention' in I. Forbes and M. Hoffman (eds) *Political Theory, International Relations and the Ethics of Intervention*, London: Macmillan: 111–20.

Volkmer, I. (1999) *News in the Global Sphere*, Luton: University of Luton Press.

Waltz, K. (1997) 'Evaluating Theories', *American Political Science Review*, 91(4): 913–17.

Welch, D. A. (1992) 'The Organizational Process and Bureacratic Politics Paradigms Retrospect and Prospect', *International Security*, 17(2): 117–18.

Wheeler, N. (1992) 'Pluralist and Solidarist Conceptions of International Society: Bull and Vincent on Humanitarian Intervention', *Millennium Journal of International Studies*, 21(2): 130–60.

Wheeler, N. (2000) *Saving Strangers: Humanitarian Intervention in International Society*, Oxford: Oxford University Press.

Whitney, C. R. (1995) 'Conflict in the Balkans: In Brussels Disunity Imperils French Proposal for Bosnia Force', *New York Times*, 18 July.

Williams, K. (1993) 'The Light at the End of the Tunnel' in J. Eldridge (ed.) *Getting the Message: News Truth and Power*, London: Routledge: 87–315.

Wintour, P. and Beaumont, P. (1999) 'Revealed: The Secret Plan to Invade Kosovo', *The Observer*, 18 July.

Wolfsfeld, G. (1997) *The Media and Political Conflict*, Cambridge: Cambridge University Press.

Woodward, B. (1996) *The Choice*, New York, NY: Simon and Schuster.

Zaller, J. (1992) *The Nature and Origins of Mass Opinion*, New York, NY: Cambridge University Press.

Zaller, J. and Chui, D. (1996) 'Government's Little Helper: US Press Coverage of Foreign Policy Crises, 1945–1991', *Political Communication*, 13: 385–405.

INDEX